VISUAL DATA

# Visual Data

## *Understanding and Applying Visual Data to Research in Education*

*Edited by*

Jon E. Pedersen
*University of Nebraska*

and

Kevin D. Finson
*Bradley University*

SENSE PUBLISHERS
ROTTERDAM / TAIPEI

A C.I.P. record for this book is available from the Library of Congress.


ISBN 978-90-8790-514-9 (paperback)
ISBN 978-90-8790-515-6 (hardback)
ISBN 978-80-8790-516-3 (e-book)


Published by: Sense Publishers,
P.O. Box 21858, 3001 AW Rotterdam, The Netherlands
http://www.sensepublishers.com

Cover design by Carrie L. Finson


*Printed on acid-free paper*

# TABLE OF CONTENTS

# INTRODUCTION

Beauty is in the eye of the beholder. So, too, is understanding. Virtually any two individuals can "see" the same thing, yet draw different conclusions regarding what meaning it has for them. Such outcomes can be perplexing, particularly to educators who try to provide for their students visual aids to help explain what seems to be even simple phenomena. More complex representations seemingly exacerbate the situation. Unless a visual impairment exists, most of us utilize our sense of sight as our predominant sensory input pathway. However, the visual sense is more than simply the functioning of the eye. It involves the neural connections between the eye and the brain, as well as the way(s) in which the brain processes the stimuli and information it receives. Although much of this occurs as the natural way the human brain and sensory systems function, some of it occurs because of what one has learned and how one learned it. In geology, for example, one person might look at a rock and see a history of advancing and receding shorelines with their accompanying deposition of silts and sands with definite wave or current patterns, while another person might look at that same rock and see little more than a colorful striped stone. In other words, one person understands what he/she sees much differently than will the other.

The visual inputs we receive can be collectively called visual data. Precisely how one defines visual data is a key question to ask. That is one of the questions we asked each author who wrote a chapter for this book. If one comes to a decision with respect to what visual data are, then the next question becomes, "What are visual data like?" Then, "What do they mean?" As with any data, we can collect it and compile it, but if we don't have some way to bring meaning it, it has little value to us. The answers may not be as straightforward as one might assume at the outset. Coming to understand what visual data tell us has been called "visual literacy." In fact, enough people are interested in understanding visual literacy that they've formed an organization whose purpose is to specifically do just that: The International Visual Literacy Association (you can find out more about them at http://www.ivla.org).

Leave it to be said there are those educational researchers who have questioned whether visual data are truly relevant and whether they can lead us to any better understanding of cognition. The collective opinion of the authors in this book would say otherwise. One need not look too far back into history to begin sensing that there is, indeed, something to it. The issue is whether or not we can determine what that "something" is. Tests have existed for decades that attempt to measure

*J.E. Pedersen and K.D. Finson (eds.), Visual Data, 1–3.*
© 2009. *Sense Publishers. All rights reserved.*

one's use of visual data in assessing cognitive ability or intellectual maturity (e.g. the Goodenough-Harris Drawing Test), visual-spatial aptitude, geometrical application, visual thinking strategies, and so forth. Research has revealed that individuals with good visual-spatial skills are those who pursue careers in architecture, art, engineering, mathematics, science, etc. (Lord & Holland, 1997). Visual data have also been used in other career areas that might not immediately surface in one's thinking, such as psychologists' use of subjects' drawings (particularly children's perceptions of themselves and their roles relative to their families) or with subjects who draw their pain (headaches in particular).

The extent to which visual data permeates what we do as educators is such that it may be difficult to identify every discipline in which it emerges. In this book, we have tried to provide a forum for authors from a cross section of common disciplines: visual arts, English, literacy, mathematics, science, social science, and even higher education administration. In his chapter on visual arts, Harold Linton takes us into the realm of colors and their impact on our psyche. He takes us from the use of colors in paintings of mountains to color coordination in the workplace and homes. Harold draws from something fun that many of us have experienced when looking at a particular colored image for a minute, then looking away only to see the reverse colors, and discusses the importance of applying this to the operating room. Several authors have addressed visual data revealed through drawings made by subjects ranging from young children to adults. Charlie Barman explains what he discovered when leading a nationwide U.S. study on elementary children's perceptions of scientists. Kevin Finson discusses how the Draw-A-Scientist Test came to be, and how it and its use has evolved. Jon Pedersen includes an examination of teachers' perceptions of themselves teaching science, and what that means for science methods and science education. Nate Carnes attempts to take a look at the extant research literature on the use of drawings, and seeks to identify how those studies fit together, if they do, or what discrepancies exist between them and where they occur. He leads us to think more about the increasingly complex and multi-dimensional contributions within each of the research discourses emerging from the literature, and tries to unveil important issues that demand our attention.

Shifting somewhat from drawings and visual arts, André Mack and Margaret Niess delve into visual data in mathematics, with particular focus on computer graphics and how those tools have evolved, have been used, and the promise of their future use. The plethora of visual data that comes to us requires that we mentally have or develop an efficient way of organizing and handling those data. David Hyerle addresses this issue in his exploration about thinking maps (related to concept maps, but different) and graphic organizers. Similarly, when we read or make use of literacy tools, we need to have cognitive processes in place that help us make sense of what it is we are reading. Hence, the focus of Patricia Chrosniak's thought about the use of visual data in the discipline of literacy and reading.

Limitations cause us to exclude some noteworthy chapters that could be written about other aspects of visual data. For example, much could probably be written about visual data use in psychology. We could explore not only what the discipline has to say about visual data, but how those data are used and what psychologists believe they mean. Certainly, a chapter could be written about the use of visual data in the arena of special education. We know children, in particular, key in on colors and shapes, and recent research has revealed interesting behaviors in eye contact with children having autism. Something could be said about the importance of graphic or visual data for non-readers of any age, as well as for those speaking different languages. And even though we've touched on the visual arts in this book, more could be said about that, as well as something about the performing arts. We could continue to generate lists such as this, but the point is that visual data are among us, and what we learn from them is really up to us.

## REFERENCES

Lord, T. & Holland, M. (1997). Preservice secondary education majors and visual-spatial perception: An important cognitive aptitude in the teaching of science and mathematics. *Journal of Science Teacher Education*, 8(1), 43–53.

HAROLD LINTON

# CHAPTER 1
# THE COLORIST'S DATA©

As an artist and designer, I create visual form with special emphasis on color in art and architecture. My education in the visual arts at Syracuse and Yale Universities peeked my curiosity about visual perception and the discovery of fresh visual concepts crucial to the work of the artist and designer. During the late 1960s and early 1970s, I was exposed to the pedagogy of Josef Albers through his teaching assistants and students who worked with him during his tenure as Chairman of Graphic Arts at Yale, 1950–1958. Albers' method of pedagogy developed during his teaching design at the Weimer Bauhaus, 1920–1925, and expanded into painting at the Black Mountain College in North Carolina, 1928–1940. Albers' approach was to explore the nature of color governed by an internal and deceptive logic. Problems posed to his students motivated their powers of self-discovery and cultivated an understanding of visual perception. Another influence during my education was Arnold Bank who taught design and calligraphic arts from 1960– 1984 at Carnegie-Mellon University, Pittsburgh, Pennsylvania. Bank challenged his students through problem-solving exercises to analyze form, discover vital metaphors, and create beauty in the production of relevant letterform in design. At Syracuse University, I studied design with Lee Ducell who served for many years as principal sculptural designer for Minoru Yamasaki. Lee challenged his students to pursue countless iterations during the process of design conceptualization. He insisted that visual data as visual note taking be thoroughly integrated in the design process and that numerous correlations and comparisons between two and three-dimensional concepts be experienced during the search for meaningful form. Phrasing and rephrasing was the theme of the studio in the search for elegant form, personal discovery, and a meaningful design statement.

When I began teaching color in architecture in the 1970s, the significance of Faber Birren's published works on color in architecture had been well established. His work evolved throughout his career from studies in color theory into explorations of color applied to the architectural environment. Birren's ground breaking work as visual consultant to industry during World War II helped reduce accident rates in manufacturing plants throughout the United States and provided a footprint for generations of artists and designers to follow who wished to pursue a new specialization in design called "color consulting." In 1982 Faber Birren reviewed my first manuscript relating color and light to the 3-D foundation studio course in architecture and wrote to my publisher in support of my first publication,

*J.E. Pedersen and K.D. Finson (eds.), Visual Data, 5–29.*

*Figure 1.* Architectural façade color study from *Color Model Environments: Color and Light in Three-Dimensional Design*, Van Nostrand Reinhold Company, Inc., New York, NY, 1985. Photo: Courtesy of Harold Linton.

*Color Model Environments: Color and Light in Three-Dimensional Design*, Van Nostrand Reinhold and Company, New York, N.Y. (Figure 1). Tom Porter, Professor of Architecture, Oxford Polytechnic Institute, Oxford, England, was another important mentor of mine. Like myself, Tom had migrated from a background in fine arts and design into teaching visual design and drawing courses in architecture. His seminal book, *Color for Architecture*, published by Van Nostrand

*Figure 2.* Ruoholahti Architectural Color Proposal. Future Apartment Tower Site Development: Ruoholahti Harbor Area. Helsinki, Finland. 1997. Photo: Courtesy of Harold Linton.

Reinhold in 1976, mapped the most important parameters of color theory and color applied to visual experience in the built environment. The following images are examples of color investigation from my students in color design from the University of Art and Design (UIAH) Helsinki, Finland, 1997 (Figures 2–5).

Today, I actively pursue research in human perception, the visual elements and principles of design, and the effects of color applied to three-dimensional form and space. All of my early influences have inspired my work over three decades of research, practical experience, teaching, and authorship of numerous books on color in design. I have been able to assimilate the theory, planning methods, technology, challenges of problem-solving, research, and visual communications involved in the practice of color consulting and color design.

Today, the artist/designer functions predominantly with visual data. The world we relate to and the problems we solve require solutions created from the considered use and application of visual form and ideas. In public fine arts projects, I create dimensional wall constructions made from bending hardwoods and upholstering canvas to these frames. Planning is a key attribute in all of my public art. To fully explore through drawing and models what the nature of a piece of art will be like before embarking on the construction process is imperative. Included here is a series of images taken from one of my planning sketchbooks that trace in a few examples of the progress and evolution of my thinking and planning for a construction for the new Muskegon County Airport, Muskegon, Michigan. The role of the computer in my work does not replace hand drawing but is one tool I use in specific ways to test color ideas and compositional studies (Figures 6–13).

7

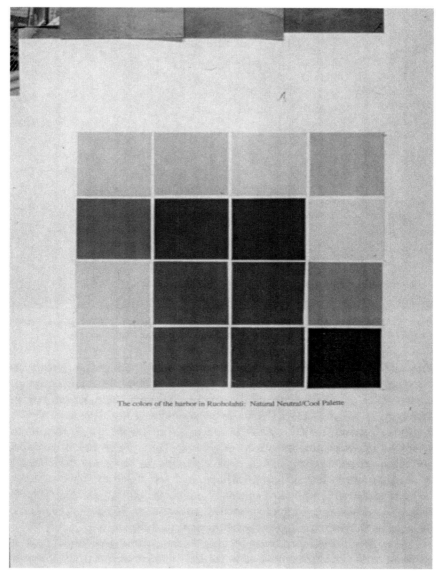

The colors of the harbor in Ruoholahti: Natural Neutral/Cool Palette

*Figure 3.* Color palette analysis from harbor site stone, earth, and site context. Photo: Courtesy of Harold Linton.

During the closing decades of the 20th century, the methods and tools of recording color and applying color concepts to real projects expanded due in part to technology but also to refinements and collaborative thinking between science, technology, material science and the ever-growing education of the public about color in their world. I serve the architecture profession through applying my expertise to support the guiding the visual concept of building design. My

*Figure 4.* Students working in teams testing color composition ideas on building facades. Photo: Courtesy of Harold Linton.

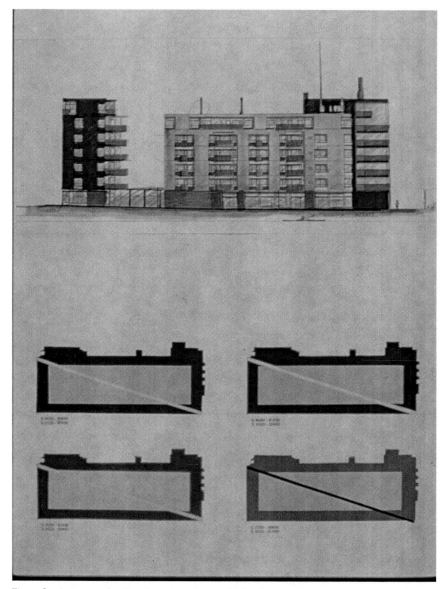

*Figure 5.* Apartment facade color scheme in pencil with alternatives studies in color design papers. Photo: Courtesy of Harold Linton.

background as artist and designer is populated with a diverse sensibility made up of a broad awareness and a refined visual perception. It includes knowledge of design and its history, an intimate understanding of design process and visual planning, expertise with industrial color materials and methods of application. My background incorporates knowledge of new technologies for visualization, an awareness of design context and cultural identity, a background in physiology and

*Figure 6.* Author's Sketchbook: *Arcs of the Concord.* Photo: Courtesy of Harold Linton.

psychology as it relates to human perception and human welfare, and an ability to problem-solve and respond creatively to design concepts with innovative ideas (Figures 14–16).

Over the years the definition of my role as a colorist within the built environment has broadened. As a historical note, the role of the color designer striving to complete the work of the architect did not really appear until the 1950s, shortly after the end of the Second World War. Historically, in Europe, it was industrial architecture that first made broad use of and supported the work of colorists. A little

11

*Figure 7.*  Photocopy collage of early influential ideas. Photo: Courtesy of Harold Linton.

later in the 1960s, the appearance of huge apartment complexes that tended to be somber and repetitive in appearance created the need to personalize these buildings with color. In France, beginning in the early 1970s, new multi-disciplinary teams including urban planners, architects and colorists came together to build new cities. It became evident that colorists had found themselves in a new, experimental territory and there was neither formal education nor school for color applied to architecture. Colorists and architects used traditional studio media for planning color for architecture, i.e., drawing tools, paint and paper to visualize

*Figure 8.* Site documentation of airport departure lounge. Photo: Courtesy of Harold Linton.

color, as well as different planning methods one could describe as fumbling and speculative that progressively became more concrete.

From the burgeoning corporate giants of the entertainment industry in the 1980s and 1990s, a new architecture of urban renewal and the ubiquitous urban mall, office buildings and office parks, restaurants, environmental graphic design and signage, the practical role of color in the landscape and design of our time is flourishing. The creative processes of architects, visual artists and designers, theoreticians, and those of a more analytical and rational method are together opening a new and essential chapter. The wealth of color design accomplishments

13

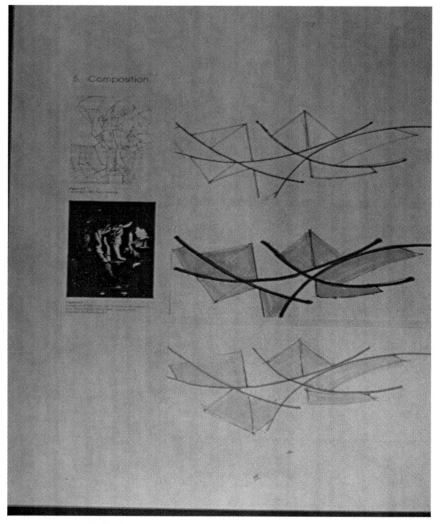

*Figure 9.* Studies in composition hand drawings. Photo: Courtesy of Harold Linton.

in the last half of the 20th century have engaged the public and sparked more than passing interest in color in architecture. A few examples of current methods of color design are included that reflect new trends in professional practice and design education, and beckons us to imagine what lies ahead: a future where the expectation will be for color throughout the built environment.

Actually, the world of visual data for the colorist continues to evolve just as technology advances and new industrial materials enter the marketplace. My understanding of new possibilities and processes supporting color science, technology, materials, and methods are all in a constant state of refinement and change. The language (visual data) of color and the integrally related science of

*Figure 10.*   Formation study in color marker. Photo: Courtesy of Harold Linton.

light (natural and artificial illumination) are intertwined subjects and important elements in planning the appearance of exterior and interior environmental color design. Knowledge of the unique characteristics of color and light and their associated vocabulary, science, materials, and artistic goals are critical in the daily work of color design planning and related communication with professionals across the fields of architecture and the allied design disciplines.

In architecture, one example of the colorist's work begins with the use of a light meter. Readings taken from stones native to the seascape along the Mediterranean coastline are used to chart a color palette indigenous to the site that can

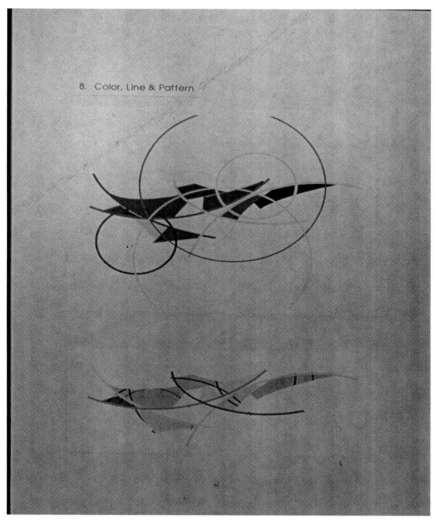

*Figure 11.* Computer analysis of geometry of construction. Photo: Courtesy of Harold Linton.

be applied to the creation of paint colors. The new paint colors can be applied, thereby helping to integrate the appearance of the building into the shoreline as opposed to allowing it to stand as it once did – a polychromatic eyesore contrasted against 18th century historic architecture.

Another example taken from the medical field includes the practice of surgeons wearing green operating gowns in order to arrest the visual effects of the "after-image" phenomenon while performing surgery. "After-image" is associated with the physiology of the eye. When the eye is exposed to bright hues for prolonged periods of time it reacts by producing the complimentary color in one's vision. It works similarly to shooting a camera's flashbulb off in front of one's eyes – the complimentary hue produced that follows one's vision is typically

16

*Figure 12.* Computer analysis of color and pattern. Photo: Courtesy of Harold Linton.

a violet and may last in one's vision for as long as 30 seconds obstructing or blurring one's view before fading from view. Arresting an after-image requires one to divert their gaze to a near complimentary hue to the subject hue. Therefore, surgeons often glance toward their green surgical clothing or sleeve or the green wall in the surgery suite to neutralize the after-image effect created from one's view of bright red human tissue. This practice extends their time and ability to focus on tasks requiring extraordinary acute observation, physical coordination, and dexterity.

17

*Figure 13.* Final constructed work installed in airport lounge. Photo: Courtesy of Harold Linton.

*Figure 14.* Colordesign3d.com. Author's web site demonstrates architectural color projects and concepts, publications, and fine arts. Photo: Courtesy of Harold Linton.

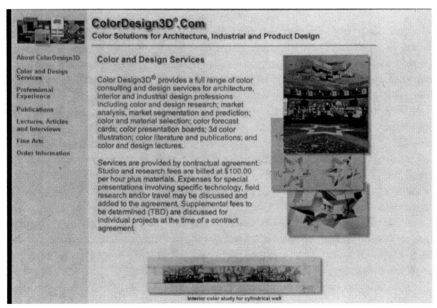

*Figure 15.* Colordesign3d.com. Author's projects in color design for architecture. Photo: Courtesy of Harold Linton.

*Figure 16.* *Design Ideas* catalog. Author's color concepts for metal, glass, and home products. Reprinted with permission of Design Ideas, Inc. Photo: Courtesy of Harold Linton.

And finally, the concept of "whiteness" and how human beings adjust psychologically to interior space under variations in interior light is a fascinating subject.
The concept of quantity and quality of interior illumination can vary greatly from
one type of environment to another. Human beings adapt to an extraordinary range
of high to low effects of light (quantity) and various temperatures of light from
warm to cool (quality) in consideration of the environment appearing to be light
hued and neutral white.

Practicing color design and exploring areas of research that have for decades
remained unchallenged have been a source of fertile ground for my work. My
research has been published in several books on color. *Color Forecasting: A
Survey of International Color Marketing*, published by Van Nostrand Reinhold
and Company in 1994 was written to help designers and artists understand the
selection process and industry practices in creating color palettes for industrial
materials and products. Membership in color forecasting organizations, i.e., The
Color Marketing Group, enables one to learn about the processes of color selection and product development. My background crossing fine arts and architecture
helps me to work across disciplines and contribute to a diverse set of projects and
problems affecting the visual outcome of our environment (Figures 17–20).

I am intrigued with the work, research, and methodology of historic and contemporary colorists. The recent work of Jean-Philippe Lenclos of Paris, France
has been influential to the profession of architecture and the color designer. His
firm, Atelier 3d Couleur, provides color consulting and design services to every
sector of the design community internationally. There are several formative examples as influential ideas from Atelier 3d Couleur that have contributed to my
overall development. Among these concepts of color design are the thorough
exploration of planning, of innumerable testing of ideas and recording one's
color experimentation in sketchbooks and journals to be used if necessary on
presentations for clients. A great understanding of the problem at hand is gained
through rehearsal and rephrasing of color composition, a point that both Lenclos
and Albers agree upon and have fostered in their students (Figure 21).

Another influential example is certainly the *Interaction of Color* by Josef
Albers published by Yale University Press in 1963. The treatise was composed
of original silkscreen color prints created largely by Albers and his students at
Yale. The accompanying text is poetic and reflective of the great power of Albers
in discussing color relationships and orchestrating visual analysis in search of
solutions to design problems.

During the 1940s and 1950s, Faber Birren did so much to consider the visual
circumstances of our environment and underscore the potential for collaborative
thinking between artist and architect. He strived to cultivate an understanding
through his writing that effective design solutions for the public welfare stem
from experts working collaboratively. Birren's groundbreaking work for industrial plants during the Second World War dramatically reduced accident rates in
the manufacturing sector of the country. Tom Porter's *Color for Architecture* is a
hallmark publication that threw back the curtain on the richest of all possibilities
of color in the built environment: the history of high cycle use of color in ar-

*Figure 17.* Author's work included in special edition of Metropolis Magazine devoted to the color forecasting industry. *Metropolis*, February/March 1999 issue, copyright 1999 Bellerophon Publications, Inc. Permission granted by Metropolis. www.metropolismag.com.

chitecture. His research has greatly contributed to my awareness of the power of collaboration between art and architecture. He has been a champion in engaging cross-disciplinary thinking, writing, and art/design practice.

My own beliefs have evolved over time to underscore visual planning (sketching, drawing, note-taking) as the cornerstone of effective communication for the development of color design concepts and ideas. The act of self-discovery is integral to the process of visual planning. New solutions to problems arise when one

*Figure 18.* "The Color Guard", article about color forecasters for industrial products. *Metropolis*, February/March 1999 issue, copyright 1999 Bellerophon Publications, Inc. Permission granted by *Metropolis*. www.metropolismag.com.

is able to see alternative schemes, and compare and analyze their deficiencies and advantages.

The connective tissue between my planning and presenting a project solution to the public, private sector, or an individual client has always been my ability to intuitively think through a project and unearth creative solutions that intrigue the public. Visual note taking for me eventually coalesces into large-format sketchbooks for each project. (Note: A few pages from the *Arcs of the Concord* project sketchbook figures 9–16 are included).

*Figure 19.* Color palettes for home products and industry change over the decades and are influenced by numerous factors such as cultural trends, environmental concerns, political changes, fashion news, and the entertainment field. *Metropolis*, February/March 1999 issue, copyright 1999 Bellerophon Publications, Inc. Permission granted by *Metropolis*. www.metropolismag.com.

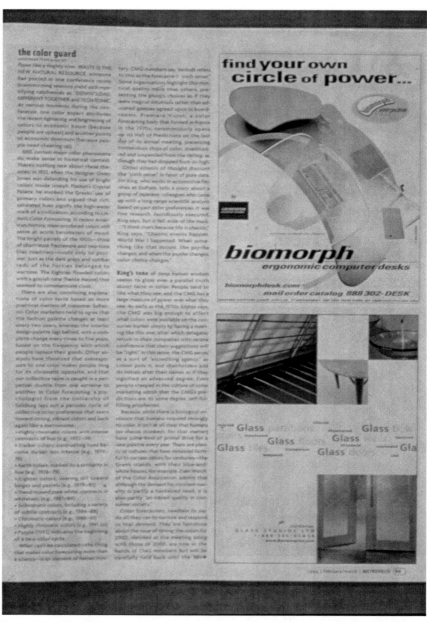

*Figure 20.   Color Forecasting: An International Survey of Color Marketing* by Harold Linton included data on color trends in automotive design and industrial sectors. Copyright © 1994 by Harold Linton. Reprinted with permission of John Wiley & Sons, Inc.

*Figure 21.* Installation of recent public commission entitled, *Fortunes of Nature*, Grand Valley State University, Grand Rapids, Michigan, 2001. Photo: Courtesy of Harold Linton.

I am consistent in research on topics in color and architecture that interest me and that I believe have interest in the public sector. A recent book that strays from the exclusive subject of color but relates to my interests in planning, graphic design, and architecture is *Portfolio Design Third Edition*. The surprise of this best-selling book for architecture and allied disciplines has been its translation into three foreign languages and its continued popularity in its third English edition (Figures 22 and 23).

As an author and educator (as well as artist and designer), I don't look at issues in isolation. I am more inclined to analyze multiple relationships and explore solutions broadly. Knowing the right questions to ask is as important as a particular skill in visualization. It takes time to learn how to cultivate one's ability to penetrate a subject and move through it to a comprehensive understanding of a problem. I don't think this is learned in school as much as we try to impart the process. During professional practice it becomes increasingly self-evident who has the ability to tackle projects in depth.

Being fluent in technology has been integral to moving fluidly back and forth through applying creative thinking to design projects. The impact of advanced technology on the design professions is dramatic and important. We communicate more efficiently with more precise tools about the nuance of color and light and their role in planning the built environment. Color design, in particular, benefits from advanced technology in computer software and hardware. Color organizing systems such as Munsell Color System (United States) and the Natural Color System (Sweden) afford colorists and design professionals ample opportunity to work with color problems and communicate findings directly to the client.

*Figure 22.    Portfolio Design Third Edition.* Cover. Copyright © 2003 by Harold Linton. Reprinted with permission of W. W. Norton and Company, Inc.

Munsell GretagMacbeth manufactures important tools such as controlled lighting chambers, color measuring instruments, color vision tests, industry standard guides, educational products, food color standards, atlases, and more tools that provide a continually refined method of measuring and communicating color solutions. All of this is to say that the colorist's ability to work across the communities of science, design, fine arts, and industry are well established by virtue of the tools available and their application to solving everyday problems in the field.

I believe that the profession of the color consultant today is a new and evolving field of serious academic preparation and industry specialization. As new color educational courses and degree programs make their way into higher education, the benefits of training in color design and communication becomes more prevalent throughout industry and manufacturing.

The challenge to educate the client, however, is a constant obstacle in our profession. Developing methods of introducing color design concepts and relevant ideas to clients is part of the challenge of my work. Perhaps there is a book lurking beneath this idea as one could possibly find material for writing about the most unique and unanticipated themes. Colorists like architects draw conversationally. Perhaps crayons at lunch are a playful yet casual way to open a dialog.

Other challenges are abound in our profession. Myriad interpretations of visual data/information can confuse and puzzle clients. The more clever one can find ways of simplifying and conveying information about a problem to the client, the

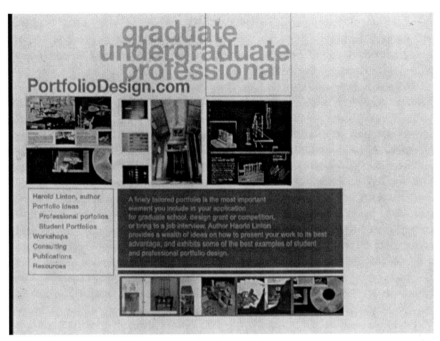

*Figure 23.* Portfoliodesign.com. Author's web site devoted to helping students organize their work into well-design professional presentations. Photo: Courtesy of Harold Linton.

better able they are to walk arm in arm toward discovering solutions. For the client to understand the over-arching project in all of its manifestations is a goal worthy of the designer's creative energy and imagination. It's called client education.

At the root of the profession and being a teacher, nothing is more important than research and education. Success in education is certainly measured in different terms. It does relate in part to cultivating a readership. My work in color and design has found an audience in the profession of architecture. I have developed a relatively strong audience among students of architecture and allied design disciplines. My research in color as it relates to forecasting palettes for industry has helped designers and lay people better understand the depth and breadth of planning that occurs in color design for mass markets. Perhaps the profession has benefited by having new resources available for the public and industry that can be easily accessed as a source of information. The experiment to create a new MA degree program in Color and Design at the University of Art and Design (UIAH) Helsinki, Finland was a milestone in my professional experience. Although the program was short-lived over two years due in part to difficulty in finding an appropriately prepared student body, the exposure I received to the state of the profession of color design and consulting in Europe was irreplaceable and has yielded numerous benefits.

My work in the field of visual communications especially in architecture and architectural illustration has been received well in collaboration with a groundbreaking academic program in higher education that I helped to create and launch in the 1990s entitled, Bachelor of Fine Arts in Architectural Illustration, at Lawrence Technological University, Southfield, Michigan. Since then, the program has been renamed, *Imaging*, with respect to a sizable curriculum component of digital illustration courses integrated into the program.

It has also been gratifying to see *Portfolio Design Third Edition* climb to become a popular and useful professional reference, especially used by students and young professionals in architecture and related design fields. The content of this project involved creating a roadmap with supporting documentation of the possible approaches to designing effective graphic presentations of one's own work in architecture. First published in 1997 by W.W. Norton, New York, New York, *Portfolio Design* has been translated into three foreign languages: Spanish, Korean, and Chinese (2006) (Figures 22 and 23). Currently, my research delves into color consulting for industry and architecture that involves research in material science, new product line development, and color design workshops. I am also exploring concepts in graphic design for professional presentations including discussion of the interface of advanced technology with graphic design and multimedia.

In closing, I would suggest to those in education who wish to employ color content in their own disciplines, no matter how diverse the subject content may be, one of the best approaches to integrating color and design into a curriculum is through a breadth of context. Howard Gardner's seminal work on eight areas of intelligence tells us, as educators, students learn in different ways and through different experiences. Color imbedded in the art curriculum is not necessarily the only place to integrate art and design content. Why do students naturally know far more about the attributes of subtractive mixing (paint and dyes) than additive mixing (light and illumination)? Probably because they have had many more opportunities to work with paints and pigments throughout their education than they have been able to work with stage lights, television monitors, and illumination technology. Therefore, the practical opportunity to broaden a program of instruction is to better integrate (color) subject matter in multiple disciplines so it becomes part of a broader educational experience. Growing a visually literate culture requires planning and a strategy for implementation – both of which are exciting and worthwhile challenges.

## REFERENCES

Albers, J. (1963). *The interaction of color*. New Haven: Yale University Press.
Birren, F. (1950). *Color psychology and color therapy*. Citadel Press.
Linton, H. (1985). *Color model environments: Color and light in three-dimensional design*. New York: Van Nostrand Reinhold.
Linton, H. (1986). *Harold Linton: Paintings 1976–1986*. Cataloguing-in-Publication Data (Exhibition Catalog), Muskegon, Michigan.
Linton, H. (1989). *Color in architectural illustration*. New York: Van Nostrand Reinhold.
Linton, H. (1991a). *Color consulting: A survey of international color design*. New York: Van Nostrand Reinhold.
Linton, H. (1991b). *Architectural sketching in marker*. New York: Van Nostrand Reinhold.
Linton, H. (1993). *Sketching the concept: Perspective illustration for architects, designers & artists*. New York: Design Press/McGraw-Hill.

Linton, H. (1994). *Color forecasting: A survey of international color marketing.* New York: Van Nostrand Reinhold.

Linton, H. (1996). *Portfolio design,* 1st Edition. New York: W. W. Norton & Company.

Linton, H. (1999). *Color in architecture: Design methods for buildings, interiors, and urban spaces.* New York: McGraw-Hill Professional Books.

Linton, H. (2000a). *Portfolio design,* 2nd edition. New York: W. W. Norton & Company.

Linton, H. (2000b). *Diseno de portfolios.* Barcelona: Gustavo Gili S.A.

Linton, H. (2003). *Portfolio design,* 2nd edition. Seoul: Kimoondang Publishing Corporation.

Linton, H. (2004a). *Portfolio design,* 3rd edition. New York: W. W. Norton and Company.

Linton, H. (2004b). *Marketing your architecture firm.* New York: W. W. Norton & Company.

Linton, H. (2004c). *Urban reflections: Illustrated world cities.* Melbourne: Images Publishing Pty., Ltd.

Porter, T. and Mikellides, B. (1976). *Color for architecture.* New York: Van Nostrand Reinhold.

DAVID HYERLE

# CHAPTER 2
# BEYOND THE WALL OF TEXT: THINKING MAPS®
# AS A UNIVERSAL VISUAL LANGUAGE FOR
# TRANSFORMING HOW WE SEE KNOWLEDGE,
# THINKING AND LEARNING

Learners construct knowledge as they build cognitive maps for organizing and interpreting new information. Effective teachers help students make such maps by drawing connections among different concepts and between new ideas and learners' prior experience

Linda Darling-Hammond, *The Right to Learn* (1997, p. 74)

Neuroscientists tell us that the brain organizes information in networks and maps. What better way to teach students to think and organize and express their ideas than to use the very same method that the brain uses.

Pat Wolfe, Foreword, *Student Successes with Thinking Maps* (2004, p. xi)

## A BREAKTHROUGH IN EDUCATION?

Have you noticed that over the decades there have been no major breakthroughs in the practice of teaching and learning? Almost daily now, we hear of breakthroughs such as hybrid cars, medical cures for a range of diseases, new farming techniques, micro-credit banking for growing economies in developing countries, nanotechnology implants, search engines such as Google and sites that facilitate social networking such as *myspace*, *facebook* and *youtube*. There are also discoveries of the multiple dimensions beyond three in the "outer space" of the stars and of the complex circuitry of the "inner space" of our brains. So why are there few if any breakthroughs in education? I believe that this is because so few educators, researchers, and foundations funding innovation are focused on communication between teachers and learners, and how information and knowledge is *represented* by teachers and students in order to transform learning. As investigated in this writing, the lack of innovation is directly related to the paradigm of linearity: knowledge is transmitted through linear strings of words and numbers, in spoken or written forms. As offered below through the Thinking Maps language, one pathway to a significant breakthrough in teaching and learning may come when

*J.E. Pedersen and K.D. Finson (eds.), Visual Data*, 31–49.

educators deeply consider the insights offered by Linda Darling Hammond and Pat Wolfe: the brain maps and networks information and that effective teachers need to explicitly support students' minds as they create cognitive maps in order to learn.

Unfortunately, the great "breakthrough" expectation of the past generation since the advent of the World Wide Web and personal computers has been the hope of "networking" technology, somehow elevating students' thinking and learning into a qualitatively new realm. Yet, computers in classrooms, like the promise of other teaching machines of the past, have brought a quantitative over-load of processed content and unlimited unprocessed content, but no significant, direct improvements in students' abilities to process and evaluate information or how to think through the complexity of problems that come with living in the 21st century. As a matter of fact, most educators would probably agree with this oddly contradictory notion: many of our multi-tasking children cannot stay focused and independently think through multi-step problems, and thus easily become bored by school unless they are "entertained."

Alas, education, like philosophy, may not be amenable to breaking news on the cable channels, unless it is the *failure* of educators to transform teaching and learning in this new century. The solutions offered to the problem of "failed" schools deal with everything but close scrutiny to the core dynamics of teaching-learning that remain mired in a strange integration of disproved "old school" behaviorist models and idiosyncratic "new school" progressive teaching tech-niques. Many educators, concerned political and business leaders, educational entrepreneurs, and even parents in search of solutions have all but given up on a belief that there could be a breakthrough in how we understand the teaching-learning processes and thus have given up the search for tools for transforming how we teach and learn. Instead, many folks turn to a range of financially draining and unproven "solutions" that have very little to do with the fundamental relation-ships of *how* learners learn and teachers teach. These solutions include "smaller schools," content knowledge teaching and assessments via computers, isolated educational "heroes" who miraculously transform their own classroom or school, charter or private voucher systems, privately run schools, or worse, the growing business of after school test taking programs that show but a momentary blip in test scores. Some in the business world believe the answer lies in making schools work as businesses, led in part by "data-driven" decision making. Instructionally, in the rush to raise test scores, many schools also turn to one-shot workshops on how to implement "best practices" responding to specific testable items. Over the past few years we see that federal accountability measures offering negative reinforcements back educational teachers and administrators into a blind alley of test item analysis. This is a sad state of affairs.

It must be said that from the perspective of the short stretch of "modern" history, we are just now getting started in answering this question. We may be in a methodical climb toward a cumulative understanding of the processes of learning that may slowly break through existing barriers. In the United States, we only began offering "adequate" education to more than the elite in our society

just a few generations ago. Those who could learn and/or those who were priv-
ileged enough to be given a formal education were the chosen few. Only in the
last few generations have we even attempted to fully educate *all* girls, children
of color, those in poverty, and those with diverse and/or debilitating emotional
and cognitive needs. But there is only halting progress and much backsliding as
we try to "close the gap" between the financial haves and have-nots. Of course,
some still don't have even an "adequate" learning environment. Jonathan Kozol
well documents that the financial-resource inequities bound up in our class-based
society, often divided by race and racism, still exists as schools are presently re-
segregating. Given the needs of those at the bottom of the equity-resource ladder,
and those immigrants needing to learn more than basic literacy, I believe we need
to move with urgency *and* insight.

Certainly there have been many significant changes in the modern era of
education in the United States: cooperative learning, process writing, social-
emotional learning, a shift away from a singular Intelligence Quotient to Howard
Gardner's theory of "multiple intelligences." Most recently there is great interest
in the neurosciences and translations of brain research into practice. Certainly
new brain research may offer a scientific basis for rethinking teaching and learning. But I ask: why haven't there been any breakthroughs in *directly* improving
learning by all students? Maybe this is because, as Neil Postman once defined
it, education is basically a *conserving* activity, keeping roughly thirty years behind what researchers have proven would make a difference in classrooms. But
this is no longer acceptable in an accelerating, "flat world" global community,
as described by Thomas Friedman, wherein we have moved away from the
need for the conveyor belt *manufacturing mind* to the thinking, problem-solving,
information-knowledge creation, *networking mind*.

Are there no breakthroughs to be had? Yes. But there are significant barriers
in *how we think* and represent information and knowledge that prevent us from
seeing how to transform teaching and learning. What could be the barrier to a
breakthrough in learning?

### THE LINEAR "WALL OF TEXT" AS THE BARRIER

Let's consider that there is a barrier that is limiting our perceptions of how
knowledge looks – or more precisely, in our way of *representing* knowledge and
thinking – that is preventing a breakthrough in transforming how we actually see
learning. Ironically, this barrier is deeply and invisibly grounded in what also
has been the greatest strength of our "advanced," literate, technological society:
literacy has been defined almost exclusively by what I call the linear *Wall of Text*.
I first woke up to this dilemma in the mid 1980s when reading this passage by
Novak and Gowin:

> Written and spoken messages are necessarily linear sequences of concepts
> and propositions. In contrast, knowledge is stored in our minds in a kind of
> hierarchical or holographic structure. (Novak and Gowin; 1984, p. 15)

The *Wall of Text* is the strictly linear representation of information and knowledge as found in textbooks – and from teachers' presentation in verbal and written form – of information and concepts. Teachers' *representations* of knowledge as linear and thus students' efforts at the generation of spoken and written lines of texts are radically limiting teaching, learning, assessment and most damaging of all, thinking. This barrier frames each of us like blinders on racehorses galloping forward to the finish line. Our wider view beyond the blinders and our peripheral vision, is limited by this: The linear Wall of Text as the honored and nearly exclusive way of representing our thinking in the learning process unnecessarily defines our fundamental, holistic, differentiated patterns of thinking and the nonlinear concepts we are learning into the singular, highly routinized sequential forms of communication we call speaking and writing and numerating.

This is a challenge that may make most of us who are educators and academics, who have lived by the text, quite uneasy. It is downright *heretical* to those who believe that *text* as we know it is the apex, the penultimate representation system of the human mind. Text – the page and the spoken word – have been traditionally understood as *sacred*.

Let me make this easier to swallow. What is suggested here is *not* to throw out the Wall of Text, but to seek to find ways to represent the nonlinear thinking that is richly embedded and hidden between the lines of text, to see visual representations as dynamically living side by side text, conceptual patterns buried within text, and to offer rigorous tools for surfacing these nonlinear ideas on a moment to moment basis in classrooms. There are many who have made this point that we must move beyond our extreme focus on linear thinking in education and business, including those who have given us tools and visions for new ways of seeing the world, such as Peter Senge, Tony Buzan, Margaret Wheatley, Frijof Capra and David Bohm. Edward Tufte, whose extensive writings on visual representations, has even fully analyzed the use of PowerPoint and reveals the inherent mind numbing bulleted linearity upon which this "presentation" software rests as it is used in classrooms to boardrooms some 15,000 times every day (Tufte, 2006). The problem clearly stated by these leaders and now brain researchers is that we as human beings *do not think in text*: our brains and mind think in nonlinear networks of information. Our brain-body system also, by most guestimates offered by neuroscientists, receives 75–90% of its information visually through our eyes. The brain "maps" information, *not* text blocks. This information calls out for visual mapping of information that is congruent with thinking processes. It is now clear that in the information overload, high-technology, knowledge-creation landscape of the 21st century, educators and business leaders must support our students in moving *from* seeing knowledge as bound by static text *to* seeing knowledge as also dynamic and richly patterned points of visual information in map form.

The difficulty, at least in the daily life of classrooms and the institutions of schooling and the workplace, has been in bringing forth a practical, theory rich, elegant model for what nonlinear thinking would *look like* for teachers, students and administrators from pre-kindergarten to college and into the workplace. Thinking

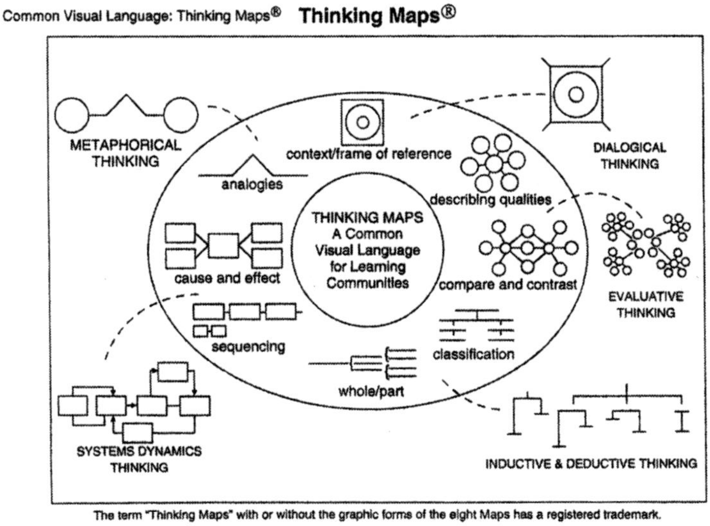

Common Visual Language: Thinking Maps® **Thinking Maps®**

The term "Thinking Maps" with or without the graphic forms of the eight Maps has a registered trademark.

*Figure 1.* Thinking Maps Language.

Maps, a visual language for learning, is one pathway for opening the mindset to a new way of seeing. For as David Bohm has written:

> If we could learn to see thought actually producing presentations from representations, we would no longer be fooled by it. (Bohm, 1983, p. 69)

## A HISTORY OF THINKING MAPS AS A LANGUAGE OF VISUAL TOOLS

Below we will look at examples of such a proven model in schools, a common language of visual-spatial-verbal tools called *Thinking Maps*, as a representation system supporting high quality thinking, communication in the classroom, interpretation of text and, importantly, the dynamic relationship between and among teachers and learners. Thinking Maps is a practical and theory-embedded language of eight *interdependent*, dynamic graphics based on, respectively, eight fundamental cognitive processes.

When I first conceived of this language in 1986, I knew it was emerging from a wide array work in the field by others and supported by many researchers and practitioners who had laid the groundwork for this kind of language. I believed then that it was a critical starting point and leverage point for learners and teachers alike in creating a bridge between the complex patterning of our unconscious brain structures to the conscious processes of our minds making sense of the world around us. This has proven to be the case over the past fifteen years as these tools have been implemented successfully in 5,000 schools where the whole faculty has gone through in depth professional development (Hyerle, 2004).

From what context and frame of reference did this language of Thinking Maps emerge? As a novice teacher, I was caught up in an educational movement – the "thinking skills" movement – that rose in the mid-seventies to the late eighties and then was incorporated into many progressive teaching practices since that time in the United States, and to a lesser degree internationally. That was a time when "higher order" thinking as described by Benjamin Bloom's Taxonomy of Educational Objectives (Bloom, 1956) was beginning to deeply influence education. Higher-order questioning and the explicit facilitation of thinking was *the rage*. This sounds odd, of course, since wouldn't one consider "thinking" and the facilitation of thinking to be foundational to the learning-teaching processes of the late twentieth century as our society moved into the information age? I believe that this movement towards a "thinking process" approach to teaching, learning, and assessment was the first sustained, theoretically deep challenge to the dominant view of learning based on the principles of behaviorism and the strict western, logical deductive mindset. The movement toward the explicit "teaching for, of, and about thinking" was well articulated and practiced by many educational leaders and classroom teachers at the time. Art Costa, a leader among many in the field, guided many of us at that time and into the present to see that the direct coaching of thinking skills and Habits of Mind was essential to bringing about a new paradigm of learning, teaching, and leadership. (For the cumulative knowledge and comprehensive documentation of the thinking skills movement, see Developing Minds, edited by Art Costa (ASCD: 1985, 1991, 2000).)

By 1986, after leaving the classroom and working for several years leading professional development in schools based on a range of thinking skills approaches, I was asked to write a workbook for middle school students that would enable them to explicitly learn fundamental thinking skills and to transfer them across all disciplines. I was then using a model of six thinking skills initially developed by Dr. Albert Upton, of Whittier College in California. A graduate student of Upton's, Richard Samson, had modified this fundamental model reflecting the interplay of thought and language, Dr. Richard Samson. The theoretical foundation and the core thinking processes identified were central to my development of Thinking Maps (Upton, 1960; Upton and Samson, 1961). Their work described in detail how these fundamental processes of thinking were not merely "lower order" cognitive processes, but when used interdependently and at different levels of complexity through language, they became the essence of and pathway to higher orders of thinking.

Though not central to his work, Upton did include several traditional "diagrams" that he used to link thought and language: tree diagrams for hierarchical classification, flow charts for sequencing, and brace maps for showing physical parts of whole objects. This is where the model of Thinking Maps crystallized for me and I had a glimmer of a language for learning based on the explicit mapping of cognitive patterns unique and universal to human experience. I asked myself, "What would it look like to link each fundamental cognitive process to a dynamic visual tool?" I could see that a relatively few visual representations could be used broadly as unifying representations of thinking with written forms ... as a visual language that was *congruent* with thinking patterns that virtually *embodied* cognitive processes. I surmised, that if thinking occurred in patterns, and these patterns ranged from hierarchies to causal loops to comparatives, don't we need tools that explicitly represent different types of thinking? Text alone would not do.

I also sensed that individuals within a community of learners could co-construct and collectively show their evolving thinking processes from a blank page – not only in spoken or written text – but also as interdependent *visual patterns*. As David Bohm has written, "many worlds are possible – it all depends on representation, especially the collective representation. To make a 'world' takes more than one person, and therefore the collective representation is the key ..." (Bohm, 1983, p. 69). I thought, we don't need a few disconnected graphics, we need a language of interdependent visual tools that would work together as a language for personal, interpersonal, and collective thinking across cultures. I soon realized that it was crucial to have each unique graphic primitive look and expand in a way that was most congruent with the respective definitions of each fundamental thinking process. The visuals had to be dynamic thus mimicking the neural networking actions of the brain and mind, and that they needed be used together as we unconsciously unite our isolated thinking processes into holistic forms. In *Expand Your Thinking* (Hyerle, 1989) I brought forward, tentatively, a universal visual language for thinking of cognitive maps that could be used together for improving thinking, learning, and communication.

The first full expression of the work was published in a training guide for teachers, *Designs for Thinking Connectively* (Hyerle, 1989). Thinking Maps was therein described as a common visual language of eight interrelated cognitive skills, each with a clear definition and terminology, and most importantly, each with a graphic primitive that was congruent with the process for ease of use, expansion, and communication. The *graphic primitive* for each map is the basic form from which each map may grow in an organic way, from simple to complex, while sustaining the integrity of the graphic, much like iterative patterns of leaves growing on a tree from year to year. For example, the graphic primitive for a Flow Map consists of a rectangle and an arrow. From this starting point for mapping a sequence, the Flow Map may expand in any direction – with smaller substage boxes – with an infinite number of boxes and configurations of relationships. Parallel flows, feedback loops, and even Flow Maps within more expansive sequences may be represented. This language of eight graphic primitives offered teachers and students across schools and schools systems a language for working and thinking collaboratively in linear and nonlinear ways, with simple to complex problems. Students would become independent thinkers who could adapt the maps to their own unique, developing cognitive abilities, thus enabling them to transfer their thinking across disciplines and to the fundamentals of reading comprehension, writing processing, and mathematical problem solving. Having a visual representation of thinking, teachers would also have an additional way to access and *assess* not just *what* students were thinking, but *how* they were thinking.

## Graphic Primitives and Definitions

| primitives | Thinking Maps and the Frame | expanded map: |
|---|---|---|
| | The Circle Map is used for seeking context. This tool enables students to generate relevant information about a topic as represented in the center of the circle. This map is often used for brainstorming. | |
| | The Bubble Map is designed for the process of describing attributes. This map is used to identify character traits (language arts), cultural traits (social studies), properties (sciences), or attributes (mathematics). | |
| | The Double Bubble Map is used for comparing and contrasting two things, such as characters in a story, two historical figures, or two social systems. It is also used for prioritizing which information is most important within a comparison. | |
| | The Tree Map enables students to do both inductive and deductive classification. Students learn to create general concepts, (main) ideas, or categories headings at the top of the tree, and supporting ideas and specific details in the branches below. | |
| | The Brace Map is used for identifying the part-whole, physical relationships of an object. By representing whole-part and part-subpart relationships, this map supports students' spatial reasoning and for understanding how to determine physical boundaries. | |
| | The Flow Map is based on the use of flowcharts. It is used by students for showing sequences, order, timelines, cycles, actions, steps, and directions. This map also focuses students on seeing the relationships between stages and substages of events. | |
| | The Multi-Flow Map is a tool for seeking causes of events and the effects. The map expands when showing historical causes and for predicting future events and outcomes. In its most complex form, it expands to show the interrelationships of feedback effects in a dynamic system. | |
| | The Bridge Map provides a visual pathway for creating and interpreting analogies. Beyond the use of this map for solving analogies on standardized tests, this map is used for developing analogical reasoning and metaphorical concepts for deeper content learning. | |

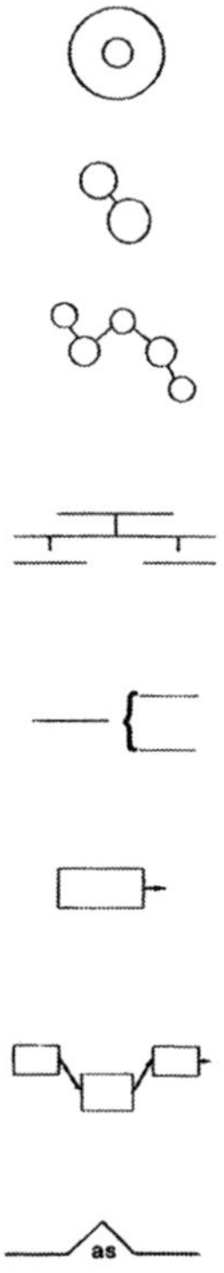

**The Frame**

The "metacognitive" Frame is not one of the eight Thinking Maps. It may be drawn around any of the maps at any time as a "meta-tool" for identifying and sharing one's frame of reference for the information found within one of the Thinking Maps. These frames include personal histories, culture, belief systems, and influences such as peer groups and the media.

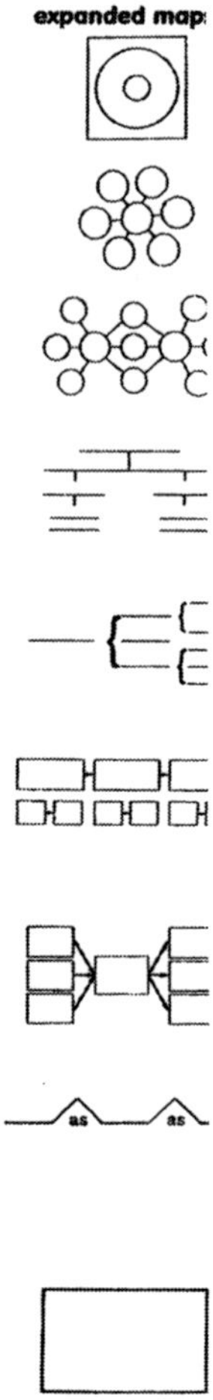

*Figure 2.* Thinking Maps® graphic primitives and definitions.

## THINKING MAPS AS A SYNTHESIS OF VISUAL TOOLS

I was certainly aware during the development of the Thinking Maps language that it was emerging from a range of cognitive science research, but also from the vast array of visual tools used over the previous decades. Upon first look, many times educators and researchers have misconstrued the Thinking Maps language as merely a simplistic variant of Tony Buzan's Mindmapping®, or a set of isolated "graphic organizers" for duplication, or just as an interesting array of semantic maps. This is understandable since the field of visual tools had not been well defined. My own wide experimentation with visual tools and soft-

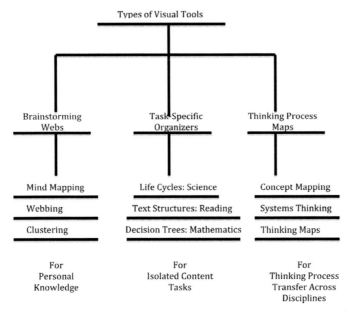

*Figure 3.* Types of visual tools.

ware programs has been exciting and at times overwhelming as I have worked with many different kinds of tools based on different theoretical frames, such as: Mindmapping®, graphic organizers, flow charting and hierarchical trees, causal loop systems thinking, concept mapping, inductive towers, Total Quality tools, and even traditional forms such Euler Circles and Venn diagrams.

I embraced these different forms, but also wanted to make sense of the variety and purposes of each. In my literature review for my dissertation (Hyerle, 1993) I offered background on the range of visual representations and focused on the purposeful use of each. A comprehensive revision of this book with up to date research and practical guidance in how to implement and use visual tools is available in *Visual Tools for Transforming Information into Knowledge* (Hyerle, 2009, in press). I informally grouped these different types of tools under the conceptual banner "visual tools" and identified three basic categories (see Figure 3).

My dissertation was later published in a refined form by the "Association for Supervision and Curriculum Development" and distributed to the 115,000 members as *Visual Tools for Constructing Knowledge* (Hyerle, 1996). In this book, I offered a detailed introduction and analysis of these different visual tools, noting the strengths and limitations of each in education and how each visually represented information and different theories about the structure of knowledge: *brainstorming webs*, *task-specific organizers*, and *thinking process maps*.

*Brainstorming webs* represent creative, generative, associative construction of knowledge. These tools are highly dynamic, holistic, often begun from the center of a blank page, idiosyncratic, and used for generative thinking. Tony Buzan's development of Mindmapping® technique (Buzan, 2003) was central to informing the development of different visual brainstorming tools.

*Task-specific organizers* (often called "graphic organizers") often reflect a more analytic, deductive view of the construction of knowledge. These tools are relatively static graphics used for isolated content or process learning tasks. They often show up as blackline masters in published programs which students are asked to fill in. Graphic organizers support a formal scaffolding of content learning and sometimes thinking processes.

*Thinking process maps* are based on the direct facilitation of conceptual learning and common patterns of thinking. These tools are often theoretically rich, grounded in fundamental conceptual-cognitive processes and often lead to visual languages such as concept mapping developed by Novak and Gowin based on hierarchical knowledge and "systems thinking" diagrams based on a "causal feedback" view of knowledge.

The most influential research and practice in the field came from the works of Tony Buzan (Mindmapping), Novak and Gowin (concept mapping), and Peter Senge and the late Barry Richmond (causal loop systems thinking and STELLA Software). This is because even though each of these approaches defines "thinking" differently, each one of these methods is theoretically strong, perceives the learner as in charge of the construction of the visual map, and attempts to scaffold conceptual learning rather than prescribed structures of "given" information. Each of these approaches is rigorous in that each animates a visual language based on graphic primitives that are easy to use but that then evolve toward complexity as learners become more fluent with the tools. The learning community such as a school or business then honors the deeper facilitation of individual and collective thinking over time. It is now clear that there are several principles of Thinking Maps as a language that derive from these leaders in the field.

## BREAKTHROUGHS IN SCHOOLS

Since 1990, a small group of educators came together with me to focus on implementing Thinking Maps across whole schools and school systems. The model of implementation focused on training all teachers and administrators in the use of this language for improving student learning, teacher performance, and tangentially, for collaborative leadership. The work has been fully documented in a wide-ranging book with chapters by sixteen different authors, *Student Successes with Thinking Maps: School Based Research, Results, and Models for Achievement Using Visual Tools* (Hyerle, 2004). The results show the success of students across every discipline and at the elementary, middle, high school and college levels. The Thinking Maps have been used across schools in England and in the United States, including in large city districts such as New York City, which serves students representing close to 150 different languages and dialects. The work has also had extensive piloting in Singapore (with Chinese, Malayan, and Indian cultures mixing with a traditional English pedagogy) and with smaller pilots in Japan,

Mexico, and New Zealand. Teachers across these various learning communities have expressed that there was nothing counterintuitive about the use of the maps across these cultures and languages, as the cognitive skills are not grounded solely in language or a particular culture, but in the processes we as humans use every day around the world for communicating, solving problems and survival.

There are endless examples and documented results of Thinking Maps – from kindergarten to college to school leadership, from literacy development to mathematical and scientific problem-solving – that can be found in the resource materials used for training teachers: *Thinking Maps: A Language for Learning* (Hyerle & Yeager, 2007), and in the research offered at the nonprofit foundation, *Thinking Foundation* (www.thinkingfoundation.org). Beyond direct impact on reading comprehension and writing process, two areas that are beginning to show great promise and significant results are in the fields of special education and second language acquisition. It is clear from the qualitative and quantitative results that the Thinking Maps, because they are based in fundamental cognitive patterns and are visually accessible by all students, provide scaffolding for students with language disabilities as well as a bridge between primary and secondary languages.

## PRINCIPLES GROUNDING THINKING MAPS AS LANGUAGE

Every language across the disciplines – such as English, numerical systems, musical notation, and integrated languages such as the table of the elements in science, have a few common elements: consistent graphic primitives that are flexibly used in order to develop simple to complex ideas and communication in a certain "language" community. Thinking Maps is a meta-language for thinking that works across each of these languages and enables teachers and learners to communicate patterns of thinking.

There are at least five principles of Thinking Maps that have surfaced as we work in schools that reveal the transformational use of these tools:

1. there are a relatively few, universal cognitive structures;
2. visual patterns need to be congruent with these cognitive structures;
3. graphic primitives enable definition and expansion of each map;
4. the visual representation supports the integration of content and process through form;
5. the knowledge mapped out is always influenced by the map maker's frame of reference.

These are abstract principles that are discussed below, so using two examples from the field will support bringing these concepts down to earth. The first example has been previously published in *Student Successes with Thinking Maps* (Hyerle, 2004) and shows how students in a first grade class initially responded to their teacher who was asking them comprehension questions about a story they had read, "How Leo Learned to be King." A full analysis of this class-

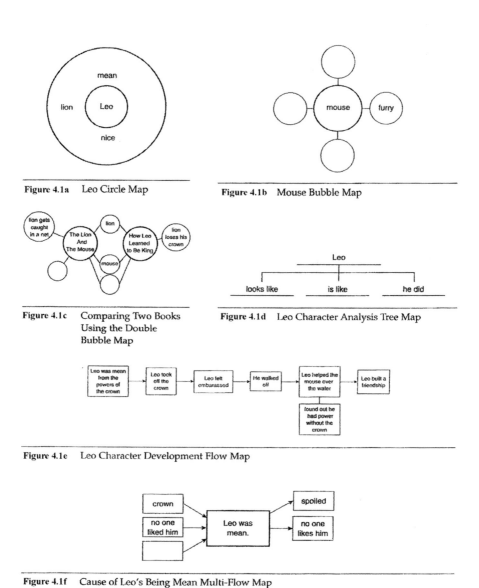

Figure 4.1a    Leo Circle Map

Figure 4.1b    Mouse Bubble Map

Figure 4.1c    Comparing Two Books Using the Double Bubble Map

Figure 4.1d    Leo Character Analysis Tree Map

Figure 4.1e    Leo Character Development Flow Map

Figure 4.1f    Cause of Leo's Being Mean Multi-Flow Map

Figure 4.1g    Bridging Qualities of Characters Across Text

*Figure 4.*    Thinking Maps® for reading comprehension.

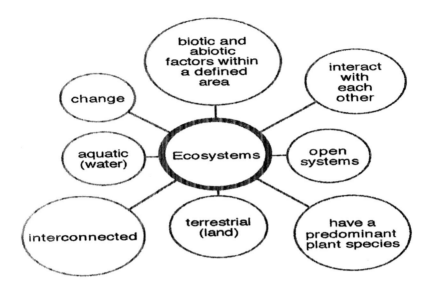

*Figure 5a.*

room activity and the video clips of the classroom interactions may be viewed at www.thinkingfoundation.org.

As you scan the different maps in Figure 4, please note that they were written on the white board by the teacher and transposed here for clarity. Here is the context: After the students read the book about how a lion turned mean as he gained power as the King, the class talked about the text, and the teacher, Ms. Crystal Smith, asked her students this question: "How would you organize your thinking about this book?" Seven of the eight maps were generated by the students to show how they were thinking and organizing their ideas: context information about Leo (4.a); describing the mouse (4.b); comparing the book to another book (4.c); categorizing character analysis information from the text (4.d); a sequential flow of how Leo developed as the story progressed (4.e); what caused Leo to become so mean as a king (4.f); and bridging by analogy from one story to a common quality of two characters (4.g). After the teacher asked for just a few bits of information in map form from the students, she asked that they each go back to their desks and choose which map or maps helped them the most in understanding the story, and to create a map independently and begin writing from their map about the story.

A second sample of student work is an array of Thinking Maps generated using Thinking Maps Software by an eleventh student at Niles North High School, a suburban school outside of Chicago. Jacki Naughton, a biology teacher at the school, taught all of her students how to use Thinking Maps for scientific problem solving, but also for note taking. The students learned how to work through the Wall of Text by mapping out key concepts as they studied a typical high school

43

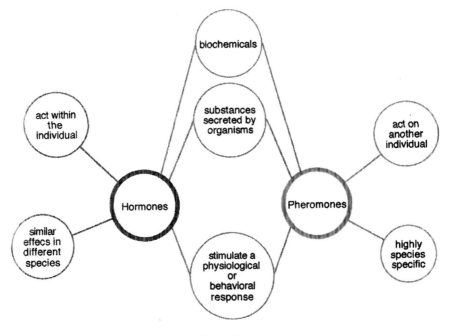

*Figure 5b.*

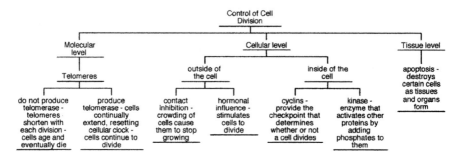

*Figure 5c.*

textbook. The maps shown here in Figures 5a–d are just five of over 40 Thinking Maps created during the term by this student using Thinking Maps Software as she read the text: properties of an ecosystem (5.a); comparison of hormones and pheromones (5.b); categories of control of cell division (5.c); the causes and effects of telomere response (5.d). This student had become so fluent with all of the Thinking Maps that she could face a complex text and seek the essential conceptual patterns of content knowledge being delivered by the textbook author.

Given these two examples – one by a group of novice map users from first grade reading a fictional story and one by an expert, individual student from the eleventh grade – what can we understand in the way of the five principles noted above that reveal Thinking Maps as a language for learning?

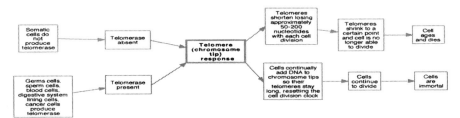

*Figure 5d.*

Principle 1: There are universal cognitive processes. Though controversial, I have come to believe over the past twenty years of practice and research in different parts of the world, that there exist uniquely human, universal cognitive processes[1] that are a primary foundation for learning and language development. As in the examples, the map links thinking and language use at the deepest level. Every human categorizes information, but will categorize information *differently* depending upon cultural frames of reference and language. In the two examples above we see that these cognitive patterns *transfer* across the study of literature and in the sciences, across age levels and across informal and formal category structures. The first graders could generative informal categories using a Tree Map for grouping ideas about a character, and the eleventh grade student uses the same map to formally define categories about the control of cell divisions. The cognitive skill of categorization – just as we have seen with the other seven processes – is unconsciously at work in the human mind. Importantly, as shown quite well in both examples, the cognitive skills are also used interdependently when we are interpreting and analyzing information and transforming linear text structures into knowledge.

Principle 2: Visual Patterns are Congruent with Thinking Processes. Visual maps representing processes are congruent across a range of these linear and holistic cognitive patterns. As shown in the two examples, with the exception of sequencing, the cognitive processes that animate the Thinking Maps are not grounded in linear, sequential thinking. As discussed above, written and spoken forms of language, though complex and elegant, communicate nonlinear forms of thinking in strictly linear terms. In unison with Thinking Maps, clarity of communication of thinking patterns and content knowledge is enhanced. For example, when an author is writing about categories in the animal kingdom, a hierarchical

---

[1] As a challenge to this belief in cognitive universals, I would suggest a reading of Richard Nisbett's "The Geography of Thought." He states that he once held the belief that there are common thinking processes across cultures, and then was convinced by research that this was not the case. Yet, I believe that this issue is more a matter of definition of "thinking" because Nisbett goes on to reveal, chapter after chapter, that every culture classifies information, makes comparisons, sequences, and understands causality – *but in different ways*. The Thinking Maps model is based on this assumption: every human being thinks using these universal processes and that these processes emerge and are represented in different ways within the context of specific cultures and languages. Because we all have common cognitive processes, any human being has the capacity to learn, to learn a second language and to adapt in a new culture. The Thinking Maps enables any learner from any culture to map their own patterns from universal cognitive primitives.

tree map more clearly represents the complexity of the category structure and thinking than paragraph after paragraph of formal prose attempting to describe category structures. In the examples shown, the students were easily able to show what they know about the comparisons, cause-effect reasoning, and descriptors and are drawn from across the linear content text. Thinking Maps offer an additional, more congruent representation of different forms and patterns of thinking than linear writing, also unveiling the hidden conceptual structures within written and spoken language. Thus, Thinking Maps create a rich dynamic between the written code and the cognitive code, thus enhancing a deeper comprehension of concepts in text.

Principle 3: Graphic Primitives for each Map. Thinking Maps begin with simple, unique graphic primitives and expand, overlap and embed one within the other, reflecting the complexity of depth and breadth in and among cognitive processes. As with any language, graphic primitives are essential for communication. For example, the letters in the alphabet or the numbers 0–9 are the basic, interdependent graphic primitives that engender infinite ways of communicating ideas and mathematical concepts. With the Thinking Maps language, there are eight graphic primitives that generate infinite iterations. When some or all of the maps are used together, the thinker may move to greater complexity. The eight parts of speech of the English language offer a rich but imperfect analogy to Thinking Maps: from the eight parts of speech, the writer or speaker may generate endless strings of sentences. So, too, may a thinker generate endless maps reflecting patterns of thinking. The two examples above, when observed side by side, show how the maps may be used at a novice level and then grow in complexity as the cognitive development of the learner evolves. The power of the novice to expert use has been revealed when we conduct leadership training with teams from school districts – including the superintendent and board members. They are using the Thinking Maps for complex problem solving and strategic planning at the same time that their first graders are using the very same tools in their classrooms.

Principle 4: Integrating Content and Process through Form. Knowledge in and across disciplines exists and grows over time through the interplay of content (what), process (how), and form (pattern). Educators have expended endless energy on the relative importance of teaching for "content" versus teaching for "process" learning. This dichotomy is false and there is a middle way that unites the two in a triad. When using Thinking Maps, learners are simultaneously constructing and *forming* patterns of *content* knowledge and skills using cognitive *processes*. As you look back at the examples, you may ask yourself, "Are these representations of content or process?" This is a trick question, because the answer is *both*. For example, when a first grader identifies multiple causes and effects of Leo the lion king being "mean", and the eleventh grade student patterns the causal relationships in a "telomere response" then they are showing the "form" of the "content" as well as applying the cognitive "process" of cause and effect reasoning.

Principle 5: Frames of Reference. Understanding and growth occur through the personal, interpersonal, cultural, and institutional frames of reference and the wider field which surround and influence perceptions. The field of frame semantics is relatively new, but it draws on the understanding that our background culture, language, and personal experiences deeply influence how and what we perceive (Lakoff and Johnson, 1980). A central tool of the Thinking Maps model is the "Frame of Reference." As a learner is mapping out a view of knowledge, he or she may also draw a rectangular shape around the outside of the map being constructed. Within this "metacognitive" Frame, the learner notes what is influencing his or her perception of the knowledge being constructed. For example, the first grade students might have been asked to think about what in their life reminds them of Leo the Lion, or the mouse that was dominated by the lion. The high school student, when describing an "ecosystem" using the Bubble Map, could have reflected on the ecosystems that she moves through and lives in, and how these descriptions fit her background and cultural frame of reference. The ecosystem of a suburb of Chicago frames one's understanding differently than living in the city center, or in a rural part of the United States or on the savanna in Africa. Each of the maps, uniquely created by hand or on computer by students, surfaces the learners' content knowledge as well as their point of view, thus supporting their cognitive understandings. When students use the Thinking Maps with fluency they also deepen their critical thinking by establishing a reflective, metacognitive stance in the world.

## ENDNOTE

There is an unspoken barrier and cognitive dissonance between what is going on in the brain and how we ask our students, and ourselves, to represent our best thinking. As discussed above, most cognitive scientists and educators interested in facilitating thinking and learning processes have primarily focused on assessing spoken and written *representations* of thinking. These representations, like Potemkim villages of the mind, are linear facades of the actual *forms* of thinking; whereas, we know as human beings that our worlds of perception, emotion, and cognition are fundamentally *nonlinear in form*. We teach about concepts and systems and our brain naturally "maps" patterns, storing information in networks across our unique "hemispheres" and "territories" of the brain-mind-body connection. Information is distributed across the brain and linked, weblike, *in form*. The problem is that those studying thinking processes and teaching for so-called "higher-order thinking" have not had a *nonlinear representation* system, or a *language* for showing what and how they know something other than by linear strings of words and numbers. When teachers and administrators participate in a year long process of professional development with Thinking Maps, they are learning how to present contents and processes in a more authentic way than through the normal auditory-linear presentations found in most classrooms. Most importantly, the focus of this professional growth is on the direct teaching of all of their students, across their school, in becoming fluent with the tools for life long learning.

If knowledge continues to be defined by processes of short term information retention in linear strings of words, we are all in trouble in this age of information as decisions will be made in episodic ways, devoid of problems approached as richly patterned, complex and systemic. This is the state of education for students from an "advanced" culture in what Thomas Friedman calls the "flat world" which is now dominated by "knowledge creation" and communication across a range of cultural frames of reference.

As the ageless Albert Einstein famously said, the significant problems we face today cannot be solved at the same level of thinking we were at when we created them. I thought of this quote when, at the end of the movie, *An Inconvenient Truth*, about threats of global warming, Al Gore implored us to think differently about this problem that affects every person on the planet. He asked us not only to think differently about our own ecosystem (as an eleventh grade might do in a science class), but the earth as one ecosystem. I believe that he was suggesting that we not just change *what* we think about this issue that requires an understanding of complex, interdependent variables and systems. This offering was more about challenging us to consider *how* we think in the 21st century. It isn't that we need to think harder, or longer, or more analytically or creatively. We have to do more than think "outside" the box. We need to think in another world of representations in order to surface a different way of thinking about the Walls of Text that are held as books in the hands of learners, or in "hand-held" downloads from the other side of the world. We cannot simply ask our students, as digital natives, to think differently about patterns of relationships, systems, and interdependencies if we do not offer them practical tools for seeking and showing patterns of their own thinking.

## REFERENCES

Alper, L., & Hyerle, D. (2007). *Thinking Maps: A language for leadership*. Cary, NC: Thinking Maps, Inc.

Buzan, Tony (1994). *Use both sides of your brain*. London: Dutton.

Bloom, B.S. (Ed.) (1956). *Taxonomy of educational objectives. Handbook I: Cognitive domain*. New York: McKay.

Bohm, D. (2004). *On dialogue*. Oxon, England: Routledge Classics.

Capra, Frijof (1996). *The web of life*. New York: Simon and Schuster.

Costa, Arthur (Ed.) (1991, 2000). *Developing minds*. Alexandria, VA: Association for Supervision and Curriculum Development.

Costa, Arthur (1991). Foreword. In J. Clark (Ed.), *Patterns of thinking*. New York: Allyn and Bacon.

Costa, A., & Garmston, R. (2002). *Cognitive coaching, A foundation for renaissance schools*. Norwood, MA: Christopher-Gordon Publishers, Inc.

Darling-Hammond, Linda (1997). *The right to learn*. San Francisco, CA: Jossey Bass.

Friedman, Thomas (2005). *The world is flat*. New York: Farrar, Straus and Giroux.

Gore, Albert (2006). *An inconvenient truth*.

Hyerle, David (1989). *Designs for thinking connectively*. Lyme, NH: Designs for Thinking.

Hyerle, David (1989). *Expand your thinking*. Stamford, CT: Innovative Sciences, Inc.

Hyerle, D. (1996). *Visual tools for constructing knowledge*. Alexandria, VA: Association for Supervision and Curriculum Development.

Hyerle, D. (2000). *A field guide to using visual tools*. Alexandria, VA: Association for Supervision and Curriculum Development.

Hyerle, D., & Yeager, C. (2007). *Thinking Maps®: A language for learning training resource manual*. Cary, NC: Thinking Maps, Inc.

Hyerle, D., & Yeager, C. (2007). *Thinking Maps® training of trainers resource manual*. Cary, NC: Thinking Maps, Inc.

Hyerle, D. (2008, in press). *Visual tools for transforming information into knowledge*. Thousand Oaks, CA: Corwin Press.

Hyerle, D. (Ed.) (2004). *Student successes with Thinking Maps®*. Thousand Oaks, CA: Corwin Press.

Kozol, Jonathan (2005). *The shame of the nation*. New York: Crown Publishers.

Lakoff, G., & Johnson, M. (1980). *Metaphors we live by*. Chicago: University of Chicago Press.

Nisbett, Richard E. (2003). *The geography of thought*. New York: Free Press.

Novak, J., & Gowin, R. (1984). *Learning how to learn*. Cambridge, MA: Cambridge University Press.

Piercy, T.D., & Hyerle, D. (2004). Maps for the road to reading comprehension: Bridging reading text structures to writing prompts. In D. Hyerle (Ed.), *Student successes with Thinking Maps®* (pp. 63–74). Thousand Oaks, CA: Corwin Press.

Richmond, B., Peterson, S., & Vesco, P. (1987/91). *STELLA*. Lyme, NH: High Performance Systems.

Senge, Peter M. (1990). *The fifth discipline*. New York: Currency and Doubleday.

Thinking Maps®: Technology for learning [Software]. (1998; 2007). Cary, NC: Thinking Maps, Inc.

Tufte, Edward R. (2006). *The cognitive style of Power Point: Pitching out corrupts within*. Cheshire, CT: Graphics Press.

Upton, Albert (1960). *Design for thinking*. Palo Alto, CA: Pacific Books.

Upton, A., Samson, R., & Farmer, A.D. (1961). *Creative analysis*. New York: E.P. Dutton.

Wheatley, Margaret J. (1992). *Leadership and the new science*. San Francisco: Berrett-Koehler Publishers, Inc.

KERRI KEARNEY

# CHAPTER 3
# PARTICIPANT-GENERATED VISUAL DATA:
# DRAWING OUT EMOTIONS

Both as qualitative researchers and practitioners, we have long been interested in exploring relationships between human emotion and change. In qualitative research, we have sought ways to document individual perspectives that triangulate interviews and observations. Our initial efforts were in the field of organizational change, and those efforts led to a better understanding of organizations at the individual unit of analysis and how those individual pieces affect the functioning of the larger organization during times of change. As practitioners, we simply looked for what worked – what worked to move the people component of change forward as quickly and efficiently as possible because, in the day-to-day, time is often the most precious resource. The initial research provided a foundation for learning that was critical to us in carrying our work forward into other areas and it, therefore, provides the foundation for this chapter.

Almost completely as a result of "what worked" in the field, drawings emerged quite early in our research processes as a very helpful tool. Our interest in visual data focused primarily in the area of participant-generated drawings used to facilitate emotional recollection and data collection (Kearney & Hyle, 2003, 2004). No matter the specific focus of the research questions, the underlying question remained relatively consistent: What role does individual emotion play in the ability of individuals to absorb, regroup, and move forward during times of imposed change? Ultimately, with the assistance of participant-produced drawings, we believe we will be able to better outline strategies that will help individuals and, when working with organizationally-based change, the organization more successfully (defined as both efficient and effective) move through change.

## THE DISCOVERY OF THE POWER OF DRAWINGS IN THE ORGANIZATION

When the organization as you have known it seems to have turned on its end with no clear ties to anything that seems familiar, it is human emotion that boils up and over the usual boundaries of "good" behavior. When emotional outbursts and individual emotions seem to be the primary drivers for decision making and human interactions, when even common sense seems to have departed in the midst of an organization's struggles to find footing in a whole new world, organizational consultants begin to look for something, *anything* that will help re-frame the chaos

*J.E. Pedersen and K.D. Finson (eds.), Visual Data, 51–58.*

into something remotely understandable . . . something controllable. Such was the state of things when one of us first turned to drawings. Much like lancing a boil that lets the poison out so that healthy healing can begin, employee-produced drawings initially served simply as a way to get everything out on the table for discussion. The only known fact was that the organization could not survive on the current path. The driving belief was that it was better to deal with this reality than continue to pretend that we were not immersed in the slow and painful dance of certain organizational death.

It was during this time for the organization that drawings first proved themselves as a valuable tool for releasing emotion and allowing individuals, and therefore the organization, to process and move forward. Later, as researchers, we decided to use the drawings methodology as a "study within a study" on organizational change. While drawings may be a more common data collection tool today than in the past, they remain a non-traditional methodology and there was little in the literature to guide us. So, we set out to forge our own path and, while the research continues, thus far we have had extremely promising results.

## THE ORIGINAL STUDY

In the original organizational change study, we used participant-produced drawings as a part of a larger study which examined the emotional impact of change on individuals in an educational institution, in this case the loss and eventual replacement of the organization's leader (Kearney, 2002; Kearney & Hyle, 2003). We used participant produced drawings for two reasons. First, we had a problem (organizational change that led to losses by the individuals in the organization) that necessitated the surfacing of emotions-based data, traditionally a difficult type of data to collect. As described earlier, previous organizational development experience suggested that drawings were a way to tap quickly into the emotional lives of participants; there was also some support in the literature (Vince, 1995; Vince & Broussine, 1996; Zubroff, 1988). Second, the use of drawings as a catalyst for unstructured interviews, an integral part of the study design, freed participants to frame their own experiences without the constraints of the biases we brought to the study. As noted by Denzin and Lincoln (1994), "the open-ended interview rests on the assumption that the researcher will ask questions that are culturally meaningful to the subject" (p. 410). The photograph or drawing-based interview uses participant-produced images as a guide. This suggests strong collaboration between researcher and participant and, as such, "the marriage of visual methods and ethnography seems natural" (p. 410).

### From the First Study to the Present

Our first experience with the use of participant-produced drawings as a research methodology produced a great deal of excitement as we quickly saw that this research would lend support to the previous anecdotal experiences. Our first methodology article, written from this study, quickly found a publisher and thus our journey into the study of participant-produced drawings was solidified.

### Defining and Redefining Visual Data

Although our use of "visual data" has thus far been limited to participant-generated drawings, our definition of "visual data" has become much broader, and our interests in this area have continued to expand. As students of qualitative inquiry, we know about self and other-generated photographs and video, field notes documenting observations and other traditional "visual data" sources. But as students of organizations, we know and have been influenced by others who have also successfully used drawings as a part of data collection in organizations – some for research purposes (Nyquist et al., 1999; MacLure, 2002; Meyer, 1991; Trower, Austin & Siorcinelli, 2001; Zubroff, 1988). The work of others who have used drawings to bring to the surface important thoughts and emotions as a part of organizational interventions (Vince, 1995; Vince & Broussine, 1996), also have influenced our work as they affirm the same experiences we had in an organization prior to beginning research in this area.

Of particular influence are Nossiter and Biberman, who conducted in 1990 a study specifically for the purpose of examining the usefulness of drawings as a research methodology. They concluded that drawings "focus a person's response" and lead to "respondent honesty and parsimony" (p. 15). Further, they noted the willingness of respondents to draw and the joy expressed in completing the activity with the observation that the activity may have increased respondent response rates. Meyer (1991) also found that the request for drawings seemed to increase response rates, noting that every CEO contacted in his study completed the requested diagram but 7 of 22 "failed to return an accompanying questionnaire" (p. 227).

Drawings may also be a more specific or direct route to the emotions and unconscious responses or feelings underlying behaviors during change (Vince, 1995). Imagery can "bridge the gap between the apparently individual, private, subjective, and the apparently collective, social, political" (Samuels, 1993, p. 63). In his 1988 study, Zubroff found that, for clerical workers experiencing organizational change, "pictures functioned as a catalyst, helping them to articulate feelings that had been implicit and hard to define.... These simple drawings convey feelings that often elude verbal expression" (pp. 141–142).

The works of these specific researchers were our earliest influences in terms of designing a research study using participant-produced drawings. Of course, others have since added to the knowledge these researchers originally offered.

### Changes to Focus and Practice

In a follow up study to the leader loss research described earlier, we replicated much of the original study to see if the original results were also replicated. While this study produced increased understanding of the world of organizational change, specifically leader loss, it also reaffirmed the role of the drawings methodology. In some respects, however, we found that the drawings become more powerful when used in situations of the greatest felt loss (and associated emotion). In other words, where the loss is not perceived to be of high personal impact, drawings are helpful but not critical in surfacing the individual's experience – people appear to perceive there to be less risk in talking openly. Where emotions are running high, however, we find participants less forthcoming (they appear to perceive there to be higher personal risk to open sharing) and participant-produced drawings, in our experience, are unmatched as a vehicle for accessing emotions-based data.

Our research efforts in this area have also continued to affirm some of our earliest findings about the drawings methodology. While we certainly remain open to research, our own or others', that conflicts with our experience to date, at this point we have accepted several currently known "truths" about the drawings methodology.

*Creation of an emotions pathway.* Participant produced drawings "create a path toward participant feelings and emotions, making them viable tools for researchers who seek access to this type of data" (Kearney & Hyle, 2004, p. 376). Vince (1995) also found that "drawings are good at revealing the underlying emotional experience" (p. 12) even when no reference to feelings or emotions is made in the request of participants to draw. It has also been our great fascination that, when teaching the drawings methodology to researchers in the classroom, even their prior knowledge of how the methodology works does not seem to inhibit the power of the drawings process itself.

*Succinct presentation of the individual's key experience(s).* "The cognitive process required to draw leads to a more succinct presentation of the key elements of participants' experiences" (Kearney & Hyle, 2004, p. 376). This phenomenon has been in evidence both in follow up formal studies that used the drawings methodology as well as when graduate students studying research have been asked to draw as a part of their personal learning process. The mental process required by drawing appears to help participants to "sort their experiences to date into succinct pieces and attach meaning to them" (p. 376).

*Drawings interpretation.* Our experience has repeatedly and consistently taught us that the participant, not an outside "expert", must interpret the drawings themselves. Although some authors (Nossiter & Biberman, 1990) have suggested that drawings could be analyzed and interpreted by graphic artists and clinical psychologists, our experience is that only the individual can explain the true meaning of his or her drawing. Informal "tests" with licensed psychologists and others have shown us that, while they may often be right, the instances of misinterpreting the meanings of the drawings are too great to be trusted for research purposes. When drawings are used as an entrée to a long interview, we also agree with Vince (1995) that the power of drawings is "not only in the diagnostic power of the images themselves, but also in the contextual and collaborative discussions and developments that emerge as a result of them" (p. 12).

An example of our earliest experience with this phenomenon is seen in Figure 1, which depicts a flock of birds in flight.

*Figure 1.*

The participant herself noted that this part of her drawing might easily be mis-interpreted. In explaining the birds, the participant said, "You would probably think of this as serene. No! I hate to fly ... It scares me to death ... But that's my feeling of insecurity." To fully understand the meaning of her drawing, further explanation about her personal fears was needed from the participant herself. (Kearney & Hyle, 2004, p. 377)

This need for the participant him- or herself to interpret the drawing, rather than any "expert," has been a consistent finding in our work.

## DRAWINGS AS TRIANGULATION

Drawings serve as an important additional source of data. Again and again, draw-ings have demonstrated to us (and to participants) their ability to elicit more from the participants than what would have been captured via more traditional data collection methodologies. Drawings also confirm other verbal reports and observations. Our experience has consistently been that integration of visuals with verbal reports can be a useful form of triangulation, which lends further credibility to study results (Merriam, 1998).

### Continuing or Future Drawings Research

Other findings and observations in the use of participant-based drawings in both the original and subsequent studies have led to a number of issues to be addressed through future research. In general, there simply needs to be much more re-search completed about the application of the drawings methodology for research. However, three specific questions continue to be of particular interest to us.

*The importance of knowledge about the drawings methodology.* How impor-tant to participation is it to withhold information about the drawings methodology prior to being in a one-on-one interview with participants? In other words, will the knowledge they will be asked to draw encourage or inhibit willingness to participate in the study?

In our original study, we experienced an overall reluctance from participants asked to draw. Participants did not know drawings would be a part of the interview when they agreed to participate. Follow up interview data showed that the primary issue behind participants' reluctance was concerns about their artistic abilities – a personal characteristic. The literature, however, reports that participants responded to requests to draw with "enjoyment" and subsequently became quite "engaged" in the activity (Nossiter & Biberman, 1990; Meyers, 1978). Derry (2002) also reported only one resistor. Vince and Broussine's (1996) requests for drawings were directed to participants in various group settings and they also reported positive responses to the request.

Our follow up efforts to the original study produced both resistors and participants who gladly embraced the drawings exercise. From our experiences and the available literature, it seems the only common finding is that the drawing activity itself evokes powerful responses from some participants. There is not yet sufficient evidence, however, to allow researchers to predict respondent reactions with any accuracy.

*Structuring the instructions to draw.* What is the optimum amount of structure to provide in the instructions to draw? While the provision of little structure in the instructions to draw allows participants to frame their own experiences, therefore potentially combating researcher bias, it also does not allow for comparison of the perspectives of participants who may choose to address clearly different aspects of the change (see Kearney & Hyle, 2004, for more information). The timing of the drawings methodology, whether early in the interview experience or well after the interview has begun, also has produced mixed responses from participants. Derry (2002) found that placing the drawings request later in the interview, conceivably after a relationship has been built between researcher and participant, may elicit a more positive response from the participant. However, our concern remains that by later in the interview, researcher biases, no matter how well we attempt to remove them, may have already exerted some influence on the participant. The real question deals with the optimum balance between eliciting a positive and open response to the request to drawing with the desire to offset researcher biases. To date, we have been unable to reach any real conclusions about how this issue is best approached in any particular situation.

*Practical outcomes and impacts of drawing.* A question that continues to nag us, even from our original study, is that of the individual and organizational impact of the surfacing of what are sometimes very strong emotions through the use of drawings. Thus far, we have not stayed within the organization to provide additional individual or group processing support of the emotions that resulted from the drawings process itself. However, anecdotal and informal reports by participants have suggested that the drawings themselves help to move the individuals, and therefore the organization, forward. With some practical facilitation, we believe it is quite possible that drawings may open an opportunity for organizational intervention that could be critical to speeding the processing of change at the individual level. It is also a remaining ethical question as to whether some type of debriefing process should also be incorporated with the use of participant produced drawings.

*Our Contributions*

In other reports of the use of drawings in organizations (Meyer, 1991; Nossiter & Biberman, 1990; Vince, 1995; Vince & Broussine, 1996), conclusions about the efficacy of drawings were reported primarily from the researchers' observations and analyses of participant responses as well as researcher analysis of the drawings themselves. This is valuable information and an important perspective. However, we chose to ask the participants themselves how the request to draw changed their responses and affected the information they shared. Recognizing that both the participants' and the researcher's perspectives on the drawing methodology are culturally rule bound, we believe that their use in this study provides an important foundation for our findings.

*Current Research and Other Projects*

Experience is the greatest of all teachers. While we have persisted with the study of the efficacy of participant-produced drawings, we have expanded their use to similar problems occurring in other contexts. These efforts are in addition to the continuation of our work of the study of the impact of leader loss on individuals in the organization, a focus that we have never since addressed without the use of participant-produced drawings.

Currently we have an additional organizational change/leader loss article that is under review for publication. In addition, data collection using the drawings methodology has begun for a third study on leader loss. In this study, participants will be questioned in a follow up interview about their experiences with the drawings process in a more detailed and targeted fashion than any known to date by us or other researchers. We believe their perceptions are critical for furthering the understanding of the use of the drawings methodology by qualitative researchers.

A related but different study, for which data collection will soon begin, involves the study of the transition of collegiate athletes from their known identities as athletes to their new identities post-eligibility. The drawings methodology is expected to be critical for eliciting the emotional experiences of these athletes, experiences that to date have not been well surfaced in the literature. While the focus of this study, in general, remains the impact of change on the individual, this particular population presents some unique challenges.

Collaborative efforts with researchers in the K-12 education field have begun to lead to some interesting findings about the perspectives of educators, both "front-line teachers" and teacher educators, about their responses to accountability in the schools – a profound change in education that has led to very high individual emotion for many. Likewise, in related collaborative research, the drawings methodology is being used as a major methodological component for a presentation intended to answer a somewhat provocative question posed by a recent education conference: "Why do kids hate school?" (Mathers & Kearney, 2006). The use of the drawings methodology in this instance returns drawings to their original place in using them for children rather than adults. However, we expect that results will continue to bridge this understanding and, therefore, provide us further insight into our use of this methodology with adults.

Finally, it would be remiss not to note that a "practice" article that denotes the strong ties of faculty research to faculty practice is in process. While not a research study in and of itself, it is hoped that it delivers to the field a strong message about the importance of bringing what we are learning in research, in this case the drawings methodology, to our work as practitioners. Experiences with the targeted use of drawings to determine student readiness to learn (e.g. for an international group of students making an initial cultural adjustment to the United States) to assessing the well-being of students who have experienced recent losses of their faculty mentors have shown us that drawings are powerful both as a part of and separate from their role as a research methodology. This belief will continue to fuel our efforts to bridge what we learn about the power of drawings from research to the practice that, hopefully, positive impacts the human race.

## REFERENCES

Denzin, N.K., & Lincoln, Y.S. (1994). *Handbook of qualitative research*. Thousand Oaks, CA: Sage.

Derry, C. (2002, April), More than words can say? The value of drawings in qualitative research, Using visual images in research: Methodolgical issues and innovations, Symposium conducted at the annual meeting of the American Educational Research Association, New Orleans, LA.

Kearney, K.S. (2002). *A study of the emotional effects on employees who remain through organizational change: A view through Kubler–Ross (1969) in an educational institution*. Unpublished doctoral dissertation, Oklahoma State University.

Kearney, K.S., & Hyle, A.E. (2003). The grief cycle and educational change: The Kubler–Ross contribution. *Planning and Changing, 34*(1&2), 32–57.

Kearney, K.S., & Hyle, A.E. (2004). Drawing out emotions in organizations: The use of participant-produced drawings in qualitative inquiry. *Qualitative Research, 4*(3), 361–383.

MacLure, M. (2002, April). *Mimesis and illusion in art and research*. Paper presented at the annual meeting of the American Educational Research Association, New Orleans, LA.

Mathers, J.K., & Kearney, K.S. (2006). *The impact of no child left behind: Drawings from the field, once removed*. Essays from the Second Annual Conference of the Academy for Educational Studies, Missouri State University, Springfield MO. Manuscript submitted for publication.

Merriam, S. (1998). *Qualitative applications and case study research in education*. San Francisco: Jossey-Bass.

Meyer, A.D. (1991). Visual data in organizational research. *Organization Science, 2*, 218–236.

Nossiter, V., & Biberman, G. (1990). Projective drawings and metaphor: Analysis of organizational culture. *Journal of Managerial Psychology, 5*, 13–16.

Nyquist, J.D., Manning, L., Wylff, D., Austin, A., Fraser, P.K., & Sprague, J. (1999). On the road to becoming a professor: The graduate student experience. *Change, 31*, 18–27.

Samuels, A. (1993). *The political psyche*. London: Routledge.

Trower, C.A., Austin, A.E., & Siorcinelli, M.D. (2001). Paradise lost: How the academy converts enthusiastic recruits into early-career doubters. *AAHE Bulletin, 53*, 3–6.

Vince, R. (1995). Working with emotions in the change process: Using drawings for team diagnosis and development. *Organisations & People, 2*, 11–17.

Vince, R., & Broussine, M. (1996). Paradox, defense and attachment: Accessing and working with emotions and relations underlying organizational change. *Organizational Studies, 17*, 1–23.

Zubroff, S. (1988). *In the age of the smart machine: The future of work and power*. New York: Basic Books.

KEVIN D. FINSON

# CHAPTER 4
# WHAT DRAWINGS REVEAL ABOUT
# PERCEPTIONS OF SCIENTISTS:
# VISUAL DATA OPERATIONALLY DEFINE

Everyday, wherever we are, we are bombarded with sensory information. For those of us who have eyesight, we rely to an extraordinary extent on our visual sense to tell us about the world around us. Over ninety percent of our sensory inputs come via visual sense. The format and speed at which visual stimuli come to us can impact the way our brains handle the information. Some of us can simply process the information more efficiently and more quickly than others. The way we each perceive visual stimuli may vary to some extent as well. For example, the wife of a couple I know has a particular blouse that she calls blue and he calls green. Visual stimuli fill our environment. However, visual stimuli themselves are not visual data.

We can gather all sorts of information that results from the presence of visual stimuli. This information is visual data. We can observe, detail, record, analyze and evaluate it; and we can gather information about the ways in which the brain processes those stimuli and how we physiologically and mentally (psychologically) respond to them. We can do all this, of course, with varying degrees of organization. Even unorganized information can be visual data. The more organized the visual data is, the more useful it is to us as researchers and practitioners. We can perform a variety of analyses on those data, and we can design and conduct experiments with variables that yield more visual data. It is true that one can collect all sorts of visual data, as is the case with almost any data obtained from any one of many sources, but unless one then uses it for a purpose and applies it, it is really of little value.

In the case of the type of visual data that is of interest to me – drawings of scientists – without a clear protocol to follow in analyzing the drawings and then using the results to inform us with respect to treatments or curricula development, etc., all we really have at hand is a nice set of drawings. Refrigerators across the country are covered with nice drawings made by young children, but those collections tell us little about the cognition going on in their minds, and so the usefulness of the drawings is limited. But if we approach examining those drawings with a purpose and a protocol, then we have visual data. It is then that we can begin to ascertain not only the fine motor skills of the artist, but also something about how he/she perceives the world around him/her. One might argue that the

*J.E. Pedersen and K.D. Finson (eds.), Visual Data, 59–77.*

data are still there, whether or not we perceive them or employ any protocol. In a way, that is true. However, disorganized data are not very helpful if we really want to find ways to improve learning or whatever it is we're about.

## GETTING STARTED WITH VISUAL DATA

*The Starting Point*: For me, my foray into visual data research began in earnest in 1990 when I was co-directing a National Science Foundation funded program called "Young Scholars." That program was designed to bring rising eighth graders to campus for an intensive three-week summer program immersing them in experiences in each of the major science disciplines and mathematics. Among the experiences were included whole group laboratory explorations and one-on-one explorations with a faculty mentor on a project mutually agreed upon by both the student and faculty member. Students had opportunities to sit face-to-face with researchers and field scientists and technologists to learn about their careers and interests.

We selected rising eight graders as our target audience because the research literature we had been reading for years provided increasingly persuasive evidence that it is during the middle school years that students begin making up their minds about what they wish to pursue as vocations, and consequently what courses they will take in high school and later in college. We were also convinced by the literature that too few students were selecting the sciences and mathematics as vocations, and this was particularly true for female and minority students. Hence, we admitted into the program thirty students each summer, of whom twenty were female.

*Fundamental Problems and Issues*: As many researchers do, we were interested in "where the students were at" both when entering and exiting the program. So, we carefully selected several instruments to use with the group, including one that measured attitudes toward science and another that assessed locus of control. However, we felt that these measures could not tell us what we really wanted to know: did the three week experience actually have any positive impact on these students, and was that impact one that led students to actually desire to select science or mathematics as a career option?

Our quest to address that question led us to additional research literature describing how strongly the perceptions one has about something actually influences one's decision to either pursue or not pursue it. So, our question now became, "What are the perceptions of scientists that these students hold, and in what way(s) are those perceptions manifested in the students' choices of areas of study and careers?"

At about this juncture, we discovered an article written by Chambers (1983) that dealt precisely with that question. Chambers reported the development of an instrument that was patterned after Goodenough's work with the *Draw-a-Man Test*. The *Draw-a-Man Test* was a psychological tool that allowed one to assess, in part, the psychological state of the person making the drawing. We were aware of snippets of research scattered here and there that spoke about psychologists having clients make drawings or paintings, and then analyzing them to more effectively diagnose the client's mental state. Along that same line, we literally stumbled across a report from the late 1980s (Wickelgren, 1989) in which medical practitioners at Faulkner Hospital's Graham Headache Center (Boston) found a way to utilize this psychological connection in treating their patients who suffered from migrane headaches. The doctors had their patients draw their headaches. To their surprise, similar and clearly identifiable features emerged in a number of the drawings made by classical migrane sufferers. This sent the doctors seeking a psychological link between the images and the organization of a specific group of cells within the brain's visual cortex, an area of the brain known to be intensely affected by many migrane attacks, and an area the doctors were then attempting to impact with targeted treatment.

Chambers' instrument was similar to Goodenough's, but focused specifically on scientists, particularly elementary children's mental images of scientists. Chambers described how a drawing of a scientist made by a child on a blank sheet of paper could be examined to identify specific attributes about the drawing, and therefore, the child's mental image of a scientist. Taken together, many children's drawings could reveal that a certain set of attributes consistently appeared in drawings. Chambers called these "stereotypical images." Thus, Chambers' work brought Goodenough's work into the realm of science education. The *Draw-a-Scientist Test* (DAST) had emerged.

So it became evident to us, from a psychological perspective, that drawings could certainly reveal significant information about someone's deeply embedded ideas or mental images, even if that person was unable to or had difficulty writing or speaking. All this led us to consider how we could use the *DAST* with our students. We knew Chambers had dealt with over 4,800 drawings, and we believed there needed to be a more systematic method of analyzing drawings than that heretofore used. We felt the need to more easily quantify the stereotypical images contained within drawings so that statistical analyses could be directly employed with the data and inter-rater reliability could be quickly established. As a result, we devised a checklist that included the seven most-often occurring images Chambers identified, plus some additional ones we derived from the research literature. We called each of these images an "element," and devised a protocol to use with the checklist. The checklist and protocol together were named the *Draw-a-Scientist-Checklist (DAST-C)*. Using our Young Scholars students, we were able to pilot test and validate the instrument.

## WORKS MOST INFLUENCING MY RESEARH

There were two pieces of research that initially provided the impetus for my research and most influenced its direction: that of Chambers (1983), which was briefly discussed in the previous section, and that of Schibeci and Sorenson (1983). Chambers' influence centered on the distillation of seven specific elements that consistently appeared in drawings of scientists. These seven elements were (1) the presence of lab coats (usually white), (2) eyeglasses, (3) facial hair, (4) symbols of research (e.g. scientific/laboratory equipment), (5) symbols of knowledge (e.g. books, filing cabinets), (6) technology (products of science, such as rockets), and (7) relevant captions (e.g. formulae, "eureka"). Chambers went further and looked at attributes of each of those elements that may also have significance: (a) size of objects compared to the size of the scientist, (b) signs or indications of danger, (c) light bulbs, (d) basement or underground laboratories, (e) male/female figures, (f) and mythical images such as Frankenstein or Jekyll-Hyde. Notable in Chambers work was that of the 4,807 drawings made by elementary (grades K-5) children, only 28 showed female scientists. Since there was an astonishingly consistent appearance of these seven elements and their attributes in so many drawings, Chambers called them "stereotypic images." Hence, we have the stereotype of a scientist: someone who is not like the normal, average everyday person who is a friend or neighbor. The drawings and subsequent analysis of them were named the *Draw-a-Scientist Test* (*DAST*).

Besides translating Goodenough's *Draw-a-Man Test* into the *DAST*, another of Chambers' more significant contributions was the idea that detailed information in the mind of a child could be obtained even if that child lacked the ability to write or verbalize what was in their minds. This opened up an entirely new avenue of deriving information from a source often overlooked by science education researchers: young children. Further, since many people, both young and old, seem to like to sketch or draw (some call it "doodling"), it provided a very natural and non-threatening method of finding out what someone thought. Data could be obtained from even the most primitive of drawings, so artistic talent wasn't a requisite skill. The tools needed for conducting the *DAST* were simply a blank sheet of paper and a pencil or marker. The simplicity of the "instrument" was amazing.

A study published by Schebeci and Sorensen (1983) also provides impetus to my interest in visual data research. Their work, as I perceived it, bolstered the utility of the DAST. Their study was conducted in Australia with the purpose of examining the potential of the DAST as a quick and reliable means of determining what images of scientists were held in the minds of elementary students. Their results led them to conclude the DAST was a reliable, valid and useful instrument.

Perhaps a third work influenced me as well, and may have influenced Chambers and other researchers to come later. This third work was that of Mead and Metraux (1957). They had 35,000 high school students write an essay to describe what they believed a scientist looked like. Analysis of the essays revealed characteristics paralleling the elements Chambers identified in the DAST: elderly or middle-aged males in white lab coats and eyeglasses in a laboratory performing dangerous experiments. Hence, the work of Mead and Metraux has come to be seen as the seminal work that really started the whole "draw a scientist" research paradigm. This work also led us, in our work with the 8th graders in 1990, to include students' verbal and written descriptions along with their drawings of the scientists. Our analysis of the three types of data led us to conclude that the drawings by themselves could serve as a reliable means of ascertaining an individual's image of a scientist.

## PRIMARY AIM OF MY RESEARCH

Researching drawings of scientists made by people of all ages is of interest to me, but more so is a focus on the drawings of children and students up through college age. Initially, just corroborating that elements continuously appeared in drawings was enough. However, this could only carry one so far, and then self-evaluation stepped in and made me assess whether this was all there is to it, or if there was some deeper and more significant information to be derived from scribbles and sketches. If the furthest one could go with this line of research was just an examination of the types and frequencies of various drawing elements, then the research itself could be little more than one of those cutesy curiosities that appears on one's radar from time to time. Through the 1990s, science educators across the country were publishing articles about students' drawings. Even though some studies looked at comparisons between different groups, such as ethnicity, gender, etc., they were basically stuck on just examining types of elements and the frequencies with which they occurred in sets of drawings. Needless to say, some depressing thoughts began to creep into my psyche.

As I was reviewing the work I had thus far done with drawings, I began to reconsider the psychological aspects of what was going on in the minds of the persons making the drawings. There were other measures out there that were used to glean information about learners' psychological state, attitudes, self-efficacy, and so on. So I began to wonder if the drawing data could be linked in some way to any of those other measures. This, in turn, started me thinking about even more difficult questions, such as what are the connections and interactions between drawing data and these other measures, exactly when in one's life stereotypic images begin forming in the mind, which media are most effective in one's formulation of those images, and how does media affect them? Indeed, these seemed to be more significant questions than ones like, "How many drawings showed a scientist wearing a lab coat?" These questions posed problems that would be much more difficult to research, but were certainly worth pursuing.

The primary aim of my visual data research has thus become that of trying to determine answers to these more complex questions. In many ways, these are fuzzy questions because there are so many variables that simply cannot be controlled, because media in its various forms is so pervasive in today's society, and because there are so many mental operations occurring at any one time in one's brain that finding anything stronger than correlations (i.e. cause and effect) between one's mental images of scientists and psychometric measures of attitudes, self-efficacy, etc. is largely inferential, at best. Nevertheless, it is this very set of questions that I've challenged my colleagues to investigate (Finson, 2002).

## THEORETICAL CONSTRUCTS

The theory providing the underpinnings of using drawings to derive data about individuals' perceptions of scientists is relatively straightforward. We develop ideas about things, or form concepts about them, sometimes with very little factual information. As we gain more information, our conceptions become more sophisticated as we assimilate it into our mental schema. As humans are prone to do, we internalize these ideas and come to hold tightly to them, and letting go of them or changing them is a difficult thing to do, and not always without risk.

The information we use at the beginning of concept formation is important to consider, particularly with respect to its source, type, and quality. However, no matter how good the information is, we will interpret it based on our own previous experiences, observations, and learning. In doing so, the same piece of information may be interpreted by one person to mean one thing and by someone else to mean another. In other words, our experiences color the way we perceive information that comes to our senses, and even can influence what information we are open to receiving. Consequently, we may develop concepts that are considered "accurate" and readily acceptable with regard to scientific thinking, or we may develop concepts that incorporate inaccuracies or misinterpretations, but which make perfect sense to us as long as we view them through the lens of our own experience and level of understanding. Clark (1988), in working on belief systems of teachers, noted that beliefs were apparently "eclectic aggregations of cause-effect propositions from many sources, ... generalizations drawn from personal experience, ... values, biases, and prejudices" (p. 5). Goodman (1988) thought that teachers are influenced by "guiding images" from past events, that these events created "intuitive screens" through which new information is filtered, and thus impacts one's perspectives. With respect to perceptions of scientists, we use our own personal experiences, prejudices, etc. as filters to discern information that contributes to what we perceive scientists are like. Taking this line of reasoning a bit further, the beliefs one has about something significantly influences the perceptions one has about that something (Calderhead & Robson, 1991). The information that we use to define what our particular beliefs are is aggregated over time and experiences, and eventually we draw from those relatively isolated bits and pieces of information to form perceptions or mental pictures – conceptions (Nespor, 1987). This process is called *episodic memory*. The biggest problem with episodic memory is that the aggregation of memories we have about one thing can have exaggerations or inaccurate interpretations (or even irrelevant information) sprinkled throughout the mix, much like adding a few grains of salt to sugar and contaminating its sweetness. All in all, the perceptions individuals have of scientists are not necessarily a reflection of reality (Pion and Lipsey, 1981).

So what type of information is it that leads us to begin developing a particular conception of what a scientist is (or isn't), and where does that information come from? Part of the answer is readily apparent, and part of it is much fuzzier. One clue is found by considering the seven stereotypic elements Chambers (1983) identified. Where do we find images of scientists wearing lab coats? Or working in laboratories with bubbling liquids? An obvious answer is media. Keep in mind that media includes both print and graphic forms. Since the 1950s, our world has become increasingly media-driven. Gardner (1980) suggested that students are exposed to cultural models through media, and such exposure significantly contributes to their mental schema. Schebeci (1986) took a step further and stated that modern television is a major player, that many television programs and movies portrayed scientists as amoral, insensitive, and obsessive. Flick (1990) found that television programs like the Children's Television Workshop produced positive influences on children's views of the scientific enterprise. Arquette and Horton (2000a) examined the role of television programming on the self-identify of young viewers as well as gender identity (2000b). Hence, television's influence can be inferred to be significant in the formation of concepts about scientists.

The same may be inferred about the influence of movies, although perhaps more indirectly. Although not directly investigating conceptions of scientists, a few studies have clearly shown that movies contribute to the images young children have about themselves and the world around them. For example, Butler (2005) reported research conducted at Dartmouth's School of Medicine that revealed preschoolers' exposure to movies rated PG-13 and R resulted in those children's behaving more and more like the characters in the movies. In a somewhat related way, Baker-Sperry (2003) examined how our view of Cinderella has changed since the Brothers Grimm first printed it. By inference, this changed view has been reinforced by movies, cartoons, and other graphic media. Essentially, in the original Cinderella, the wicked step-sisters were physically attractive persons. However, over time, society has come to equate wickedness with ugliness, so the stepsisters are now almost universally portrayed as homely, if not ugly looking individuals.

One can even find media influences through such seemingly innocuous items as video games. Shaffer, Squire, Halverson, and Gee (2005) studied the effects of video games on students' learning. Basically, they concluded that media such as video games allow players to learn by inhabiting virtual worlds. In these virtual worlds, learners develop situated understandings, learn what are (at least within the virtual context) effective social practices and shared values, and form powerful identities. All this occurs without much external guidance. Consequently, the learner begins to become a part of the virtual culture, and this is used by the learner to govern how he/she responds in the non-virtual (i.e. real) world. The key, then, is whether the cultural identity gained from video game use is one that is acceptable in non-virtual society. As a consequence, the conclusions one draws from experiences of virtual immersion may not be ones that are necessarily appropriate in the real world.

Taken together, these studies (and others) logically lead one to conclude that the way scientists are portrayed in media is a significant contributing factor in the formation of one's concept of what a scientist looks like and does. Supporting the stereotypic perception of a scientist is literature such as the classics *Frankenstein* and *Dr. Jekyll and Mr. Hyde*, short stories, and actual people we can observe (doctors, dentists, etc.) who perform their work often indoors and wearing lab coats, etc. The sources of information that tell us what scientists look like are many, are varied, and are pervasive.

## CONNECTIONS TO OTHER PSYCHOLOGICAL MEASURES

To revisit our original problem, we needed to investigate factors that could positively influence 8th graders to pursue science as a career choice. The *DAST-C* was a useful tool for some of those pursuits. To underscore the need for this line of study, one can refer to several studies that indicate an individual's perceptions, attitudes toward, and self-efficacy relative to science and scientists can impact one's likelihood of pursuing science as an area of study and vocation (Kahle, 1988; O'Brien, Kopala, & Martinez-Pons, 1999; Zeldin & Pajares, 2000). Since perceptions of scientists is a mental image or psychological construct, it seems reasonable that it may have connections with other psychological constructs such as those noted in those other studies: locus of control (LoC), self-efficacy and self-concept, and attitudes.

Sumrall (1995) interviewed 358 grade 1-7 students after giving them the *DAST*. His intention was to determine the reasons why the students drew the scientists they did. Analysis of the interviews yielded 12 groups of reasons that included, among other things, LoC. His conclusions were that Euro-American males had the highest percentage of self-image drawings, which was directly related to their LoC. The data did not show this to be true for other groups. Ross (1993) found significant differences ($p < 0.001$) between male and female high school students ($n = 14,825$) in their internal LoC, showing female science majors had higher LoC than did either male science majors or female non-science majors. In similar studies, Finson (2001), and Schibeci, (1989) also found that drawings of scientists made by students were connected to their LoC and self-efficacy. In studying self-efficacy and self-concept, MacCorquodale (1984) and later Ross (1993) examined drawings of scientists made by 2,442 junior high and high school students.

Among the factors they focused on were self-image and occupational aspirations, noting that females having low self-concepts with respect to science are less likely to enter science programs in college than are their high self-concept counterparts. Fourth graders' perceptions of self and of scientists as well as self-efficacy were studied by Bohrmann and Akerson (2001), who found appropriate interventions could change the self-efficacy of students, and in particular female students. Among the factors investigated by Mason, Kahle, and Gardner (1991) were the attitudes of 549 high school biology students who were asked to draw scientists. Among their findings was that an effective intervention program could positively impact the attitudes of students and the stereotypical slant of their drawings of scientists. Smith and Erb had similar findings earlier in 1986.

## WHAT'S BEEN LEARNED FROM THE WORK OF OTHERS

Over the past 55 years, we've actually learned quite a lot about people's mental images of scientists. Basically, we can refer to these pieces of knowledge as systemic issues. They are systemic in the sense that most are not limited to a single individual or group. In fact, this is one of the more fascinating aspects about *DAST* work. So many factors will vary depending on the particular subgroup one studies, but perceptions of scientists vary little. The systemic issues relative to drawings of scientists and the perceptions they reveal include age and grade level, culture and race, gender, media influences, socioeconomic group (from both income and rural-urban perspectives), and time. For each of these systemic aspects, people's perceptions of scientists remain amazingly stable.

If one were to ask both first graders and college students to draw a picture of a scientist, the images that emerge would generally include the traditional stereotypical elements. Even though the sophistication of the drawings and details may increase with age or grade level, the same stereotypical elements would be present in each set of drawings, regardless of age (Beardslee & O'Dowd, 1961; Rosenthal, 1993). Perceptions of scientists are also very similar across cultural borders and across international boundaries. Studies by Rodriqugez (1975) in Mexico, Krajkovich & Smith (1982), Chambers' (1983) study in China, and Rampal's (1992) study in India each revealed the stereotypical image of scientists was held in common in such varied cultures across the globe.

Perhaps the most research has focused on gender issues. In virtually every study reported in the literature, females have a more unfavorable view of scientists than do males, and more females than males do not see themselves entering the sciences as vocations (Yager & Yageer, 1985; Fort & Varney, 1989; Mason, Kahle, & Gardner, 1991; Odell, Hewitt, Bowman & Boone, 1993; Sumrall, 1995). Some studies (MacCorquodale, 1984; Ross, 1993) found the same basic outcomes, but also noted females rating themselves as highly competitive tended to be those who took "hard sciences" as college majors, had higher LoC, and were more willing to delay family formation. Additionally, in 1990, Dickson, Saylor and Finch wrote that people normally draw images of their same gender when clinical psychologists ask them to draw a person. This holds regardless of personality measures and family composition. However, this does not appear to hold true when people are asked to draw a scientist. Hence, females tend to draw male scientists.

The influence of media has already been discussed in the section on theoretical constructs. However, to augment that information, Gardner (1980) suggested that cultural models to which students are exposed; including television, movies, and comic books; can significantly contribute to students' mental schema. Shebeci and Sorensen (1986) suggested that television reinforced the stereotypical image of scientists in viewers' minds, and Flick (1990) discussed the influences of television on younger children.

With respect to race, the extant research has demonstrated that the stereotypical image of scientists cuts across racial and ethnic lines. Shebeci and Sorensen

(1993) studied Australian elementary children's perceptions of scientists. One group of students was predominantly Black and the other Caucasian. Caucasian children included more stereotypical elements in their drawings, but both groups drew scientists who appeared White. In 1995, Sumrall found obtained the same results in the U.S. South, as did Odell, Hewitt, Bowman, & Boone in 1993 in the U.S. Midwest. Finson (2003) compared drawings of scientists made by Caucasian, Native American, and African American eighth graders. Virtually all the drawings in that study portrayed Caucasian scientists.

Factors of socioeconomics were included in the study conducted by Schebeci and Sorensen (1993) that involved elementary students from rural western Australia and urban metropolitan Perth. Results showed no significant differences between groups in the stereotypical images they drew.

Perhaps most amazing of all systemic aspects of perceptions of scientists is that the classic stereotypical image has withstood the test of time. The early study by Mead and Metraux (1957) revealed common features in students' drawings, and Chambers (1983) later crystallized those features into stereotypical elements. Etzioni and Nunn (1974), Hills and Shallis (1975), Rodriguez (1975), Ward (1977), Krajkovich and Smith (1982), and Barman (1996) each demonstrated that these stereotypical elements consistently appeared in drawings made in a span of over fifty years. The only notable and statistically significant change that has been observed is a reduction in the frequency at which mythic, Frankenstein-type images surface in drawings (Barman, 1999).

## INTERVENTION EFFORTS

If one of the overarching goals of science educators is to encourage students to enter science-related professions, then it stands to reason that we should be concerned with the persistence of stereotypical perceptions of scientists that deter talented youngsters from pursuing the sciences. Through drawings of scientists, we can readily identify if students hold such perceptions. The trick is to determine how best to target and intervene to positively impact those perceptions.

Intervention approaches have varied over the years. Some have focused on providing students, particularly middle school age students, experiences with role models. Most role model interventions have involved female scientists, but some have simply included scientists whose work takes place outside the laboratory (Smith & Erb, 1986; Bodzin & Gehringer, 2001). Other interventions involved teacher training (Mason, Kahle, & Garnder, 1991; Reap, Cavallo, & McWhirter, 1994; Huber & Burton, 1995; Bohrmann & Akerson, 2001). Some included exploration of careers options in the sciences and science-related fields (Finson, Beaver, & Cramond, 1995), others were comprised of focused discussions with students after drawings were made (Moseley & Norris, 199). Still other programs, such as that described in Finson, Beaver, and Cramond (1995) employed combinations of these approaches. To some extent, each approach has been found to yield positive results: students' stereotypical images of scientists become less stereotypical. In some cases, the stereotypical images disappear altogether. However, the duration of these interventions must be extended. Simple one-shot, single-exposure experiences are insufficient to elicit the changes desired in students' thinking. Interventions need to become more widespread as well. Most of the interventions reported in the research literature have been limited to relatively small groups of students. Taken together, even though loosely coordinated, they can have some positive results. Barman's (1999) report of fewer mythical elements in drawings may be an indicator that at least some of these intervention efforts have started to have the kind of impact science educators hope for, but it is still too early to tell if this is really the case. As of the time this is being written, there exists no coordinated concerted statewide or nationwide intervention effort to hit stereotypical perceptions of scientists head-on.

## APPLYING AND USING INFORMATION GLEANED FROM DRAWING

The specific ways visual data from drawings can be used is really dependent upon your particular needs. Similarly, the visual data collected are dependent on what it is you are trying to find out, and upon the group from which you attempt to get them. So, from the outset, you need to have a clear idea in mind with respect to these matters. Once you have solidified your thinking about your needs and the group(s) from which you will get data, you should develop a research agenda. This agenda needs to include planning the different types of data you desire and how you expect to get them. You should plan how you are going to treat the data (analyze it, manipulate it, etc.) once you have it, as well as what you are going to do with the results you obtain.

Suppose you are a teacher in middle school science and you are wondering if you can somehow justify inviting outside speakers to your classes or temporarily altering the curriculum to focus on specific science careers. One place to start could be to have your students each make a drawing of a scientist. The reason for selecting this mode of data collection is that your students will likely enjoy making drawings, it takes a relatively short amount of time to do, and those drawings can reveal to you what stereotypical images of scientists your students possess. Once you have the drawings, you can then uses the *DAST-C* (checklist) to score the drawings, and learn what your students envision when they think of scientists. If your students' drawings are like most groups studied in the last several decades, they will predominantly show middle-aged males working indoors with bubbling liquids. This information in and of itself can then lead you to decide there is a need for inviting female scientists to your classroom as role models, and a need to help students learn about careers not limited to those in chemistry. Hence, you have started to mentally plan your intervention strategy. Following the implementation of the interventions you've planned, you may find it useful to conduct a posttest, having students again draw a scientists. Then you can analyze the posttest drawings and compare the results to the pre-intervention drawings to see whether your interventions impacted students, and to what degree they did so. Although this "action research" is repetitive of so many studies reported in the research literature, it still holds value to you in your decision making process about your science curriculum. You may find it useful to utilize the *DAST-C* each year with each new class of students.

Other measures can be used together with the *DAST-C* to yield other important information about your students. If you have the skills, you can collect data from these other measures and make statistical comparisons between them and those from the DAST-C. For example, you may be concerned about your students' attitudes toward science, so you locate an attitudes instrument appropriate for the age group and have students complete it at the same time they complete their drawings. You may be concerned about your students' self-efficacy or locus of control, since high and positive values of these measures are indicative of students who are more prone to pursue additional science coursework and science careers. Statistically, you would probably limit your statistical comparisons to correlations since, even though there is evidence that all these measures are related, no direct cause-effect linkage has been established between them. Depending upon the results, you may wish to plan interventions that specifically target improving attitudes toward science or self-efficacy, such as Science Olympiad types of activities, mentoring by "real life" role models in science fields, etc.

More sophisticated researchers may wish to tackle planning and conducting studies that focus on the more difficult aspects of visual data from drawings. Perhaps you may try to move beyond the correlational relationships level and delve more into cause-effect relationships between drawings and other measures. There is a host of potential studies yet to pursue, many of which remain unaddressed in the literature.

- At what age or grade level to stereotypical images of scientists begin to form?
- How rapidly do stereotypical images of scientists form once they begin forming?
- How are stereotypical images of scientists reinforced?
- What are the specific factors influencing stereotypic perceptions?
- Where do stereotypical images of scientists come from?
- How persistent and enduring are perceptual changes that occur as a consequence of various targeted intervention strategies?
- What linkage exists, if any, between stereotypical images of scientists and cognitive growth or achievement with respect to science skills and content?
- How do changes in attitudes, or self-efficacy, or locus of control affect changes in stereotypical images of scientists?
- Does a teacher's tendency to be predominantly expository or constructivist in orientation impact the degree to which students' drawings of scientists include stereotypical elements (see a pilot study on this in Finson, Pedersen, & Thomas, 2006)?

As the direction of your research into drawings of scientists proceeds, there are a couple of key points to keep in mind. First, past research (Kahle, 1988; Hammrich, 1997; O'Brien, Kopala, & Martinez-Pons, 1999; Pajares, 2000) is clear that individuals who have negative perceptions of science or scientists are unlikely to pursue science courses of study and subsequent careers in science. Often, the images people have of scientists are distorted views of what actual scientists are like (Pion & Lipsey, 1981), and many people simply cannot see themselves taking on the role of being a scientist. This may occur because females tend to view scientists as predominantly males, because minority students often perceive scientists as being White, because most students think scientists work in dangerous laboratory conditions, or because of any number of other things. Second, knowing what we do about the first key point, stereotypical images are really themselves neither good nor bad. Real scientists, for example, sometimes wear white lab coats and goggles to protect themselves, and to see them without such attire would raise safety concerns. We can have students wear lab aprons and safety goggles when doing work in school laboratories, thus paralleling what one might see in the images drawn by students. Such images would not necessarily be bad, but are still stereotypical by definition. Hence, the context in which stereotypic images are held is important to consider.

## EXAMPLES OF MY WORK AND METHODS

My personal work with drawings used to assess individuals' perceptions of scientists started with the development, piloting and field testing of the *Draw-a-Scientist Test Checklist* (*DAST-C*) (Finson, Beaver, & Cramond, 1995). This has been one of my two largest contributions to the field thus far. My second significant contribution has been a historical review of fifty years of drawing a scientist, looking at what we've learned and not learned from it (Finson, 2002). My other work in the field has looked at refining *DAST-C* procedures and protocols, examining students' self-efficacy as inferred through their drawings of scientists, comparing the perceptions of scientists of three racial/ethnic groups, and comparing students' *DAST-C* data with the teaching styles of teachers as measured by the *Draw-a-Science Teacher Teaching Test* (*DASTT-C*) (Thomas, Pedersen, & Finson, 2001). In each of these studies, the *DAST-C* has been carefully and consistently used. A number of other researchers interested in visual drawing data have used the *DAST-C* to create related instruments useful for other populations, such as mathematicians, engineers, and pre-service science teachers. My latest foray with drawing data is designing a study to examine the influences of media on students' perceptions of scientists.

The use of the *DAST-C* itself is very simple. Subjects are given a blank sheet of paper and a drawing utensil (pencil, marker, etc.) and are told to, "Draw a picture of a scientist." This prompt is always the same. Students will sometimes ask for clarification about what I want, but I simply repeat the original prompt. Some colleagues have changed the prompt, using phrases like, "Draw a picture of a scientist doing science." However, I try to emphasize that such changes in the prompt are really asking a different question, and the results derived from it will necessarily be different (or at least must be interpreted differently) than would be the case if the original prompt was used. Adding the phrase "doing science" essentially begs the question. It automatically limits the drawer to thinking of a scientist in a particular setting performing a particular act. The beauty of the original prompt is that students will often draw scientists at work in a laboratory in pre-intervention drawings, but post-intervention drawings show regular-looking people sometimes on the beach, in Bermuda shorts, shopping, and so on. This is noteworthy because such post-intervention drawings indicate students have come to view scientists as normal, everyday people. The changed prompt does not allow for this to occur.

Once the drawings are made, I next take the checklist itself to score them. For large sets of drawings, I may use a scoring summary sheet so that I don't need an individual checklist sheet for each drawing. A summary sheet lists the checklist elements along the left margin, and has a series of columns across the page – one column for each drawing. However, I only use this judiciously since the checklist allows for notations about qualities in the drawings that are not addressed by the checklist elements. These qualities might include the wildness of the scientist's eyes or hair, the type of clothing he/she is wearing, the variety of scientist shown, or something else of interest (e.g. Native American 8th graders do not draw animals in cages, and African-American 8th graders often only draw the heads of their scientists). In the actual scoring of a drawing, if any one checklist element is present, that element gets checked. If the drawing shows any additional parts that are that same element, the checklist is not checked again. There is only one check per element, regardless of how many instances of it occur in the drawing. Once all the elements have been considered (either checked or not), the number of checkmarks are added. The checklist has both an "upper" and "lower" subscale as well as a "total" score. The upper subscale score is based solely on the historical, classic stereotypical elements as identified by Chambers (1983). The lower subscale includes elements we thought should be considered in drawings, and which were often mentioned but not addressed. In our development of the Checklist lower subscale, we wanted to be sure the elements were common, or stereotypical. Consequently, in there is a "mythic" element rather than a choice of mythic and normal (mythic would be stereotypical, normal would not be). Subscores and/or the total Checklist score can then be treated with statistical procedures as the researcher deems appropriate. The Checklist is shown in Figure 1.

Figures 2 and 3 are sample drawings made by 8th graders. Figure 2 is a drawing made before any intervention program occurred, and Figure 3 is a drawing following an intervention program. Using the Checklist, Figure 2 would have a total score of 8 while Figure 3's would be 1. From these scores, it is easy to see that Figure 2 is more stereotypical than is Figure 3. Specifics about the way these two figures are scored can be found just below the two figures. What to do with these values is then up to the researcher.

In Figure 2, the image has a lab coat, eyeglasses, symbols of research (beakers and test tubes and lab counter) that are normal in size compared to the person, and symbols of knowledge (pens in pocket). This results in an upper checklist score of 4. The image also is of male gender, Caucasian, doing work indoors, and middle-aged or elderly scientist. This results in a lower score of 4. The total score

**Rater:** _____   **STUDENT NAME:**       **ASSESSMENT**   1   2   3

*DRAW-A-SCIENTIST CHECKLIST*

1. Lab Coat (usually but not necessarily white) ....................................................  _____

2. Eyeglasses ....................................................................................................  _____

3. Facial Growth of Hair (beards, mustaches, abnormally long sideburns)............  _____

4. Symbols of Research (scientific instruments, lab equipment of any kind)........  _____
   a. Size of Scientific Instruments/Equipment in Relation to Scientist:

       1)  Small...............................................................  _____
       2)  Normal............................................................  _____
       3)  Large...............................................................  _____

   b. Types of Scientific Instruments/Equipment:

5. Symbols of Knowledge (principally books, filing cabinets, clipboards,
   pens in pockets, etc.)....................................................................................  _____

6. Technology (the "products" of science) ............................................................  _____
   a. Types of Technology (TV, telephone, missiles, computers, etc.)

7. Relevant Captions (formulae, taxonomic classification, the "eureka!" syndrome)

---

### ALTERNATIVE IMAGES

8. Male Gender......................................................................................................  _____

9. Caucasian ........................................................................................................  _____

10. Indications of Danger.......................................................................................  _____

11. Presence of Light Bulbs...................................................................................  _____

12. Mythic Stereotypes (Frankenstein creatures, Jekyll/Hyde figures,
    "Mad/Crazed")................................................................................................  _____

13. Indications of Secrecy (signs or warnings of "Private," "Keep Out,"
    "Do Not Enter," "Go Away," "Top Secret," etc.)............................................  _____

14. Scientist Doing Work Indoors .........................................................................  _____

15. Middle Aged or Elderly Scientist ....................................................................  _____

**NOTE:**     Several indicators of the same type in a single drawing count as ONE indicator
           (e.g. Two scientists each with eyeglasses counts as one, not two).

16. Open Comments (dress items, neckties/necklaces,l hair style/grooming, smile or
    frown, stoic expression, bubbling liquids, smoke/steam, type of scientist –
    chemist, physicist, etc., -- etc.):

**UPPER / LOWER SCORE:**   ⧄       **TOTAL SCORE:** _____

© 1990 Kevin D. Finson, John B. Beaver, & Bonnie L. Cramond

*Figure 1. Draw-a-Scientist Test checklist (used with permission of authors).*

*Figure 2.* Pre-intervention drawing.

*Figure 3.* Post-intervention drawing.

for the drawing is, therefore, 8. The image also is one with a smiling scientist who is probably a chemist. In Figure 3, the image has none of the elements listed on the checklist, so the upper score is 0. The image is that of a male, but there are no other lower checklist elements, resulting in a lower score of 1. The total score for Figure 3 is 1. As with Figure 2, the image in Figure 3 is smiling and apparently well-groomed. Note the lack of a lab coat, pens in the pocket, and any laboratory equipment.

The possible range of Checklist scores is 0 to 15. My experience with students' drawings is that scores of 8 and above are relatively "high" and therefore should be interpreted as "stereotypical." Scores of 5–7 are average, and scores of 4 and below are non-stereotypical (some might call them "normal").

## REFERENCES

Arquette, C., & Horton, J. (2000a). The development of gender stereotypes: The role of television programming on young viewers self identity (ERIC Document Reproduction Service No. ED443411).

Arquette, C., & Horton, J. (2000b). The influence of current television programming on the maintenance of female gender identity (ERIC Document Reproduction Service No. ED443416).

Baker-Sperry, L. (2003). The pervasiveness and persistence of the feminine beauty ideal in children's fairy tales. *Gender and Society, 17*(5), 711–726.

Barman, C.R. (1996). How do students really view science and scientists? *Science and Children, 34*(1), 30–33.

Barman, C.R. (1999). Students' views about scientists and school science: Engagning K-8 teachers in a national study. *Journal of Science Teacher Education, 10*(1), 43–54.

Beardsley, D.C., & O'Dowd, D.D. (1961). The college-student image of the scientist. *Science, 122*(3457), 997–1001.

Bodzin, A., & Gehringer, M. (2001). Breaking science stereotypes. *Science and Children, 39*(1), 36–41.

Bohrmann, M.L., & Akerson, V.L. (2001). A teacher's reflections on her actions to improve her female students' self-efficacy toward science. *Journal of Elementary Science Education, 13*(2), 41–55.

Butler, P. (Producer) (2005, October 3). *Primetime America.* Chicago, IL: Moody Institute.

Calderhead, J., & Robson, M. (1991). Images of teaching: Student teachers' early conceptions of classroom practice. *Teaching and Teacher Education, 7,* 1–8.

Chambers, D.W. (1983). Stereotypic images of the scientist: The Draw-a-Scientist test. *Science Education, 67*(2), 255–265.

Clark, C.M. (1988). Asking the right questions about teacher preparation: Contributions of research on teacher thinking. *Educational Researcher, 17*(2), 5–12.

Dickson, J.M., Saylor, C.F., & Finch, A.J. (1990). Personality factors, family structure, and sex of drawn figure on the Draw-a-Person Test. *Journal of Personality Assessment, 55*(1 & 2), 362–366.

Etzioni, A., & Nunn, C. (1974). The public appreciation of science in contemporary America. *Daedalus, 103*(3), 191–205.

Finson, K.D. (2001). Investigating preservice elementary teachers' self-efficacy relative to self-image as a science teacher. *Journal of Elementary Science Education, 13*(1), 31–42.

Finson, K.D. (2002). Drawing a scientist: What we do and do not know after fifty years of drawings. *School Science and Mathematics, 102*(7), 335–345.

Finson, K.D. (2003). Applicability of the DAST-C to the images of scientists drawn by students of different racial groups. *Journal of Elementary Science Education, 15*(1), 15–26.

Finson, K.D., Pedersen, J., & Thomas, J. (2006). Comparing science teaching styles to students' perceptions of scientists. *School Science and Mathematics, 106*(1), 8–15.

Flick, L. (1990). Scientists in residence program improving children's image of science and scientists. *School Science and Mathematics, 90*(3), 204–214.

Fort, D.C., & Varney, H.L. (1989). How students see scientists: Mostly male, mostly white, and mostly benevolent. *Science and Children, 26*(8), 8–13.

Gardner, H. (1980). *Artful scribbles.* New York: Bavi Books.

Goodman, J. (1988). Constructing a practical philosophy of teaching: A study of preservice teachers' professional perspectives. *Teaching and Teacher Education, 4,* 121–137.

Hammrich, P.L. (1997). *Confronting the gender gap in science and mathematics: The Sisters in Science program.* Report No. SE059829. Oak Brook, IL: National Association for Research in Science Teaching (ERIC Document Reproduction Service No. ED 406 167).

Hills, P., & Shallis, M. (1975). Scientists and their images. *New Scientist, 67*(964), 471–474.

Huber, R.A., & Burton, G.M. (1995). What do students think scientists look like? *School Science and Mathematics, 95*(7), 371–376.

Kahle, J.B. (1988). Images of science: The physicist and the cowboy. In B.J. Fraser & G.J. Giddings (Eds.), *Gender issues in science education.* Australia: Curtin University of Technology.

Krajkovich, J.G., & Smith, J.K. (1982). The development of the Image of Science and Scientists Scale. *Journal of Research in Science Teaching, 19*(1), 39–44.

MacCorquodale, P. (1984). *Self image, science and math: Does the image of the "scientist" keep girls and minorities from pursuing science and math?* Paper presented at the 79th annual meeting of the American Sociological Association, San Antonio, TX.

Mason, C.L., Kahle, J.B., & Gardner, A.L. (1991). Draw-a-Scientist Test: Future implications. *School Science and Mathematics, 91*(5), 193–198.

Mead, M., & Metraux, R. (1957). Image of the scientist among high school students: A pilot study. *Science, 126,* 384–390.

Nespor, J. (1987). The role of beliefs in the practice of teaching. *Journal of Curriculum Studies, 19,* 317–328.

O'Brien, V., Kopala, M., & Martinez-Pons, M. (1999). Mathematics self-efficacy, ethnic identity, gender, and career interests related to mathematics and science. *The Journal of Educational Research, 92*(4), 231–235.

Odell, M.R.I., Hewitt, P., Bowman, J., & Boone, W.J. (1993). *Stereotypical images of scientists: A cross-age study.* Paper presented at the 41st annual national meeting of the National Science Teachers Association, Kansas City, MO.

Pion, G.M., & Lipsey, M.W. (1981). Public attitudes toward science and technology: What have the surveys told us? *Public Opinion Quarterly, 45,* 303–316.

Rampal, A. (1992). Images of science and scientists: A study of school teachers' views. I. Characteristics of scientists. *Science Education, 76*(4), 415–436.

Reap, M.A., Cavallo, A.M.L., & McWhirter, L.J. (1994). *Changing perceptions of scientists among preservice elementary school teachers.* Paper presented at the annual international conference of the Association for the Education of Teachers in Science, El Paso, TX.

Rodriquez, Sala de Gomezgil, M.L. (1975). Mexican adolescents image of scientist. *Social Studies of Science, 5*(3), 355–361.

Rosenthal, D.B. (1993). Images of scientists: A comparison of biology and liberal arts studies majors. *School Science and Mathematics, 93*(4), 212–216.

Ross, K.E.K. (1992). *The role of affective and gender influences on choice of college science major.* Paper presented at the 41st annual national meeting of the National Science Teachers Association, Kansas City, MO.

Schibeci, R.A. (1986). Images of science and scientists and science education. *Science Education, 70*(2), 139–149.

Schibeci, R.A., & Sorenson, I. (1983). Elementary school children's perceptions of scientists. *School Science and Mathematics, 83*(1), 14–19.

Shaffer, D.W., Squire, K.R., Halverson, R., & Gee, J.P. (2005). Video games and the future of learning. *Phi Delta Kappan, 87*(2), 105–111.

Smith, W., & Erb, T. (1986). Effect of women science career models on early adolescents. *Journal of Research in Science Teaching, 23*(8), 667–676.

Sumrall, W.J. (1995). Reasons for the perceived images of scientists by race and gender of students in grades 1–7. *School Science and Mathematics, 95*(2), 83–90.

Thomas, J.A., Pedersen, J.E., & Finson, K.D. (2001). Validating the Draw-a-Science-Teacher-Test Checklist (DASTT-C): Exploring mental models and teacher beliefs. *Journal of Science Teacher Education, 12*(3), 295–310.

Yager, R.E., & Yager, S.O. (1985). Changes in perceptions of science for third, seventh, and eleventh grade students. *Journal of Research in Science Teaching, 22*, 347–358.

Ward, A. (1977). Magician in a white coat. *Science Activities, 14*(1), 6–9.

Wickelgren, I. (1989). Headache art lends a hand to science. *Science News, 136*(9), 136–137.

Zeldin, A.L., & Pajares, F. (2000). Against the odds: Self-efficacy beliefs of women in mathematical, scientific, and technological careers. *American Educational Research Journal, 37*, 215–246.

G. NATHAN CARNES

# CHAPTER 5
# INTERPRETING DRAWINGS
# OF PRESERVICE TEACHERS

Visual data is a broad category that includes a variety of information. Technically, "visual" originates from a Latin word, "visus", meaning sight (Merriam-Webster, 2005). So, it seems logical to classify visual data as graphic representations or products that present a picture or an image to us. Typically, these pieces of non-textual information include drawings, photographs, videotapes, and other graphic information that are primarily observed through the sense of sight. Some educators are considering the use of hypertextual and digital data that allows the viewer to gain deeper understanding of a sequence of events (Young, 2006). As computer technology progresses, the possibilities for exploring and analyzing various kinds of visual data are rapidly increasing. Additionally, single images may be combined to form a sequence of visuals to present a visual narrative (Harper, 2000). These narratives are particularly appealing to sociologists who use them to present first person accounts and cultural stories that unfold through time and space (Harper, 2000). More recently, some of my colleagues (i.e. Finson, Pedersen, Thomas, and Barman) have drawn attention to sketches and drawings that provide insight into individual conceptions and perspectives. I will highlight how their contributions have impacted my interest in drawings of science and science teaching later in my presentation.

While the attention to visual data in science education research seems relatively new, this line of inquiry has deeper historical roots in other disciplines, specifically anthropology and sociology. For example, the modern use of visual research methods dates back to the 16th century when Roger Bacon argued that observable data served as the basis of knowledge (Harper, 2000). Ball and Smith (1992) indicated that Georg Simmel initially presented the implications of human beings' competencies in visual imagery and ordinary viewing, as far as research within the social science disciplines is concerned. Simmel highlighted the huge significance of the visual mode in understanding the social dimensions of life (Ball & Smith, 1992). For several years, anthropologists have incorporated the use of visual data, primarily photography, more than any other academic discipline. Later in the 19th century, both anthropologists and sociologists used photographs to study the physical features of major racial groups (Ball & Smith, 1992). From this time period until now, inventions and the emergence of various technologies (i.e. film cameras, 16mm film projectors, television, digital cameras, the

J.E. Pedersen and K.D. Finson (eds.), Visual Data, 79–92.

World Wide Web, I-movies, and Blackberry devices) provided insights into the understanding that what the naked eye observes is often incomplete or inaccurate (Harper, 2000). Later, psychologists (i.e. Goodenough, Harris) saw potential in drawings and sketches to identify developmental and cognitive issues in young children. In my recent search on "visual data", it is evident that various engineering professions use digital data to develop new materials or technologies that expand our knowledge of the natural world and ways in which we develop new applications of existing materials. So, the parameters that define visual data are increasingly expanding and more sophisticated. In an effort to be concise, my contribution to this monograph is focused on a specific type of visual data: preservice teachers' drawings of science teaching and learning.

## PERSONAL HISTORY

During my tenure as an elementary and middle level science teacher, I believed that it was important for learners to be actively involved in their learning. As a result, I sought out and incorporated activities in which my students were physically and mentally involved. For example, I engaged my students in understanding the concept of an "electrical circuit" through the use of Mystery Circuit Boards and exploring experimental designs though the use of Estes® model rockets. This commitment to active learning served me well; my students generally felt that learning science was "fun" and had greater value to them than did than meaningless black words on pages of a textbook. On several occasions, they shared the learning activities and new knowledge that they gained with their parents who often complimented me on stimulating their children's interest in science. These positive experiences further developed my instructional philosophy that included a commitment to instructional approaches that provided students with opportunities to construct their own learning and to relate science content to their everyday lives. However, I was unable to articulate my use of effective teaching approaches. In other words, I was "unintentionally inviting" (Wong & Wong, 2004). Later, this philosophical orientation would contribute to my adoption of using the Draw-a-Scientist Checklist (DAST-C) and the Draw-a-Science-Teacher-Test Checklist (DASTT-C).

During my doctoral studies, I learned that a major piece of my instructional philosophy and my commitment to active learning experiences were consistent with the scholarly views on constructivism as a referent for science teaching and learning. Drawing from scholarly contributions that surfaced in the 1990s, it became apparent to me that there were different perspectives on constructivism. However, it was clear that there were common characteristics associated with this epistemology. Specifically, constructivists stated that authentic learning resulted from the learner's active participation in the education process, connections made with prior knowledge, and manipulation and interaction with ideas and/or objects to facilitate understanding (Arons, 1989; Howe, 2002; McDermott, 1991; Tobin, 1993; von Glaserfeld, 1992; Wheatley, 1991). Therefore, knowledge is always contextual and personal (O'Laughlin, 1992; Tobin & Tippins, 1993; von Glaserfeld, 1989, 1992; Wheatley, 1991). Information that is obtained through experiential processes is assimilated within the learner's existing cognitive schema. Inherent in the acquisition of knowledge, the learner develops the ability to interpret and apply knowledge to situations outside the context in which it was initially acquired (McDermott, 1991; Wheatley, 1991).

Despite my experiences as an elementary and middle level science teacher, I approached my first semester as a university science methods course instructor with the idea that my preservice teachers were very different from my upper elementary and middle school students. Specifically, I felt that my preservice teachers were sophisticated learners and had no need to rely on concrete experiences and did not need as many hands-on experiences to understand the concepts that I taught. Instead, I presented them with lecturers and teacher directed activities that required them to think at an abstract level. My frustration grew as it became apparent that many of the preservice teachers did not have a strong grasp of the science content that the reading assignments contained and the pedagogical knowledge that the lesson plan assignments required. In a nutshell, I resorted to instructional practices that were in stark contrast with my teaching philosophy described in the previous two paragraphs. As a result, I endured troublesome experiences with elementary teacher candidates. Unhappy with my didactic approaches and naïve view on adult learning, they fired sharp criticisms at me, indicating that my delivery of instruction was ineffective and "too advanced". Upon reflection of my mid-semester and final course evaluations, it became obvious that my instruction was "above their heads" and highly inconsistent with the manner in which they constructed images of effective elementary and middle school science education. Based on these experiences at the university level, I concluded that there was little difference between my elementary and middle school students and elementary teacher candidates with regard for the need of concrete experiences to assimilate or accommodate new knowledge.

Post-Piagetian views highlight the importance of a learner's prior experiences in making sense of new information; in other words, the age ranges that I learned for the different Piagetian stages were much less important than learners' exposure to the new knowledge. This theoretical perspective is particularly fitting for providing pedagogical knowledge to preservice teachers who have little or negative exposure to science content and instruction. Armed with this pedagogical knowledge, I responded to suggestions for improving my science methods courses, incorporating more science teaching and learning activities. Strong course evaluations confirmed the fact that preservice teachers who completed a science methods course that I taught enjoyed activities in which they were engaged and felt that they contributed to a deeper knowledge of science teaching and learning.

Furthermore, teacher education guidelines within the National Science Education Standards (NRC, 1996) continued to impact my selection of activities and instructional sequences, advocating a type of teacher preparation that included a wide range of activities that engaged preservice teachers as active learners.

Therefore, I focused on questioning skills that Carin (1997) emphasized, conceptual learning that Bentley, Ebert, and Ebert (2000) synthesized, several content standards that the *South Carolina Science Curriculum Standards* (South Carolina Science Curriculum Standards Revision Team, 1996) contained, and teaching strategies that Howe (2002) described. As a result, the interns had opportunity to share relevant experiences from their school sites, discuss the assigned readings for which they developed questions, and participate in elementary science activities that preceded additional discussions. A simulation that involved the administration of *Draw-a-Scientist Test* Checklist (DAST-C) was one of the "learned experiences" activities that appealed to my preservice teachers.

MODIFIED USE OF DAST-C

Teachers are largely responsible for establishing and maintaining learning environments that may perpetuate or change students' views of scientists (Howe, 2002; Mason, Kahle & Gardner, 1991). In addition, *Inquiry and the National Science Education Standards* (NRC, 2000) and several science education textbooks that I reviewed for use in my science methods courses devoted a considerable amount of attention to the nature of science and the work that scientists do. If elementary and middle level teacher candidates are required to learn how to teach science to their future students, then logically they must have some understanding of what science is and what scientists do. Therefore, it made sense to provide opportunity for my elementary and middle level teacher candidates to investigate their views of scientists, using an approach similar to what interviewers used in *A Private Universe* (Schneps & Sadler, 1988) designed to unveil unviable conceptions.

Although there were a number of ways that my preservice teachers could investigate their conceptions of scientists and the work that they do, the Draw-A-Scientist-Checklist (DAST) that Finson, Beaver and Cramond (1995) constructed encouraged my consideration of teacher candidates' illustrations as an impetus for changing in their conceptions of science and science teaching. As the result of their efforts to validate the DAST instrument, the authors identified eight characteristics that were considered to be "traditional images" of scientists and provided a scoring rubric that could be used to analyze two or more sets of data that the authors drew. Initially, I conducted a few informal studies to develop some confidence in using the scoring guide and gain an understanding of the extent to which my preservice teachers' perceptions of scientists were stereotypical. As Finson et al. (2005) described, I found that the DAST-C instrument was easy to administer and use. Also, the scoring protocol made it easy for me to determine the extent to which my preservice teachers made changes in their perceptions of scientists at the end of the semester. While my purpose was to highlight stereotypical images that they held at the beginning of the semester, my preservice teachers saw the usefulness of the test with their future students.

While the original DAST procedure for analysis was very consistent with the manner in which psychologists reviewed children's drawings, I became more in-

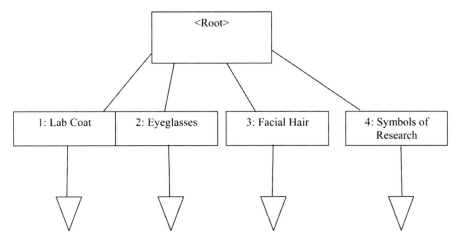

*Figure 1.* Sample representation of a NUDIST tree.

terested in the emic distinctions between the images that my preservice teachers drew at the beginning of the semester and those at the end of the semester. Because my intent was more closely aligned with an interpretive research discourse, I shifted away from the scoring protocol that Finson et al. (1995) suggested. In doing so, I consider the contents of the illustrations as non-numeric data. Because it was designed for work with non-numeric data, I used *Non-numerical Unstructured Data Indexing Searching and Theorizing* (NUDIST) computer software to help manage and analyze my descriptions of the teacher candidates' drawings instead of the numeric values that Finson et al. (1995) advocated. Since many of the drawings contained very little text, the descriptions of the illustrations were entered as text files along with the explanations that the illustrators provided, using the off-line document procedures that the instructional manual specified (*Qualitative Solutions and Research* [QSR], 1995). The categories were pre-established, using the classification scheme that Finson et al. (1995) developed. I imported these categories and entered them to a theoretical tree as nodes that served as the index system. Corresponding descriptions of the drawings were attached to the respective nodes. In addition, I entered and analyzed the interns' descriptions of sources that influenced their perceptions, using the same procedures that were used to critique the content of the drawings. The relationships among the nodes were tracked in a tree diagram that reflected the theoretical framework of the study. In Figure 1, I provided an illustration that contains a portion of the tree diagram. The arrows depict other nodes in the tree diagram that do not fit within the display. Within the NUDIST software, the researcher can view those nodes by clicking on the respective arrow.

In consideration of the themes that emerged among the NUDIST nodes, my teacher candidates had traditional and naïve views of scientists and the work that they did at the beginning of the course (Carnes, 2000). As Finson et al. (2005) found in their pilot study, my preservice teachers, most of them who were females, typically drew male figures. Furthermore, many of the figures in the drawings had stereotypical features of "mad scientists" who worked alone in a lab setting. I used this information to guide my instruction at strategic points throughout the semester, encouraging my preservice teachers to consider the human enterprise embedded in scientists' work and the diverse backgrounds of those who contributed to scientific knowledge. In doing so, we constantly revisited the extent to which we are all scientists (see Carin & Bass, 2001). At the end of the semester, the preservice teachers completed the DAST a second time and compared their illustrations to the ones that they created at the beginning of the semester. While there were significant changes in the illustrations, none of the drawings portrayed scientists as "people of color" (Carnes, 2000). The data provided some insight into the extent to which my instruction impacted teacher candidates' perspectives on scientists and the work that they do. However, the omission of interviews was a major shortcoming because the voices of the preservice teachers were relatively invisible. Therefore, my alternative to the research used to validate the DAST-C instrument fell short of capturing an interpretive tone. At the same time, the use of qualitative analysis appeared to be an acceptable alternative to visual data collection and analysis, providing similar results that can be obtained by a numeric scoring system.

The application of the NUDIST software helped unveil commonalities and differences between the drawings. The mechanics of assigning selected text units and moving them to appropriate nodes as the "theoretical tree" expanded and took shape made it relatively easy to establish relationships between the various responses. The power of NUDIST is in the ability to conduct higher level analyses that enable the researcher to construct arguments and answer research questions that invite correlations. For example, what was the common source(s) of inspiration for all of the females' drawings at the beginning and end of the science methods course? What kinds of changes, even if some of them were subtle, in the illustrations drawn at the beginning of the course and those drawn at the end of the semester? The NUDIST software is robust enough to run arguments that would answer these questions and lends itself well to a wide variety of qualitative analyses that would lead to deeper insights that go beyond the contents of the illustrations. I encourage other qualitative researchers interested in this kind of visual data to move beyond descriptive analyses.

## MODIFIED USE OF THE DASTT-C

Although my interest in preservice teachers' perceptions of science and the work of scientists continues, I have became more interested in how my preservice teachers perceived science teaching and learning for the environments in which they were about to enter. As the *National Science Education Standards* (NRC, 1996) and the Association for Childhood Education International (ACEI) guidelines indicate, it is important for teacher candidates to understand the nature of "real world" science. At the same time, these same teacher education standards give a significant amount of attention to pedagogical issues that highlight the importance of providing active learning opportunities in which children gain experience and expertise in critical thinking skills. Furthermore, the majority of the science methods courses that I teach are designed to acquaint preservice teachers with pedagogical strategies and issues. Particularly for my elementary teacher candidates, It is important for them to understand that effective science teaching practices overlap those of other academic disciplines. Following the adage that teachers teach the way that they are taught, it seemed appropriate to ascertain the preservice teachers' initial conceptions of science teaching and learning. Therefore, I became interested in their perceptions of science teaching and learning that they brought with them.

Coincidental with my reflection that led to consideration of science teaching drawings, Thomas, Pedersen and Finson (2001) developed an instrument, the *Draw-a-Science-Teacher-Test Checklist* (DASTT-C), that was useful in investigating images of science teaching while assessing stereotypical and non-stereotypical views of science teachers.. This instrument invites research participants to draw a picture of themselves as science teachers. In the most recent version of this instrument, the authors added an illustration and narrative data component. Additionally, there are prompts that encourage the illustrators to explain what the teacher and students in the illustrations are doing. The protocol for analysis requires the analyst to score the illustrations into three broad categories: the teacher, students, and the classroom environment (Thomas et al., 2001). These developers came to the conclusion that short, personal narratives might provide additional insight into certain components and aspects of illustrations that research participants drew, replacing the oral interviews that would be impractical with large groups of participants.

Thomas et al.'s (2001) development of the DASTT-C influenced my desire to learn more about my preservice teachers' conceptions of science teaching and learning in elementary and middle school environments. This activity provided an opportunity for preservice teachers to think about themselves as science teachers, a visualization that several of my elementary preservice teachers often did not make. Given existing scholarship on elementary teachers' attitudes toward science, it was unsurprising to learn that many of them either detested or were fearful of this curricular area and had a low level of self-efficacy. Furthermore, at least a few of them protested their inability to draw pictures that would adequately capture their images of science teaching and learning. Compared to the DAST-C, this test had greater appeal to me because it provided more opportunities for my preservice teachers to revisit their initial illustrations to build and organize their growing professional knowledge throughout the semester in a way that Thomas et al. (2001) defined.

Given my interest in interpretive research and the possibilities that it offers researchers to learn from research participants, a few of my MAT interns and I modified aspects of the administration of this instrument and the analysis of the data. Specifically, we made the drawing prompt less personal, asking the research participants to draw a picture of a science teacher at work (Carnes, Shull, Brown,

& Munn, 2002). In the accompanying narratives that they wrote, we felt that the illustrators had ample opportunity to identify themselves as the teacher in the illustration or another significant individual who impacted their view on science education. So, the specification that they draw themselves as science teachers was not as compelling. Furthermore we employed the use of NVivo, the qualitative analysis package that is more user-friendly than is NUDIST, although the former is very similar to the latter in several ways. In particular, NVivo supports a researcher in a way that allows her/him to explore and sensitively interpret complex data without reducing the information to numbers (QSR International, 2002). As Rich and Pataschnick (2002) noted, NVivo permits a researcher to analyze diverse kinds of data in a way that the analysis can grow into more textured and complex ways, allowing for multiple coding schemes rather than a single one. However, the downside is that NVivo was designed to code in managed textual data rather than visual information (Rich & Pataschnick, 2002).

Thomas et al. (2001), as did Thomas and Pedersen (2003), identified DASTT-C as a useful tool to help unveil episodic memories that research participants may have, particularly within the context of their own ideas, beliefs, and personal theories about how to teach elementary science. Our findings were similar, although the illustrations were not exclusively a result of previous episodes or events that influenced views on science teaching and learning (Carnes et al., 2002). Some of our research participants had difficulty recalling significant science education experiences or chose not to elaborate on them. Instead, some of them used illustrations to present their educational philosophies that they constructed. They drew from personal beliefs rooted in constructivist perspectives, even if these perspectives were inconsistent with their learning experiences. Because our examinations of the data were limited to the narratives that the preservice teachers wrote, we acknowledged the limitations of our findings and felt that interviews were necessary to get richer data and a deeper understanding.

However, time and limited availability of preservice teachers continues to be a challenge to conducting interviews and focus groups to obtain richer descriptions of the drawings and a deeper understanding of the narratives. Our MAT candidates participate in a demanding preparation program that requires a great deal of preparation for university-based courses and field experiences. In addition, some of our candidates have to maintain employment to sustain themselves, despite the fact that MAT program faculty and staff encourage them not to work. I continue to explore opportunities that would allow me to carry out some of the essential components of interpretive research (i.e. member checking, emic descriptions).

## MY PRIMARY AIM

Over the past several years, there is growing attention toward respecting the diversity of perspectives on the nature of science, science teaching, and ways of knowing. Coincidently, there is an increase in the kinds of questions about science education practices and the manner in which we seek to answer them. At the end of their review of research on science teacher education, Anderson and Mitchner (1994) advocated diversity in the manner in which we seek better understanding of science teacher education issues.

> Finally, teacher education could profit from being studied from multiple per- spectives .... for example, if one were studying competency- based science teacher education – which reflects a particular theoretical orientation – it would be helpful to look at it from psychological, social cultural, philosophical, and subject matter perspectives. Different perspectives often reflect different re- search methodologies and conducting such study with thorough attention to all of these perspectives may not be feasible. (p. 37)

To some degree, it appears that we have responded to the call that Anderson and Mitchner issued. However, Anderson (2007) applauded the diversity that exists in science education research but complained about the lack of coherence that resulted from so many different approaches. Specifically, he indicates that the frustration with reading and understanding science research results from the lack of well-defined rules that everyone follows. He seeks to present an order to understanding scholarly contributions through the lens of conceptual change, sociocultural, and critical research traditions (Anderson, 2007). The manner in which he does so is reminiscent of my learning experience with Dr. Richard Quantz, one of my doctoral instructors. While he acknowledged that there were several perspectives on education research, he helped me to begin to understand standard, interpretive, and critical discourses that impact how one reads, interprets and conducts research (R. Quantz, personal communication, 1995).

With the understanding that each research discourse has the potential to ad- vance what we can learn from visual data, I intend to gain a deeper understanding of what the illustrations mean from research participants' perspectives. For ex- ample, Golomb (2002) provides a representational theory of graphic development that may be useful in the analysis of DASTT-C products. She indicated that the debate on how to interpret children's drawings is a result of a perceived gap between children's perceptions and how they represent what they see. There are varying views among psychologists who seek to explain that children's drawings often deviate from the way in which they accurately perceive the visual world around them. Even so, my wife, a school psychologist, informed me that she and her colleagues still use drawings to gain insight into physiological, emotional, social dilemmas that students face (N.A. Carnes, personal communication, March 16, 2007). Is there a gap between preservice teachers' perceptions of science teaching and learning and what they draw? Looking at DASTT-C products from a psychological point of view, to what extent do the illustrations provide any insight into emotional or social issues that need our attention as we prepare elementary teachers to enter into the workforce? This does not mean that we should take on the task of seeking out those individuals who are maladjusted and unable to function as successful elementary or science teachers. Nor am I convinced that DASTT-C drawings will ever be insightful enough for us to determine the promise of teacher candidates' abilities to teach science. At the same time, there may be information that we are missing that would help us become more effective teacher educators.

Golomb (2002) also indicated that what children draw can be related to the developmental process of understanding and employing rules of representation. Drawing from the contributions of Rudolf Arnheim who was a renowned scholar on children's art, she indicated that pictorial representations often begin with global forms, generally consisting of a circle and line, that symbolizes something or someone that is more complex in nature. As children develop, their representations evolve from representations that are limited to personal relevance to more equivalent forms that correspond in a more structural and dynamic manner to the object or person (Golomb, 2002). Some of my informal conversations with my preservice teachers indicate that they draw stick figures for different reasons. Some individuals indicate that they are unable to draw well. So, the detail of the drawing is limited to stick figures. A few other individuals indicated that they wished to conceal specific physical characteristics of the teacher and students; in this case, the stick figures serve as a universal representation of all human beings, making it difficult to assess the drawer's sensitivity to the diversity that exists among human beings (i.e. race, sex, body type). So, does the fact that my preservice teachers often draw stick figures have anything to do with the fact that they are still in the early stages of graphic development? What is the level of correspondence between the elements that constitute the people and objects in the drawing and the actual individuals and environments that they intend to represent?

Within the discipline of psychology, the representation of space within a drawing provides an understanding of a child's concept of nearness. Some psychologists review children's drawings with interest in how the young authors represent three-dimensional perspectives. Some research indicates that most students are only able to provide perspectives that are limited to the horizontal and vertical axes. Over time, children are able to show greater coordination and discover ways to unite foreground, middle ground, and background within their illustrations (Golomb, 2002). Although it is likely that preservice teachers have outgrown these limitations, in what way do their illustrations provide insight into levels of intimacy between the science teacher and his/her students? Does the distance between the teacher and the students and between the students and each other represent the social relationships within the classroom?

## CURRENT PROJECTS UNDERWAY

Drawing primarily from the work of Goodenough, Finson, Pedersen, and Thomas, I am currently exploring the significance of the drawings that preservice teachers produce. As noted earlier, Thomas, Pederson and Finson (2001) and Thomas and Pedersen (2003) suggested that beliefs and episodic memories inspire illustrations science teaching and learning. While some of my own investigations support this inference, I am interested in further confirming or expanding on these scholarly viewpoints. In particular, Golomb (2002) indicated images that children draw are often a result representing what they conceptualize and/or is an indication of socio-cultural forces around them. In what way(s) are these contributions helpful to gaining a deeper understanding of DASTT-C data? In the analysis of a drawing, psychologists have given attention to the human form(s) that children draw, spacing that exists between humans and objects, and the arrangement of elements within the illustration (Golomb, 2002). How appropriate and revealing are these analyses for illustrations that adult learners provide? Do these elements provide viable insights into what the drawings represent or the stories that they were designed to tell? From an interpretative perspective, what additional information do adult learners, namely preservice or professional teachers, provide to help researchers better understand the significance of the drawings they produce? After all, they are more articulate than the young research participants that psychologists have used in their studies.

In addition, Thomas and Silk (1990) argued that scholarly inquiries have considered only the content of children's drawings to the exclusion of attention to the possible role that the process of the drawings might have in producing the final product. My review of the literature on science teacher drawings suggests that investigations of this form of visual data are limited in a similar manner. Also, my experiences with administering a modified version of the DASTT-C indicate that the process sometimes determines the images that preserve teachers present. For example, I recently interviewed a teacher candidate about the science teacher and students that she drew. She indicated that the stick figures with blank faces were easier to draw and that it was time efficient to do so. A disproportionately large teacher figure might suggest a teacher-centered experience. Alternatively, it might signify that the preservice teacher did not plan adequately to include a certain number of students in the picture or fit them within a floor plan that is crowded with essential instructional aids and furniture.

Considering these issues, it seems apparent to me the NVivo analysis package is a robust analytic tool that is useful for developing theoretical frameworks that emerge from non-numeric data. It has components that help the researcher input and manage data that results from DASTT-C administrations. Once the data are entered, there are multiple ways in which the researcher can analyze the descriptions of the data and append interpretations and elaborations that emerge as a result. Furthermore, NVivo's flexibility and responsiveness to a variety of research theoretical orientations allow researchers to generate more complex and rich understandings that are connected to DASTT-C data. I continue to work to improve my knowledge and ability to work with this software to provide viable answers to some of the questions I raised earlier.

Drawing from studies that date back to the mid-1950s, Finson (2002) constructed a synthesis of what we know about Draw-a-Scientist illustrations, how those studies contributed to our knowledge base, and the implications that they have for future research and science education. In the final analysis, he indicated there has been an increased focus on how individuals perceive science and scientists. It is my hope that my colleagues and I will be able to construct a synthesis of similar quality about what we have learned from Draw-a-Science-Teacher investigations, drawing from related academic disciplines and within the areas of standard, interpretative, and critical theoretical frameworks.


SPECIFIC SUGGESTIONS FOR FUTURE ENDEAVORS

Regardless of the fact science educators' attention to visual data is relatively brief, important strides have been made toward understanding how learners view science and science education. What follows are specific suggestions for educators and researchers who wish to pursue a deeper understanding of images of science teaching and learning. The first two implications lie in science teaching while the subsequent one lies in science education research. A fourth consideration crosses both areas of science education.

While my discussion of science teacher drawings focuses primarily on my experiences with elementary preservice teachers, a practicing teacher might use these illustrations within an action research project to identify instructional strategies that help students learn science more effectively while enjoying those learning experiences. For example, do the illustrations show an appreciable level of student enjoyment or boredom? Do the students draw themselves as passive listeners or active learners? What disposition does the teacher in the drawing display? What implications do these illustrations, considered together with student-written narratives, have for improving science teaching?

Furthermore, practicing teachers and others interested in science education should seek opportunities for students to engage in metacognitive practices that Anderson et al. (2001) recommend. In short, metacognitive knowledge is a dimension of the revised Bloom's Taxonomy that focuses on "Ĕ knowledge about cognition in general as well as awareness of and knowledge about one's own cognition. It encompasses strategic knowledge; knowledge about cognitive tasks, including contextual and conditional knowledge; and self-knowledge." (Anderson, et al., 2001, p. 27). In the context of drawing pictures of science teaching and learning, students can take advantage of opportunities to create illustrations that depict how they are learning science within the classroom and provide visual narratives of ways in which they learn science. The visual narratives might involve more than one illustration to highlight different activities or experiences that were meaningful to the students. The students can use these drawings to evaluate what they have learned during a learning celebration. (Ralph Peterson (1992) provides a practical overview of learning celebrations.)

Earlier in my presentation, I provided a brief overview of the use of qualitative analysis packages that facilitated my investigations of the illustrations that my preservice teachers drew. It is important for researchers who are unfamiliar with these software packages to spend some time with the tutorials, gaining an understanding of how to manage data and build theoretical frameworks that construct and chronicle understandings of science teaching illustrations. Of course, there are several other options available to those who wish to engage in qualitative research of science teaching and learning illustrations. Weitzman (2000) provides a thoughtful overview of the use of software in qualitative research. I encourage novice and experienced researchers to review his discourse.

Even though an illustration may be worth many words, it is important to understand that no single illustration of science teaching and learning tells the full story. Most psychologists use a drawing instrument with at least one other personality measure to look for a theme(s) that may be associated with a disorder or cause for concern. For example, a psychologist may have a student complete a "Draw-a-Person" test and a sentence completion exercise (i.e. "I feel happy when …") (N.A. Carnes, personal communication, April 6, 2007). Likewise, researchers should use the DASTT-C measurement with at least one other strategy that provides deeper insight into the inquiry process. The additional strategy may include an in-depth interview or focus group session(s) to understand better the significance of the research participants' illustrations. Finally, it is important for researchers to exercise caution in basing findings on single administrations of the drawing tests. The results are almost never conclusive. For example, some of my research teachers who drew the teacher at the front of the room with his/her students in straight rows indicated that the illustration depicted the beginning of the lesson only. They seemed to understand the dynamic nature of the instructional process that changes over the life of a lesson even though their illustrations did not necessarily reflect this level of insight. Therefore, the visual narratives that Harper (2000) recommended may be more useful, capturing a more complete view of preservice teachers' and children's perceptions of science teaching and learning.

## REFERENCES

Anderson, C.W. (2007). Perspectives on science learning. In S.K. Abell & N.G. Lederman (Eds.), *Handbook of research on science education* (pp. 3–30). Mahwah, New Jersey: Lawrence Erlbaum Associates.

Anderson, R.D., & Mitchener, C.P. (1994). Research on science teacher education. In D. Gabel (Ed.), *Handbook of research on science teaching and learning* (pp. 3–37). New York: MacMillan Publishing Company.

Anderson, L.W., Krathwohl, D.R., Airasian, P.W., Cruikshank, K.A., Mayer, R.E., Pintrich, P.R., Raths, J., & Wittrock, M.C. (Eds.) (2001). *A taxonomy for learning, teaching, and assessing: A revision of Bloom's taxonomy of educational objectives* (abridged edition). New York: Addison Wesley Longman, Inc.

Arons, A. (1989). *What science do we teach. Curriculum Development for the Year of 2000*. Colorado Springs: Biological Science Curriculum Study.

Ball, M.S., & Smith, G.W.H. (1992). *Analyzing visual data*. Newbury Park, CA: Sage Publications.

Bentley, M.L., Ebert, C., & Ebert, E.S. (2000). *The natural investigaton: A constructivist approach to teaching elementary and middle school science*. New York: Wadsworth Publishing Company.

Carin, A.A. (1997). *Teaching science through discovery* (8th ed.). New York: MacMillan Publishing Company Education, 75(1), 9–21.

Carin, A.A., & Bass, J.E. (2001). *Teaching science as inquiry* (9th ed.). Upper Saddle River: Merrill Prentice-Hall.

Carnes, G.N. (2000). M.A.T. interns' view of scientists. In P.A. Rubba, J.A. Rye, P.F. Keig & W.J. Di Baise (Eds.), *Proceedings of the 2000 Annual International Conference of the Association for the Education of Teachers of Science*. ED 438 191.

Carnes, G.N., Shull, T., Brown, S., & Munn, W. (2002, January). *Interacting with elementary in-*

terns' about their perceptions of science teaching. Panel presentation at the annual meeting of the Association for the Education of Teachers in Science, Charlotte, NC.

Finson, K.D. (2006). Comparing science teaching styles to students' perceptions of scientists. *School Science and Mathematics, 106*(1), 8–15.

Finson, K.D., Beaver, & Cramond (1995). Development and field test of a checklist for the Draw-a-scientist test. *School Science and Mathematics, 95*(4), 195–205.

Golomb, C. (2002). *Child art in context: A cultural and comparative perspective.* Washington, DC: American Psychological Association.

Harper, D. (2000). Managing visual methods: Galileo to Neuromancer. In N.K. Denzin & Y.S. Lincoln (Eds.), *Handbook of qualitative research* (2nd edition) (pp. 717–732). Thousand Oaks, CA: Sage Publications, Inc.

Howe, A.C. (2002). *Engaging children in science* (3rd ed.). Upper Saddle River, NJ: Prentice Hall.

Mason, C.L., Kahle, J.B., & Gardner, A.L. (1991). Draw-a-scientist test: Future implications. *School Science and Mathematics, 91*(5), 193–198.

Miriam-Webster (2005). *Miriam-Webster online dictionary.* Accessed on March 12, 2007 at http://209.161.33.50/dictionary/visual.

McDermott, L.C. (1991). Millikan lecture 1990: What we teach and what is learned – Closing the gap. *American Journal of Physics, 59*(4), 301–315.

National Research Council (1996). *National science education standards.* Washington, DC: National Academy Press.

National Research Council (2000). *Inquiry and the national science education standards.* Washington, DC: National Academy Press.

Peterson, R. (1992). *Life in a crowded place.* Portsmouth, NH: Heinemann.

QSR International (1995). QSR NU *DIST 3.0.5 for Macintoshes [Computer Software]. La Trobe University, Melbourne, Australia: Qualitative Solutions & Research.

QSR International (2002). *NVivo: Using NVivo in qualitative research* (Version 2.0). [Computer software].

Rich, M., & Pataschnick, J. (2002). Narrative research with audiovisual data: Video intervention/prevention assessment (VIA) and NVivo. *International Journal of Social Research Methodology, 5*(3), 245–261.

Schneps, M.H., & Sadler, P.M. (1988). *A private universe.* Pyramid Films.

South Carolina Science Curriculum Standards Revision Team (2000). *South Carolina Science Curriculum Standards.* South Carolina State Board of Education.

Thomas, J.A., & Pederson, J.E. (2003). Reforming elementary science teacher preparation: What about extant teaching beliefs? *School Science and Mathematics, 103*(7), 319–330.

Thomas, J.A., Pederson, J.E., & Finson, K.D. (2001). Validating the Draw-a-science-teacher-test checklist (DASTT-C): Exploring mental models and teacher beliefs. *Journal of Science Teacher Education, 12*(4), 295–310.

Tobin, K., & Tippins, D.J. (1993). Constructivism as a referent for teaching and learning. In K. Tobin (Ed.), *The practice of constructivism in science education* (pp. 3–21). Hillsdale, NJ: Lawrence Erlbaum Associates.

von Glaserfeld, E. (1989). Cognition, construction of knowledge, and teaching. *Synthese, 80,* 121–140.

von Glaserfeld, E. (1992). Constructivism reconstructed: A reply to Suchting. *Science and Education, 1*(4), 379–384.

Vygotsky, L. (1978). Interaction between learning and development. In M. Cole, V. John-Steiner, S. Scribner, & E. Souberman (Eds.), *Mind in society: Development of higher psychological processes.* Cambridge, MA: Harvard University Press.

Weitzman, E.A. (2000). Software and qualitative research. In N.K. Denzin & Y.S. Lincoln (Eds.), *Handbook of qualitative research* (2nd edition) (pp. 803–820). Thousand Oaks, CA: Sage Publications, Inc.

Wheatley, G.H. (1991). Constructivist perspectives on science and mathematics learning. *Science Education, 75*(1), 9–21.

Wong, H.K., & Wong, R.T. (2004). *The first days of school: How to be an effective teacher.* Mountain View, CA: Harry K. Wong Publications, Inc.

Young, J.R. (2006). With digital maps, historians chart a new way into the past. *The Chronicle of Higher Education, 53*(12), A33.

JOHN J. CHIODO

# CHAPTER 6
# VISUAL DATA: PROCESS AND PROCEDURES FOR EDUCATIONAL RESEARCH IN SOCIAL STUDIES

A library card is a right of passage. When I was seven years old my mother took me to the library to get me a library card. She was an Italian mother who was born on the over seas passage to the United States. She had strong beliefs as to what was good for her children. I stood there while she completed the forms and was given my own library card. Then I went over to one of the tables and sat down while she removed several books from the shelves. She sat down next to me and opened the books. My eyes scanned the pages and I marveled at the pictures. They were the art works of the great Italian painters, sculptors, and architects of the Renaissance. DeVinci, Michealango, Raphael, Chilini; they were all there. This was my heritage and I gazed at the pictures. The images are still swirling in my mind today. Sometimes when I sit and relax, I turn the pages in my mind and see those pictures over and over again.

Fast forward to an eighth grade American history classroom in Iowa. We are studying the Civil War and I have brought in some pictures for the students to observe. I am using these visuals to try to get the students to have a more in depth understanding of what it was like to have been a soldier in the war. The students are in groups and discussing the pictures. They are to pick an individual in one of the pictures and write down who they think this person is and what he possibly is thinking about. One of the students raises his hand and comments about his group's picture. "Two of the soldiers are black and they are dressed in Confederate uniforms. Why would slaves be fighting for the South when Lincoln freed the slaves?" Everyone seemed to want to give their opinion regarding the picture but they were asked to come up with some evidence to support their claims.

Fast forward again, and we are in Dayton Ohio and I am supervising student teachers for a university. Even though my content area is social studies I agree to take on an English major who was in the same school as one of my history student teachers. I observe a lesson where she is finishing discussing a short story about a boxer who trains hard but loses his match. He is aging and no longer has the ability he once had. The students are given about twenty minutes to write down their thoughts regarding the boxer. The student teacher collects the papers at the end of the class and, as I sit there shuffling through the short essays, I notice a scrap of paper with a picture on it. Instead of an essay, one of the students drew a picture of the boxer. It showed a man with bruises on his face. He was bent over,

*J.E. Pedersen and K.D. Finson (eds.), Visual Data, 93–106.*

but there seemed to be a sense of peacefulness, a sense of relief. All this in just twenty minutes; while the other students labored on several sentences.

Through the years these and other experiences have caused me to think about the fact I am not the only one who carries around vivid images in my mind. When I hear or read information, I create images in my mind that help me understand the meaning of things. In my teaching, I have also found many students seem to use the same process of visualization to solve problems. The image or picture they have in their mind acts as a guide or an outline that helps them work their way through a problem or organizes their thoughts for a presentation. Other students can view pictures or maps and almost instantly process the information they see. They are able to apply this information to solve related problems that they are given. All of this has caused me to think about (1) how I can use this as a social studies teacher, (2) how could I get students who don't visualize to use this technique, and (3) does it really have some value in the instructional process?

In the process of exploring the topic in greater depth, I began to search for a definition that would provide a structure for my own research. I started by clarifying the meaning of mental imagery and turned to Finke's (1989) definition:

The mental invention or recreation of an experience that in at least some respects resembles the experience of actually perceiving an object or event, either in conjunction with, or in absence of, direct sensory stimulation. (p. 2)

Based on this general definition of mental imagery, visual data represent the pieces of information that make up the image or the data that we extract from the image.

Our ability to use visual data is based on our capacity to perceive the visual world accurately, to perform transformations and modifications upon one's initial perceptions, and to be able to recreate aspects of one's visual experience, even in the absence of relevant physical stimuli (Gardner, 1983). Individuals may be asked to produce forms or in some way manipulate the data. However, the ability to perform these tasks may vary between individuals. A person may have an acute ability in visual perception while having little ability to draw, or transform the data. For example, a person may have a vivid visual image in their mind, but they do not have the fine motor skills to actually draw the image. Others may be able to create a verbal or a written picture of what they see in their mind, but again, lack the fine motor skills to draw the image. What we have, then, is a number of loosely related capacities that help us in our use of visual data. We can categorize these as follows: The ability to recognize instances of the same element; the ability to transform or to recognize a transformation of one element to another; the capacity to conjure up mental imagery and then to transform that imagery; and the capacity to produce graphic likenesses of spatial information (Gardner, 1983). Although these skills may be independent and vary between individuals, they also work together to some degree to enhance our ability to use mental imagery. One's ability to draw, write, or orally explain helps to bring forth the mental image in one's mind.

These skills or abilities are important in helping us become oriented to various places, be it a room or a geographic area. They help us recognize various objects or scenes when we encounter them in their original state or when the surroundings have been altered. We use them when we work with graphic representation, whether two or three dimensional, as well as real world scenes. Finally, they help us understand maps, diagrams, or geometric forms.

One of the advantages of being able to imagine an object or geographic area is that it enables us to represent complex relationships simultaneously. For example, when given descriptions of a problem, experts typically form images or construct visual diagrams in which the various features of the problem are depicted all at once (Beveridge & Parkins, 1987; Clement, 1988).

With a basic understanding of imagery and visual learning in mind, I began to explore its applications to teaching social studies. I had always been concerned with improving my students' ability to solve problems and now I wanted to apply it to my work. I reasoned that if we know that students have the capacity to use visual data, then we need to try an incorporate it into our teaching to help them learn more successfully.

As I became more interested in how we visualize things and how these so called mental images affect our reasoning, I began to think of ways to explore this area related to teaching and learning social studies. In my methods of teaching classes, we were exploring various ways to engage students in mastering various geographic skills. I became aware of the fact that my students really didn't have a clear "picture" of the earth's surface; where the continents were located and their proximity to one another. They seemed to lack basic geographic literacy – knowledge of the physical world. I recalled a statement from an article by Gritzner (1981) who said, "Individuals lacking a global 'mental map' of the world are prisoners of their own ignorance or provincialism" (p. 5).

As I immersed myself in the subject, I realized that an individual's mental map of the world is made up of a variety of images based on their broad educational experiences through the years. Yet, even with the variety of experiences that each individual has, our mental maps of the earth have some things in common. Our images are strongly conditioned by our culture and serve us in a variety of ways (Danzer, 1991). I located previous studies that focused on an individual's ability to identify various countries, cities, and physical features on maps (Kopec, 1984; Wood, 1988; McKinney, 1988) as well as a study involving undergraduate college students' ability to recreate physical features on maps (Beatty & Troster, 1987). The most notable study I uncovered was conducted by Saarinen (1987) in which he collected a worldwide sample of 3,863 student sketch maps from 71 sites in 49 countries around the world. Sketch maps are simple drawings made by students that show the physical features of the earth's surface. Saarinen was attempting to discover if there were any systematic differences in world images based on location, culture, or other factors. He concluded that people tended to center their maps on their home country rather than using standard cartographic projections.

There were also studies by Drumheller (1968), Metz (1990), and Wise and Kon (1990), who used the sketch map technique to research public school students' ability to learn world place location. These studies attempted use the sketch map technique to assess levels of progress and proficiency throughout the year. The process was used to provide teachers with information as to what areas of deficiency the students had in their knowledge of the physical world. In addition, it showed teachers what were the areas of student improvement regarding place location on maps.

With this background information, I chose to focus my research on the extent to which pre-service teachers have an accurate mental map of the world (Chiodo, 1993). If these individuals would eventually teach our children social studies (geography), one would hope they would have an accurate image of the physical world. Therefore, my study was conducted from a sample of 70 pre-service teachers (college seniors). Thirty of the individuals were students in an elementary social studies methods class and the remaining 40 were students enrolled in a secondary social studies methods class.

During the beginning of the semester, students attending their elementary or secondary social studies methods class were handed a blank piece of paper and instructed to draw a map of the world. They were told to draw and label the major land masses and to be as accurate as possible.

The major advantage of this sketch map technique is that the short and simple instructions make the test easy to administer and the technique eliminates any problems that may occur from students misunderstanding instructions. Although the sketch map technique is easy to administer, the actual task is difficult for students. It seems likely that students would rely on memories of the type of world map that most readily comes to mind and that was probably introduced in their formal education. Yet for many, retrieving this information was a difficult mental process.

Once the maps were drawn and collected, an evaluation system was developed to assess the accuracy of the drawings. Using a Likert Scale on which the number one represented a low score and five represented a high score, the maps were evaluated by the instructors. The following criteria were used to evaluate the students' maps: continents – the students were able to draw all seven continents on their map; relative location – the students were able to draw the continents in the correct hemisphere and place the continents in the approximate location with the hemisphere; correct labels – the students were able to correctly label all seven continents on their maps; and size relationships – the students were able to draw the correct size relationships between land masses. The maps were also checked to see what type of projection was used. Four special schemes were defined as a way to group the projections. They were: central focus - North and South America with Euorasia split; land masses intact; spheres; and no evident scheme. A variety of tests were used to analyze the data gathered from the student maps. Frequency distributions were developed for each of the four criteria used to assess the student maps. These included a comparison of levels (elementary or secondary) of pre-service students, a comparison of gender, and a comparison of levels and gender combined.

The data from the study revealed some interesting results. In general, all students had some problems construction a mental map of the world. The groups that performed poorest were female elementary pre-service teachers. These individuals will have the task of introducing geography to our children, yet their mental maps seemed to be the least developed of any group examined. The group that performed the best on this activity was secondary pre-service students, particularly male students. To shed some light on why this phenomenon continues to occur, the students in the study were given a one-page survey that asked them to reveal the extent of their geographic education. Students rated the extent of their geographic training in elementary, middle, high school and college. In addition, students were asked to list other sources of information, such as travel television, books, and other areas from which they obtained geographic knowledge.

Analysis of the information provided in the students' survey showed that the students who were able to perform above average on the mental map activity were students who had more than one university geography class. In addition, they enjoyed reading about geography and traveled more than students who did not perform as well on the activity. In simple terms they were better prepared formally and informally when it came to geography.

So, if we know that students in the public school are unable to visualize a reasonable image of the physical world, and likewise future teachers seem to have the same problem, what can we do to improve the situation? Or are we to remain a nation of people who don't see the world beyond our own borders? It would seem that, as educators, it would be important to develop a way to improve students' mental maps of the world. I therefore, designed a series of lessons that focused on improving students' mental maps of the world (Chiodo, 1997). Along with the lessons, I designed a research study to measure the impact the lessons had on improving the students' mental maps of the world. I wanted to find out if there was an improvement in the students' world mental maps after using the lessons. The major questions that I wanted to answer were: "Did the student's mental maps improve using the traditional mode of instruction?", "Was there a significant difference in the development of the mental world map between the students using the four protocol lessons and those instructed in the traditional instructional mode?", and "What was the reaction of the students regarding the protocol lessons?"

The students who participated in the study were enrolled in a seventh grade geography course that was part of the social studies curriculum. Two classes of 20 and 24 students were chosen to participate. Because the students were randomly assigned to the two sections of the geography course, it was assumed that a variety of abilities and experiences would be evident in both classes. The social studies program in the school district used in this study incorporates geography into the curriculum, so students had some exposure to geographic concepts and skills in grades one through six.

At the beginning of the geography class on a Friday, students were given a blank piece of paper and asked to draw and label the major landmasses, label the major oceans, and to be as accurate as possible. No maps or globes were displayed in the room while the students were completing their sketch maps. At the conclusion of the activity, the classes were told that they would have a similar activity on the following Friday and they were encouraged to study for this activity. No direct instruction was provided to the control group. Resources were available in the room and the students were encouraged to use assigned class time to study for this activity. The strategy used by the teacher was an indirect mode of instruction. He answered student questions and encouraged students to work together to complete this learning activity. The teacher for map work typically used this form of instruction. The other geography instructors who taught the course also used it. The experimental class was informed that during the following week they would have a series of short lessons that would relate to the activity they had just completed. Then they would draw another map on the following Friday.

Four lessons were designed to aid in the development of the students' mental maps (Chiodo, 1997). The design of the lessons was based on developmental aspects of learning. Drawing a world map from a mental picture requires the recall of a complex image that is composed of seven sub-parts (the continents) as well as their relationship to one another. Therefore, the lessons progressed from simple to complex images, and incorporated the concept of the grid system to develop spatial relationships. In addition, students' manual dexterity influences their ability to put down on paper the image they have in their mind. Because of this, students were not assessed on their ability to draw a perfect image of the continents.

The first lesson dealt with the basic shapes of the landmasses of the world. Students were given an outline map (outline of continents). Note: outline maps only show the outline of the continents. Outline maps are a typical geographic term of the world (Robinson projection) to draw on for the activity. The students were asked to draw geometric shapes over the continents on their world map. For example, one could draw a rectangle and a triangle to form the shape of South America. Students were then given a blank piece of paper and asked to use the geometric shapes to draw the seven continents, label them, and label the major oceans. The second lesson was designed to get students to use reference lines to improve the spatial relationship of the landmasses and thereby increase the accuracy of their map. The two reference lines used were the Equator and the Prime Meridian. The third lesson asked the students to build an image of the world map by constructing a map puzzle of landmasses. Students cut out the continents from an outline map (15–20 pieces) and then exchanged them with a partner who pasted them on a new piece of paper. The final lesson asked the students to draw individual maps of each continent.

The maps drawn by the students in both the pretest and post-test activities were evaluated for accuracy using a Likert scale similar to the one use in the previous study (Chiodo, 1993). The following general categories were used to evaluate the students' maps: continents; relative location; correct labels; and size relationships. In assessing the data, a variety of tests were used. Comparisons were made using a statistical analysis (ANOVA) between the pretests of both groups, the post-tests of both groups, and the pretest and post-test of each individual group.

Data representing the four criteria on which the maps were assessed were submitted to an analysis of variance with significance set at the 0.05 level. Analysis revealed some significant differences between the pretest and post-tests of each individual group, as well as significant differences between the post-tests of the two groups. The first test compared the pretests of both groups of students and revealed no significant difference. This verified that the two groups were similar in their ability prior to the treatment. The pre- and post-test comparisons for the control group revealed a significant difference on only one item; labeling the oceans correctly. The pre- and post-tests of the experimental group revealed significant differences on several items: contents drawn in the correct hemisphere; size and shape of the continents relative to the other continents; and the overall differences related to the means of all items. The last test compared the post-test means of the control and experimental groups and a significant difference was recorded in all four areas.

The findings from this study added to those previously conducted regarding geographic literacy. Since little has been done to help students clarify their mental maps, an implication of this study was that it is relatively easy to do this using protocol lessons that have already been developed. The teacher also indicated that the protocol lessons were not that difficult to teach and concluded that in the future he would continue to use the lessons. Finally, several students were interviewed from the experimental group regarding what they thought about the lessons. They all felt the lessons helped them in developing a more accurate mental map of the world.

My research on the use of visual data and the use of drawing was not relegated to just geography. Recently, I went back into the public school classroom and taught two sections of American history to tenth grade students. Since I had used visuals throughout my public school teaching of history and also incorporated these types of lessons in my methods class, I began to wonder about how I could delve deeper into understanding the ways I could expand its use. I had always used historical pictures as a way of getting students to interpret historical events. Students were asked to examine a picture and then answer a series of questions. Many times, students were given different pictures related to an event and asked to compare the photographs. This resulted in lively discussions where the students began to understand the interpretative aspect of history. For the evaluations of these lessons, I would have my students write essays in which they explained their analysis of the different visual interpretations.

Historical photographs were not the only form of visual data that I used. Political cartoons were a great source for visual analysis related to teaching history. Many books as well as web sites are available that contain political cartoons. Cartoons actually go back to colonial times in American history, where newspapers printed cartoons of British officials. No matter what the historical time period, my students seemed to enjoy the interpretative aspects of political cartoons.

As I reacquainted myself with teaching tenth grade history, I continued to use this teaching method with my college classes. However, I began to wonder if I could reverse the process. Could students draw their own pictures related to an event or could they develop their own political cartoons? During a unit on the Spanish American War, I gave the students an assignment where they had to develop a political cartoon related to the war. It could be in favor or opposition to the war. The results were amazing. Although the artistic level varied among the students, their ability to translate what they had read and discussed into visual data showed a great depth of understanding of the politics related to this time period (Chiodo, 2004 – NCSS Chicago).

My successes with this activity whet my appetite to continue to explore this aspect of learning. I recalled that I once attended a workshop put on by Polaroid Corporation on having students take pictures to facilitate learning in the class-room. I didn't have enough cameras for all my students, but most had access to one. Some even had camera phones that would work just fine. During a unit on the New Deal, I informed my students that one of their assignments would be to go out and take a picture of something that represented an aspect of the New Deal that was still present today (Chiodo, 2004 NCSS). Along with the picture, they had to explain in writing the relationship of the picture to the New Deal programs. Once again, my students rose to the challenge. They turned in pictures of the post office, the city jail, a baseball field, and a picture of a social security check. The most interesting was a picture of a curbstone from the downtown area. The student wrote that he found out that in several areas of the city, WPA workers put in curbstones along the streets.

My classroom success using visual data led me to wonder if there would be any difference in students' understanding of a topic in history when visual data were incorporated into their analysis of information. I decided to conduct a study comparing students' interpretation of a historical event where one group analyzed the information and presented a written interpretation and a second group ana-lyzed the information and presented both written and visual information (Chiodo, 2006). I wanted to see if there was more analysis and depth in understanding a historical event with students presenting visual information as well as written information. For my topic, I chose the battle at Lexington Green where the Minute Men fought the British soldiers prior to the U.S. Revolutionary War.

Students who participated in this study were enrolled in two eighth grade American history class, one with 19 and the other with 23 students. Since the school was in a university community, the students came from a wide variety of socio economic and ethnic backgrounds. Both classes had a range of academic abilities; however, no special education or limited English students participated in the study.

The lesson began with the students reading the textbook version of the events at Lexington Green. At this point, each student was given a variety of historical documents that included various first-hand accounts of the events as well as those that described the actual site of the battle. The students in the first period class (19 students) were told to examine all the information and then write an essay explaining their interpretation of what happened at Lexington Green. The second period class (23 students) were told the same thing; however, they were asked to ALSO draw a picture/map and write their interpretation of what happened at

Lexington Green. The students' written work was assessed by two different raters and an inter rater reliability was calculated. The essays were assessed based on the following items: length of the writing; accuracy of information; amount of detail provided, and interpretation and justification of the information presented. Since the research was viewed as a qualitative study, there was no attempt to compare the data using a statistical analysis. Rather, in the end, each student's work was view holistically in comparison to the other students'. Although there were differences in the work submitted by each student in both classes, the results showed the students who drew the picture/map and wrote their essays presented far more information and historical interpretation than the students who only wrote an interpretation of the event without drawing a picture/map. Although the drawings were generally quite crude in their development, they seemed to give the students a reference point from which they focused their comments. Their comments were also much more structured and in logical patterns. Five students from each group volunteered to discuss their written work with the researcher. The students were asked how they went about organizing and writing their written responses to the Lexington Green problem. The group who did not develop a map (first period) generally reviewed all the documents, developed some sort of hierarchy as to what information they concluded was valid, and then proceeded to begin to write their explanation of the events and defended their interpretation. The five students who were asked to draw a map and write their interpretation of the events (second period), all drew their map first based on their analysis of the historical material. They then used the map as a reference point from which they developed their historical interpretation as to what happened. The students were asked to comment on the value of the drawing activity. All five of the students thought that the drawing process helped them clarify their ideas and helped them organizes the information. As one student said, "It kind of worked as an outline for me."

Although this study was very limited in scope, the results seemed to show the having students visualize an event and draw their interpretation acted in some way as an advanced organizer for the eventual written work. Generally, the quality and quantity of the written essays were better for the students in the second period class who completed the sketch map than for the students in the first period class.

Since the vast majority of my teaching is now relegated to working with pre-service teachers, I once more began to examine what kinds to things I could do to apply visual data and the drawing process to this group of students. My research and teaching of pre-service social studies teachers had informed me the multitude of experiences my students have encountered in their schooling provides them with a foundation regarding instruction in social studies. Many educators agree that pre-service teachers bring into their teacher education programs previously constructed ideas and beliefs about students, teaching, and learning, although they are not always aware of their ideas nor able to articulate them (Anderson& Holt-Reynolds, 1995: Bird et al., 1993; Florio-Ruane & Lensmire, 1990; Hollingsworth, 1989). They seem to have vivid images of teaching. Bullough and Knowles (1991) contend students who are entering teacher education programs are seeking to confirm their own personal knowledge and images of teaching and are not interested in changing their views of what it is to be a good teacher.

There seems to be a general consensus by researchers that people filter and interpret knowledge and experiences through their belief systems and that their beliefs function as a stronger factor in change or lack of change than does knowledge (Abelson, 1979; Florio-Ruane & Lensmire, 1990: Pajares, 1992; Schommer, 1990; Snider & Fu, 1990). Keeping this in mind, it would seem logical that a teacher education program would start with an attempt to assess the beliefs that pre-service teachers hold in order to work more effectively to assist the learner in merging their knowledge and beliefs into a professional knowledge of teaching and learning.

This premise, along with my interest in mental images and sketch drawing, led me to examine the cognitive status of pre-service students' images of teaching social studies. The research was guided by the question, "What are the beliefs and perceptions of pre-service teachers entering our credential program regarding instruction in social studies?" To ascertain this information, I once again applied the use of mental imagery and drawings. Previous research in science education used drawings to understand children's' images of scientists (Goodenough, 1926; Chambers, 1983; Schibeci and Sorensen, 1993). This was later modified by Pedersen and Thomas & Finson (2001) to create a Draw-a-Science-Teacher Test Checklist. Where this previous work looked only at student drawings, I modified the procedure to include both visual images and written comments to assess the student's perceptions of social studies teaching (Chiodo & Brown, 2007). The pictures and written comments give the researcher more depth in understanding student perceptions and ideas related to teaching. A Likert Scale was used for the evaluation, rather than the yes-no rating scale used in the science test. In order for the preservice students' pictures and written comments to receive a rating, it had to meet the following requirements: if the category was present in the picture as well as mentioned in the written comments, a score of a one or five was recorded (one-direct, five-indirect); if the category was present in either the picture or written comments, a score of two or four was recorded; if the category was implied in some way via the picture or written comments, a score of three was recorded; and if a category was not present, an N/A was recorded. This rating system provided opportunities to more fully interpret the student pictures and comments. In addition, I incorporated a score sheet somewhat similar to the design that was presented by Barth (1977) in the Social Studies Preference Test. By incorporating a structure of sub scores and a total score, I was able to assess the students' perceptions on the three sub areas (teacher, students, and class organization) of the evaluation as well as an overall view of teaching social studies. Finally, Likert ratings were taken from the evaluation form and put on the score sheet to determine the student's perceptions related to direct and indirect teaching in social studies.

Fifty-two secondary social studies education majors whose ages ranged from 20 to 38 years old took part in the study. Approximately sixty percent of the students were males, while forty percent were females. Students interested in becoming middle school and high school social studies teachers are required to attend a general meeting, with the social studies faculty before entering the program. At this meeting, the students were given a blank sheet of paper and told to, "Draw a picture of yourself as a social studies teacher, teaching students." In addition, they were told, "On the backside of the paper, explain in writing what is going on in the picture." The students completed the activity in about thirty minutes.

Once the pictures were completed, they were evaluated by two researchers using the evaluation sheet. Thirteen behaviors were surveyed in order to determine the pre-service teachers' perceptions of teaching social studies. The behaviors were put into three categories: teacher, student, and environment. The teacher category contains the following behaviors: giving directions/demonstrating and activity; lecturing; using visual aids; engaging in discussion; and conducting an activity. The behaviors in the student category were: watching and listening; responding to the teacher; and responding to one another. Finally, in the environment category, the behaviors surveyed were: desks/students are in rows: teacher is centrally located; multiple positions/teacher movement; desks in groups/circle; and presence of social studies materials. After all scores were assigned, inter-rater reliability was assessed to assure the accuracy of the scoring procedure.

When the evaluation sheets were completed, the scores were transferred to the score sheet. The scores were totaled in each category and the pre-service students were either categorized as expressing direct or indirect instruction in each category. Depending on the category, low scores indicated direct teaching and high scores indirect teaching. Finally, ten students were selected randomly from the group to participate in an interview to discuss their written comments and the picture that they drew as part of the activity.

The study showed students' pictures and written comments regarding teaching social studies fell into three categories. The overall rating indicated that thirteen students' (23.3%) scores fell into the area of direct instruction, while a second group of 9 students (17.6%) were evaluated as having predominantly indirect teaching behaviors. The remaining 29 students (56.8%) were evaluated as having a mixture of direct and indirect teaching behaviors. The follow-up student interviews were used to validate the analysis of the pictures and written comments. In all cases, the students agreed with the interpretations made regarding their picture and written comments.

The findings in this research revealed that students who took part in the study had some strong beliefs and perceptions regarding social studies instruction that were based on their previous classroom experiences. The evaluation process uncovered a wide variety of student images of what teaching social studies was perceived to be. Generally, about a quarter of the students developed images and commentary related to teaching social studies that would be considered direct teaching. Another one fourth of the students saw social studies teaching more oriented to indirect teaching. Finally, the majority of the students viewed social studies teaching as a combination of different methods of instruction that varied from lecture, to group discussion, to such things as games, simulations, and individualized projects.

Throughout the interviews, students continually used the phrase "I want to be like" in reference to previous teachers they had encountered in junior high and high school. Whether their score indicated direct, indirect, or some mixture of both, this phrase was used. This seemed to be a powerful force in determining what they would be like as a social studies teacher.

The evaluation process gave the students in this study the opportunity to explore their mental images and personal beliefs regarding instruction in the social studies. This type of exploration is important in the development of pre-service teachers. Previous research suggests that educational beliefs of pre-service teachers are an important factor in their acquisition and interpretation of knowledge and subsequent teaching behaviors (Calderhead & Robson, 1991; Clandinin & Connelly, 1987; Clark, 1988; Goodman, 1988; Nespor, 1987). As teacher educators, we must be aware of the beliefs and experiences that our students bring into our classrooms regarding social studies instruction. If we are to broaden or change pre-service teachers' beliefs regarding instruction in the social studies, they need to discover that their existing frame of reference for understanding instruction is only one of several possible frames.

Considering the need for this type of reflection by pre-service students, the Draw a Social Studies Test evaluation seems to be a valuable tool that can be used by social studies instructors to help students reflect on their personal beliefs about teaching. Students can complete and score their own pictures and comments. Then, the teacher can have students compare the results and engage in a dialogue about what they think the instructional process may look like in social studies teaching.

The use of visual data can be a powerful tool in teaching and learning social studies. My progress in developing this line of research has taken me in several directions that I have discussed. Yet, I continue to think about how drawings can be applied to teaching and learning social studies in new ways. I am not a computer wiz, but I realize that the use of computers and the Internet are an intricate part of the lives of current and future generations of students. Through the use of the Internet, social studies teachers have their students search a variety of sites to examine a wide variety of print and visual data. Having students develop drawings of both the visual and written data they access via the internet may led to some interesting research studies. I simply need to sketch out the path and continue my journey.

## REFERENCES

Abelson, R. (1979). Differences between belief systems and knowledge systems. *Cognitive Science*, *3*, 355–366.

Anderson, L., & Holt-Reynolds, D. (1995). *Prospective teachers' beliefs and teacher education pedagogy: Research based on a teacher educator's practical theory*. East Lansing, MI: National Center for Research on Teacher Learning.

Barth, J. (1997). *The present and future of three traditions.* Paper presented at the annual meeting of the National Council for the Social Studies, Cincinnati, OH (ERIC Document Reproduction Service No. ED148663).

Beatty, W., & Troster, A. (1987). Gender differences in geographic knowledge. *Sex Roles, 16*(11–12), 565–590.

Beveridge, M., & Parkins, E. (1987). Visual representation in analogue problem solving. *Memory & Congition, 15,* 230–237.

Bird, T., Anderson, L., Sullivan, B., & Swidler, S. (1993). Pedagogical balancing acts: Attempts to influence prospective teacher' beliefs. *Teacher and Teacher Education, 9*(3), 253–267.

Bullough, R., & Knowles, J. (1991). Teaching and nurturing: Changing conceptions of self as teacher in a case study of becoming a teacher. *Qualitative Studies in Education, 4,* 121–140.

Calderhead, J., & Robson, M. (1991). Images of teaching: Student teachers' early conceptions of classroom practice. *Teaching and Teacher Education, 7,* 1–8.

Chambers, D. (1993). Stereotypic images of the scientist: The Draw-a-Scientist Test. *Science Education, 67*(2), 255–265.

Chiodo, J. (1993). Mental maps: Preservice teachers' awareness of the world. *Journal of Geography, 92*(3), 110–117.

Chiodo, J. (1997). Improving the cognitive development of students' mental maps of the world. *Journal of Geography, 96*(3), 153–163.

Chiodo, J. (2004, November). *Photos and photography in teaching American history.* Paper presented at the annual meeting of the National Council for the Social Studies, Chicago, IL.

Chiodo, J. (2006). Refining historical interpretation through the use of sketch drawings. Paper presented at the National Council for the Social Studies Annual Meeting, Washington, DC.

Chiodo, J., & Brown, T. (2007). Student perceptions of teaching: Assessing their mental images of teaching social studies. *Journal of Social Studies Research 31*(1), 12–26

Clandinin, J., & Connelly, F. (1987). Teachers' personal knowledge: What counts as 'personal' in studies of the personal? *Journal of Curriculum Studies, 19,* 487–500.

Clark, C. (1988). Asking the right questions about teacher preparation: Contributions of research on teacher thinking. *Educational Researcher, 17*(2), 5–12.

Clement, J. (1988). Observed methods for generating analogies in scientific problem solving. *Cognitive Science, 12,* 563–586.

Danzer, G. (1991). World maps, worldviews, and world history. *Social Education, 55*(5), 301–303.

Drumheller, S. (1968). Conjure up a map: A crucial but much neglected skill. *Journal of Geography, 2,* 140–146.

Finke, R. (1989). *Principles of mental imagery.* Cambridge, MA: MIT Press.

Florio-Ruane, S., & Lensmire, T. (1990). Transforming future teachers' ideas about writing instruction. *Journal of Curriculum Studies, 22*(3), 277–289.

Gardner, H. (1983). *Frames of mind.* New York: Basic Books Inc.

Goodenough, F. (1926). *Measurement of intelligence by drawings.* New York: Harcourt Brace.

Goodman, J. (1988). Constructing a practical philosophy of teaching: A study of pre-service teachers' professional perspectives. *Teaching and Teacher Education, 4,* 121–137.

Gritzner, C. (1981). Geographic education: Where have we failed? *Journal of Geography, 80*(7), 264.

Hollingsworth, S. (1989). Prior beliefs and cognitive change in learning to teach. *American Educational Research Journal, 26*(2), 160–189.

Kopec, R. (1984). *Where in North Carolina 1984.* United States: North Carolina (ERIC Document Reproduction Service No. ED 256630).

McKinney, C. (1988). *Pre-service elementary education majors' knowledge of world geography.* United States: Oklahoma (ERIC Document Reproduction Service No. ED 305313).

Metz, H. (1990). Sketch maps: Helping students get the big picture. *Journal of Geography, 89*(3), 114–118.

Nespor, J. (1987). The role of beliefs in the practice of teaching. *Journal of Curriculum Studies, 19,* 317–328.

Pajares, M. (1992). Teachers' beliefs and educational research: Cleaning up a messy construct. *Review of Educational Research, 62*(3), 307–332.

Pedersen, J., & Thomas, J. (1998, February). *Draw-a-science-teacher-test: Pre-service elementary teachers perceptions of classroom experiences.* Paper presented at the meeting of the National Association of Researchers in Science Teaching, San Diego, CA.

Pedersen, J., Thomas, J., & Finson, K. (2001). Validation of the draw-a-science teacher test. *Journal of Science Teacher Education, 12*(4), 295–310.

Saarinen, T. (1987). *Centering of mental maps of the world.* Tucson, AZ: Department of Geography and Regional Studies, University of Arizona, Paper series 87-7 (ERIC Document Reproduction Service No. ED 293738).

Schibeci, R., & Sorensen, I. (1993). Elementary school children's perceptions of scientists. ₁School Science and Mathematics, *83*(1), 14–19.

Schommer, M. (1990). Effects of beliefs about the nature of knowledge on comprehension. *Journal of Educational Psychology, 82,* 498–504.

Snider, M., & Fu, V. (1990). The effects of specialized education and job experience on early childhood teachers' knowledge of developmentally appropriate practice. *Early Childhood Research Quarterly, 5,* 69–78.

Wise, N., & Hecky, K. (1990). Assessing geographic knowledge with sketch maps. *Journal of Geography, 89*(3), 123–129.

Wood, R. (1988). *Geographic knowledge of university students.* South Dakota: University of South Dakota Department of Geography (ERIC Document Reproduction Service No. ED 296944).

MARGARET L. NIESS AND ANDRÉ J. MACK

# CHAPTER 7
# VISUAL THINKING, VISUAL DATA,
# AND MATHEMATICS EDUCATION

Mathematics is a discipline that depends on visual symbols when thinking about and communicating abstract ideas in writing. Early in their lives, children are taught to count, first verbally followed by communication in writing. They learn to write numerals like 1, 2, and 3 to represent number concepts of *one-ness*, *two-ness* and *three-ness*. Over multiple years of practice writing and communicating their thinking with these visual symbols, these abstract ideas represented by the visual symbols become more concrete and less abstract to them. In essence, the visual symbols embody the abstract mathematical ideas.

The transition from these early abstract visual symbols to more concrete visual representations explains the importance of the impact of visual thinking in learning mathematics. As mathematics educators, we have struggled with designing instructional methods to guide students in developing these more concrete understandings of the abstract mathematical ideas represented in the visual symbols. Over the years our thinking has evolved based on our teaching experiences, has been refined through our scholarly investigations of visual representations in mathematics, and has been clarified through our work concerning the integration of silicon-based technologies in learning mathematics. The question that has consistently haunted us throughout our careers has been, "What are students thinking as they communicate their understandings using mathematics symbols?"

Visual thinking lies at the heart of a myriad of current ideas in mathematics education highlighted by the inclusion of the *representation standard* in the National Council of Teachers of Mathematics (NCTM) *Principles and Standards for School Mathematics* released in 2000. Specifically, this *representation standard* indicates that

> Representations should be treated as essential elements in supporting students' understanding of mathematical concepts and relationships; in communicating mathematical approaches, arguments, and understandings to one's self and to others; in recognizing connections among related mathematical concepts; and in applying mathematics to realistic problem situations through modeling. (p. 67)

Through this standard, NCTM officially recognized and described the importance of students gaining an understanding of the connections among various representations – symbolic, numerical and graphical. Therefore, aside from simply

*J.E. Pedersen and K.D. Finson (eds.), Visual Data, 107–123.*
© 2009. *Sense Publishers. All rights reserved.*

recognizing the various representations, visual thinking in mathematics embodies making connections among the various representations, converting among the various representations and extending mathematical knowledge with multiple representations.

The question for our scholarly research has been connected with the thinking and understanding that students gain through the extension of their visual thinking to multiple representations within silicon-based digital technology experiences and environments. More specifically, our interest in visual thinking has been engaged with the research over the past 30 years that has explored the impact of these technologies in aiding in the development of mathematical knowledge. An overall gestalt of this research has focused on determining the impact of the incorporation of the visual data supplied by the various technologies on the development of students' mathematical knowledge, skills and dispositions.

Mathematics education researchers' concerns with visual representations presented in certain silicon-based instructional technologies and the visual thinking that they engender have created a need for robust and wide-ranging data collection devices to capture the essential nature of technology-driven classroom environments. What the students see on their display screens is just as important a source of data for educational research as what they do with the visual representations. Student-generated artifacts with technology are often dynamic and evolving, and capturing the ways in which students are responding to them in real time is usually through video recordings. Yet, one major problem for researchers is that this increased data gathering capacity has outstripped current data analysis techniques requiring new techniques for analyzing high volumes of visual data in conjunction with additional artifacts.

## VISUAL REPRESENTATIONS OF MATHEMATICS VIS-À-VIS TECHNOLOGY

"Technology is essential in teaching and learning mathematics; it influences the mathematics that is taught and enhances students' learning" (p. 1). This Technology Principle released by NCTM in 2000 was enhanced in 2006 by the Association of Mathematics Teacher Educators (AMTE) position.

> The computational and graphical capabilities of current technologies enable users to efficiently generate and manipulate a variety of representations of mathematical ideas and processes. Activities that engage students in connecting multiple representations (e.g., graphical, numerical, algebraic, and verbal), and those that invite students to analyze or create images, visualizations, and simulations provide wide-ranging opportunities for mathematical exploration and sense making. (p 1)

Together these positions support an increase in the endorsement for the importance of visualization in mathematics and mathematics education (Arcavi, 2003). More than 30 years of technological advancements have led to this incorporation of gathering and producing visual data in support of visual thinking in learning mathematics.

## LOGO MATHEMATICAL MICROWORLDS

In the early 1980s, the mathematics education community was introduced to the Logo language - a computer language that Papert (1980) described as having the capability of providing a mathematical microworld within which learners were able to explore and learn mathematics by designing instructions for a cursor called a "turtle" to move during the process of drawing specific figures or designs. In the process, these learners were engaged in visual thinking. Often in their early experiences using this computer language, students proposed instructions for the turtle such as this one to draw an equilateral triangle:

REPEAT 3[FD 100 RT 60]

Rather than being told by a teacher that the command contained an error, the actions of the turtle provided students with visual data indicating that the design was not an equilateral triangle – in fact not a triangle at all. Through this experience, students engaged in an experience that required visual thinking in a geometric microworld unlike any learning environment they had previously had opportunities to explore. Did the student learn mathematics? And, if so, what mathematics did they learn? These were certainly some of the important questions in mathematics education research in the 1980s (Clement, 1984; Clements & Batista, 1989, 1992; Hoyles, 1993; Kurland, 1984; Kurland & Pea, 1985; Pea, 1985; Pea & Kurland, 1984; Pea, Kurland & Hawkins, 1985).

Much of the early research with Logo revolved around the work of Pierre and Dina van Hiele (1959/1985, 1986) who described five levels of geometric thought, the first of which the *visual* level as a way of describing students' initial ideas in geometry. This level was pictured as the time when students reason with mental visual images. More specifically, they found that students at this level identified figures as whole, visual objects from their personal experiences without attending to the features of the object. "In identifying figures, they often use visual prototypes; students say that a given figure is a rectangle, for instance, because it looks like a door" (Clements & Battista, 1992, p. 427). These van Hiele levels provided researchers with ways to view and describe the differences in the students' geometric thinking. Thus, the Logo language provided the environment for studying students' geometric thinking. The results indicated that appropriate use of Logo engendered higher levels of geometric thinking that helped students move beyond the *visual* level. The Logo environment guided students in developing ideas about shapes that were more mathematical and precise. Logo served as a medium for communication of mathematical ideas and relationships through its visual environment; Logo supported students in their mathematical thinking and discussions as they created more efficient or elegant mathematical directions for the turtle.

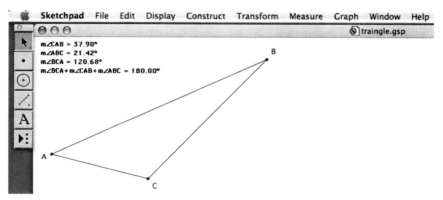

*Figure 1. Geometer's Sketchpad* creation of a triangle to explore the sum of the angles of a triangle.

GEOMETER'S SKETCHPAD AS A DYNAMIC MATHEMATICAL ENVIRONMENT

In the 1990s, technological advances promised new capabilities for learning mathematics. *Geometer's Sketchpad* supported students in making conjectures through explorations in a dynamic mathematical environment. Students were observed creating three points on the sketchpad, labeling then A, B, and C, and finally connecting A to B, B to C and C to A. In the process, they created a triangle – more accurately, a general triangle. They measured each of the angles and issued instructions to add the measures of the angles as shown in Figure 1. Relying on the dynamic nature of this environment, they moved the triangle or changed its shape by lengthening or shrinking sides and increasing or decreasing the sizes of the angles. With each move and shift of the triangle, the sum of the angles remained at 180°, prompting students to declare that the sum of the angles of any triangle was always 180°. Could there be one triangle that they did not find where the sum of the angles was not 180°? Were they able to exhaust the visual possibilities in this environment? The visual data supported students' visual thinking about the nature of mathematical proof. Does such visual data constitute a mathematical proof? Does exploration in a dynamic, visual environment increase students' understandings of mathematical content and processes? Do students gain a fundamental understanding of the nature of proof through this visual data and thinking? Such questions challenged researchers to ponder appropriate research questions and methodologies that adequately represented a sound approach to responding to such questions (Hollebrands, 2007; Laborde & Laborde, 1995; Olive, 1998; Roschelle, 1996; Roschelle & Kaput, 1996).

The results of much of the research with the dynamic capabilities of *Geometer's Sketchpad* where students are supported by the drag mode for manipulating geometrical figures has indicated that students were able to more easily investigate a class of drawings that guided them in developing conjectures from the visual representations. Concerns about students' understandings of the nature of proof has been recognized as a constraint of the technology, requiring that the teachers specifically focus their instruction toward guiding students' understandings of proof from within this visual environment. For example, Hollebrands (2007) found that students' purposes for dragging were different and their reasoning about the visual representations influenced these differences. Some of their thinking as a result of the dragging actions was found to be more reactive and random while others were used to test specific conjectures. Encouraging students to reflect on their work seems to encourage them to be more proactive in their thinking about their conjectures. Focusing their ideas about the relationships helps to them move from a focus on the visual aspects to reasoning about the geometric properties in the figures.

## GRAPHING CALCULATORS CONNECTING ALGEBRAIC, NUMERIC AND VISUAL REPRESENTATIONS

Also in the early 1990s, the computational capabilities of graphing calculators confronted mathematics educators as to whether such capabilities supported or detracted from the essential mathematics that students must learn. Among the questions educators pondered were: "What constitutes a fundamental mathematical understanding?" "Do students lose important computational skills needed for successful citizenship?" "When using the graphing capabilities, are they losing important graphing skills or are they gaining an environment within which to explore mathematical ideas?" Beginning with a linear function, students might change only one constant at a time and move to view the graphical representation of the function (see Figure 2). Does this quick access to accurate visual data for these functions help them make important connections among the algebraic and graphical representations and in the process do they gain a better understanding of mathematical content and processes? Questions about linking visual representations with algebraic representations were and continue to be explored by mathematics education researchers (Burrill et al., 2002; Ruthven, 1990).

Meta-analyses of about 80 research studies on the use of calculators (Hembree & Dessart, 1992) indicates that calculators in appropriate circumstances improve student learning, attitudes toward mathematics, and self-concepts in learning mathematics. Moreover, Drijvers (2003) described students' use of graphing calculators as aiding in "the use of realistic contexts, an exploration approach to problem situations, visualization and the integration of different representations, the experience of dynamics within a problem situation, [and] a flexible way of doing mathematics" (p. 78).

## COMPUTER SPREADSHEETS AND DYNAMIC CONNECTIONS AMONG MULTIPLE REPRESENTATIONS

Late in the 1990s, computer spreadsheets became more accessible as a potential tool for learning and teaching mathematics. While they had capabilities similar to those provided by graphing calculators, they also provided increased capabilities for dynamically making connections among algebraic, tabular and graphical representations. Figure 3 provides an example of a *Dynamic Linear Function* tool

| Function Mode | Graphic Mode |
|---|---|
| $y_1 = -5x+3$ <br><br> $y_2 = -2x+3$ <br><br> $y_3 = 2x+3$ <br><br> $y_4 = 5x+3$ | 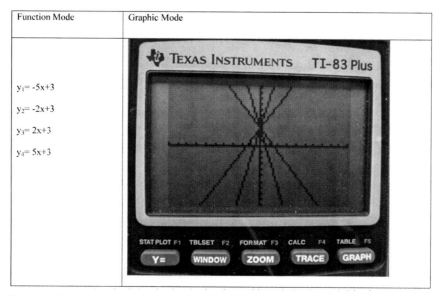 |

*Figure 2.* Visual data developed using the graphing calculator's capabilities for making connections between algebraic and graphic representations.

(Niess, 2006) that allows students to make changes in the algebraic presentations for functions *one, two, three,* and *four.* As students enter the data for the coefficients in the functions, the numeric tabular data and the visual graphical data are dynamically updated. Does this concurrent connection of the visual data with the numeric and algebraic data encourage visual thinking that ultimately engender improved understanding of mathematical content and processes? Does the process of designing spreadsheets to display visual data such as that shown in Figure 3 lead to increased understanding of mathematics? Does visual data lead to visual thinking as well as improved understanding of mathematics? Such questions focused researchers towards a consideration of the connections of learning mathematics with spreadsheets as tools for visual representations and visual thinking (Diezmann, 1997; Eisenberg & Dreyfus, 1999; Niess, 1998, 2006, 2007; Stroup & Wilensky, 2003, 2004).

Work with dynamic spreadsheets that provides an environment for students to visually investigate changes in graphs with changes in specific cell values has resulted in students developing a more accurate and robust understanding of the concepts of a variable and covariation (Niess et al., in press). Students are able to "see" that changes in the values of the cell and "see" the resulting changes in the graph. Kaput (1992) indicated that technology tools that support manipulating dynamic notations and models are important in mathematics and more specifically that "Dynamic media inherently make variation easier to achieve" (p. 525).

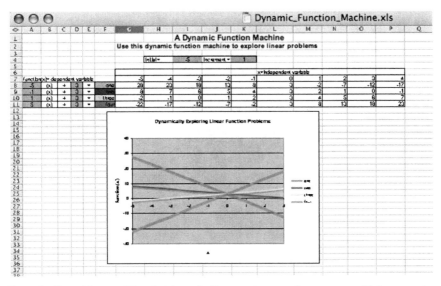

*Figure 3.* Spreadsheet rendition that dynamically supports connections among multiple representations – algebraic, numeric and visual graphics.

## NETWORKED TECHNOLOGY SUPPORTING CLASSROOM COLLABORATION AROUND VISUAL DATA

Today, newer technological tools are available in networked-supported learning environments (such as the TI Navigator network) to provide new forms of classroom interactions. Students, using networked handheld, laptop or desktop computing devices, contribute to a shared workspace that is projected for the whole class. The teacher might ask all the students to submit via their individual networked device an ordered pair of numbers where the $x$-coordinate is twice the value of the $y$-coordinate. Figure 4 renders a visual description of the graph of the ordered pairs as the students submit them. The teacher asks the students to discuss the visual display as the ordered pairs appear. At this point, eight students have entered their data and the class notices that their data seem to be forming a straight line until the ordered pair $(2, 4)$ appears. The teacher's role now is to guide the discourse about the visual data rather than saying, "There is an incorrect point up there." Instead, the students are challenged to describe what they see and are directed to the various points that are appearing. Through the class discussion and collaboration, the students detect that perhaps one point is in error. In closing, they are challenged to provide a symbolic representation of this graphical representation ($y = 2x$) that can "capture" each of the correctly entered ordered pairs.

Such networked technologies take advantage of the social space of the mathematics classroom to engage students in exploring mathematics concepts and processes dynamically and visually. According to Stroup, Ares and Hurfurd (2005), "What is new are the ways in which content now can be seen to structure

113

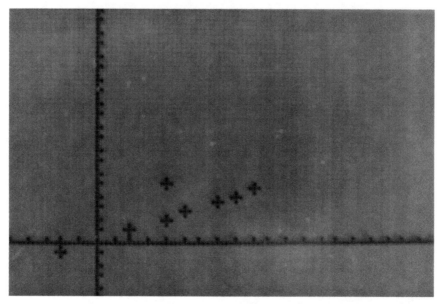

*Figure 4.* Rendition of students beginning to submit order pairs with instructions that the *x*-coordinate is twice the *y*-coordinate.

the social activity of the classroom and then reciprocally, what social conception of knowing as participation can do to help situate and advance the notion of content is enacted in classroom activity" (p. 181). In other words, these networked technologies raise the questions of exploring the relationships among content, social activity and students' mathematical achievement in different learning environments.

This newer classroom environment presents significant challenges for teachers to orchestrate the instruction in ways that change how students learn mathematics. All students are challenged to supply data and the collaborative results are described through a display of visual data in a graphical form. Teachers must carefully manage the classroom discourse to promote discussion, interactivity and collaboration in ways that also maintain a focus on the mathematics ideas and processes. Does this classroom environment support student comprehension through access to visual representations in conjunction with collaborative discourse? Does this environment support visual thinking leading to increased mathematical comprehension of the ideas? Such questions are currently challenging mathematics education researchers (Stroup et al., 2005; Wilensky, 1997; Wilensky & Stroup, 1999).

Research has demonstrated that appropriate technology-based representations can significantly affect both the quality of students' discussion and what they learn from the discussion (Cohen & Scardamalia, 1998; Pea, 1993; Ryser, Beeler, & McKensie, 1995; Suthers & Hundhausen, 2003). Furthermore, other studies have demonstrated that these activities allow a richer and more meaningful learning experience for students when studying a range of mathematical topics from the concept of function to the properties of a normal distribution. Multiple solution strategies are encouraged. Students move beyond simple success in solving a problem to an environment where they must collaboratively discuss and analyze the mathematics embedded in the visual representations.

## NEW QUESTIONS AND METHODOLOGIES FOR VISUAL DATA SOURCES

Improved technological capabilities for displaying visual data have continued to offer students new tools to engage in visual thinking that supports their learning in mathematics. Over the past 30 years, as improved silicon-based technologies have been made available for classrooms, researchers have been challenged to ask important questions about the use of these technologies in learning mathematics. Similarly, as the technologies have increased in their support of visualization opportunities, the world of mathematics education has wondered whether visualization supported or hindered increased student understanding. Is it more important to engage students in visual thinking where they interact with visual data as:

- creators of an exploratory tool (as in Logo, creating computer spreadsheets),
- users of a dynamic tool for investigation (as in *Geometer's Sketchpad* and graphing calculators), and/or
- collaborators and discussants around visual data projected by the tool (as with the classroom networked technologies)?

Or, should students be challenged to build their own mental models of these ideas?

These questions are only examples of those that have and continue to challenge mathematics education researchers. Over the past 30 years, mixed research methodologies (qualitative and quantitative) have been used in the attempt to focus on describing teaching and learning with visual mathematical representations. The issue is whether the research design adequately accounts for the multitude of variables present in the educational environments where students are engaged as they explore the visual representations using particular technologies to support their development of abstract mathematical concepts and processes.

Design experiments in educational research have gained the reputation of a reasonable approach toward not only determining if an innovation, such as the integration of various technologies in investigating mathematics, is successfully implemented, but also in formulating or extending theoretical models of teaching and learning from the feedback in the implementation process (Cobb et al. 2003). Design experiments in educational settings are conducted in actual classrooms to develop theories about student learning within the specific design. The analysis of the data is focused on the interactions of the multiple and varied elements in the socio-educational environment for developing a profile of the design in practice and is characterized by close collaboration between the teachers and researchers in the design, revisions, and implementation (Barab & Squire, 2004; Brown, 1992; Cobb et al., 2003). Purely, qualitative methodologies have also risen in popularity because of the importance of more valid in depth studies of the phenomenon of mathematics learning. Consistent with design experiment methodology, case studies analyze the classroom data to gain a comprehensive view of an innovation's impact on the functions of a *typical* classroom. Case studies add important data in the design experiment methodology in supporting multiple levels of analysis of classroom data to gain a comprehensive view of an innovation's impact on the functions of a *typical* classroom.

Consider the challenge of guiding students in gaining an appreciation for the beauty of mathematics, an affective goal in the mathematics curriculum. Can digital technology tools assist in this challenge? What part can visual data play in guiding students in this challenge? Typically, students view mathematics as a set of rules and procedures to be followed and do not think about or develop an appreciation its beauty. Figure 5 provides a task designed to develop a visual proof of the Pythagorean Theorem beginning with the development of a visual representation developed in *Geometer's Sketchpad*. Can exploration with this visual representation of a mathematical concept, such as the Pythagorean Theorem, help students gain an appreciation of the beauty of mathematics?

A case study of a teacher and class as they explore this task using *Geometer's Sketchpad* projected for whole class collaboration may provide valuable data. But this case study design-experiment is different from traditional case studies. The teacher is new to teaching mathematics with technology and new to designing lessons that engage the class in collaborative visual thinking and geometric reasoning with a purpose of guiding them in developing an appreciation for the beauty of mathematics. Capturing the students' ideas and the teacher's challenges along with the various trials with the students' responses potentially provides a rich source of data about the instructional techniques that are effectively in encouraging students to develop an appreciation for the beauty of mathematics. The method involves the researcher working collaboratively with the teacher in an iterative design process of new instructional ideas for providing students with educational opportunities for developing an appreciation for the beauty of mathematics.

Mack (2007) used such a case study design as he investigated the role of mathematical aesthetic perspectives through the classroom discourse generated in a networked-supported learning environment in mathematics instruction. Students' activities in this technological-environment visually projected the ideas as they actively generated them in the process of developing their mathematical understandings through the classroom discourse in a unit involving linear functions. Working with a secondary mathematics teacher, Mack examined the teacher's instructional practices within the context of this networked-supported classroom. Mack used a design experiment to explore the complex social interactions in the classroom discourse within the technology-enhanced environment. The case study revealed ways the teacher's mathematical aesthetic perceptions constrained her designs of the activities and the mathematical discourse during classroom implementation. The findings suggested that students' visual thinking and mathematical reasoning through the collaborative discourse as designed by

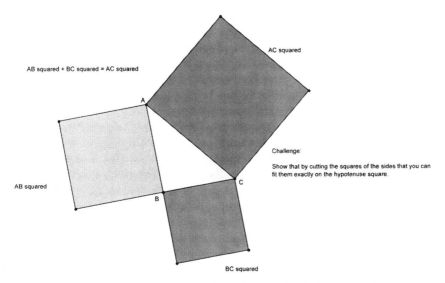

*Figure 5.* Visual task for students to develop a visual proof of the Pythagorean Theorem.

the teacher and researcher was not sufficient to support the students in associating their thinking about mathematics with an appreciation for the art of mathematics. As a result of this study, Mack challenged teachers to augment the design of the classroom activity to include more explicit connections to the aesthetics of mathematics. This case study in a design-based experiment provided a lens for looking at the pedagogical implications with an affective goal of the mathematics curriculum within technology-enhanced classrooms.

This design experiment case study provided a useful vehicle to investigate the pedagogical implications of integrating affective and cognitive goals in a technology-enhanced classroom that engaged students in visual thinking and reasoning. The teacher and the researcher worked together to design specific lessons for the teacher to implement with her students in response to the challenge presented by the teacher's lack of experience with the technology and preparation for engaging students in visual thinking in a technology-enhanced lesson. The design tested in the classroom allowed Mack to gather evidence for the identification of essential features of a model designed to prepare teachers to teach mathematics with technologies in ways that enhance their students' visualize thinking amid their mathematical reasoning.

## IMPLICATIONS FOR DATA COLLECTION AND ANALYSIS

While student learning in mathematics with the emerging technologies has characterized the incorporation of visual data, the research techniques used to study learning and teaching in mathematics has shifted over the past 30 years. From the dominance of the process-product research that used quantitative methodologies to explore the effects of isolated teaching behaviors on student achievement (Brophy & Good, 1986), educational researchers have increasingly recognized the need to identify and describe the entire educational context within which a particular phenomenon was investigated. In particular, technology-mediated classroom environments (such as in a networked-enhanced technology environment) called for more intensive investigations of how students and their teachers displayed their mathematical knowledge and understandings.

Video recordings have increasingly provided a means for gathering important visual data in the studies of mathematics teaching and learning. Moreover, some practical questions surrounding the increased capabilities for displaying visual data in exploring mathematics have challenged researchers to capture the natural learning environments emerging with access to newer and more advanced technologies. Some examples of these questions include the following: Should a video camera be used for data collection? How many? On what (or whom) should the camera(s) focus? The challenge for researchers is to adequately capture the essential nature of the classroom activity mediated by these visually rich technological environments. For this reason, the technology itself has evolved to become as much a major a player in these classrooms as the teacher and the students (Lesh & Lehrer, 2000).

Capturing the essence of the classroom obviously results in mounds of video recordings that must be analyzed in some way that accurately displays the results. Furthermore, an important potential in the design-experiment is that the teacher and researcher can collaborate in creating specific lessons for the teacher to teach; afterwards the two can reassess and design specific plans for the next lesson. The iterative nature of multi-tiered teaching experiments suggests that the researcher and the teacher review the videos in the process of considering the development of new types of activities. The videotaping role in the experiment is multifaceted: formative in guiding the development of new ideas for investigation and summative for aggregating the data from the multiple experiments.

For the summative analysis, the entire set of video evidence must be aggregated and analyzed in order to respond to the research question. Since Mack was focused on the teacher's actions, he organized his videos into three stages of lesson development and implementation: *conception, planning*, and *implementation*. Rather than spending hours and hours of watching and re-watching the videos, he used *iMovie* (Apple Computer, Inc., 2002) to digitize the videos. With the help of a video transcriber tool created specifically for the Integrated Simulation and Modeling Project (Stroup, 2002), he was able to insert beginning and ending time stamps on segments of the digitized video that referred to his specific area of interest – the aesthetic perceptions of the teacher or students. Running the video in *Quicktime*, Mack was able to stop the video, stamp the time, and create a record in his database where the individual records consisted of the critical segments of the interview, collaborations and classroom observations. Using this process, he identified over 200 records linked to the aesthetic perceptions of the teacher.

Each aesthetic-related record in the database summarized the nature of the activity in the particular clip. Each record contained fields for the *time*, ıconcept, *quote*, *level*, and *description*. Silver and Metzger (1989) argued that emotion was a cue to aesthetic enjoyment in mathematics. Therefore, Mack identified indicators that included "emotional outbursts, specific language and words like 'cool', physical gestures like 'high-fives', times the teacher called attention to specific student-generated artifacts that she thought were 'interesting', or times when she [the teacher] called attention to features of the projected whole-group artifact" (p. 65). After multiple reviews of the videos and database records, he was able to reduce the number of episodes directly related to mathematical aesthetic perceptions. Through the analysis of these data, he identified and described four levels of perspectives evident in the teacher's pedagogical approaches. Ultimately, he concluded that the teacher's pedagogical approaches needed to be more direct in guiding the students in gaining an appreciation for the beauty inherent in the nature of mathematics.

## IN CONCLUSION: IMPACT OF VISUAL THINKING ON THE AUTHORS' SCHOLARLY DIRECTIONS

Students learning mathematics are engaged in visual thinking because of the nature of the discipline of mathematics. They must interpret written symbols as they read problems they are expected to solve as demonstrations of their learning of mathematics. They use many visual symbols when communicating their solutions. The ratio of the circumference of a circle to its diameter is represented by $\pi$ (pi) and $\pi$ is an irrational number. What are the students thinking as they consider the problem of finding the circumference of a circle with a diameter of 4 inches? Do they recognize that a solution $4\pi$ is more accurate than either 4 (3.14) or 4 (22/7) since 3.14 and 22/7 are only approximations of $\pi$? What are students thinking as they communicate their solutions using these different mathematics symbols?

Visual thinking in mathematics engages students in making connections among multiple representations (symbolic, numerical, graphical). Our interest in visual thinking in mathematics intertwined with the integration of digital technologies as teaching and learning tools in mathematics has evolved over three decades with a special interest in the visual displays that aided students in making connections among the various mathematical representations. Some of our questions have been concerned with the following: What is the impact of the inclusion of visual data provided by these technologies on the development of students' mathematical knowledge, skills and dispositions? What is the impact of various technologies that provide visual data as learning tools in mathematics? What are the challenges for preparing teachers to incorporate these instructional tools when they have not learned mathematics using these technologies as learning tools?

The scholarly work of Niess has evolved from the development and assessment of curricular and instructional materials for teaching mathematics. Her work with technologies in mathematics centered on incorporating Logo programming (Niess, 1988), *Geometer's Sketchpad* (Niess, 1997), and spreadsheets (Niess, 1998) in teaching and learning mathematics. After many years of working with and observing students, she recognized the importance of visual data in guiding students toward a more robust understanding of mathematics' abstract ideas and concepts. She concluded the importance of visual data for learning mathematics resonated with another way of "listening to mathematical ideas" through the "multiple embodiments" students need when learning abstract mathematics (Dienes, 1969). Dienes proposed that learning is maximized when students are exposed to the ideas and constructs in a variety of physical contexts. The visual data presented in the evolving technologies have been instrumental among the physical embodiments for gaining access to these abstract mathematical ideas. Niess' work evolved from designing curriculum and instructional ideas to promoting and taking mathematical advantage of the visual data provided by the technological applications to engage students in visual thinking amid their numerical, algebraic and geometric reasoning.

What has been an essential part of the equation of guiding students in visual thinking as they learned with these technologies has been the challenge of preparing teachers to adopt technologies in teaching mathematics. Research has shown that teachers primarily teach what they were taught and how they were taught. Yet, these digital technologies were not available when they were learning mathematics. Their mathematics education primarily involved symbolic and numerical approaches. Their visual thinking was framed by their personal mental images rather than springing from visual data provided by the various emerging technologies. Thus, Niess directed her efforts toward preparing teachers to teach with these technologies. Her research since 1997 has focused on a description of technological pedagogical content knowledge (TPCK) as the knowledge that teachers need to teach mathematics with technology (Niess, 2005; Niess et al., 2006).

In her efforts to define TPCK Niess has analyzed mounds of video data over many years without the aid of the newer technologies that Mack used in his dissertation research. In the attempt to capture the students' and their teachers' visual thinking and mathematical reasoning, these emerging technologies have proven to be more appropriate for analyzing the multiple variables and factors the exist in live mathematics classrooms. In addition, the kinds of technological designs described in this chapter have visual artifacts that become central components of their instructional utility and require vast amounts of data from various sources, including video recordings and reproductions of the visual artifacts. The procedures for data analysis and interpretation of these large quantities of data necessitate the use of iterative, reflective analytical cycles in a manner consistent with design experimentation, beginning with a theoretical notion and leading to refinements of that notion through the subsequent empirical analysis.

REFERENCES

Association of Mathematics Teacher Educators. (2006). *Preparing teachers to use technology to enhance the learning of mathematics*. A Technology Position Statement of AMTE, available at http://amte.net.

Arcavi, A. (2003). The role of visual representations in the learning of mathematics. *Educational Studies in Mathematics, 52*(3), 215–241.

Barab, S.A., & Squire, K. (2004). Design-based research: Putting a stake in the ground. *Journal of Learning Sciences, 13*(1), 1–14.

Brophy, J.E., & Good, T.L. (1986). Teacher behavior and student achievement. In M.C. Wittrock (Ed.), *Handbook of research on teaching*. New York: MacMillan.

Brown, A.L. (1992). Design experiments. Theoretical and methodological challenges in creating complex intervention in classroom settings. *Journal of the Learning Science, 2,* 141–178.

Burrill, G., Allison, J., Breaux, G., Kastberg, S., Leatham, K., & Sanchez, W. (2002). *Handheld graphing technology in secondary mathematics: Research findings and implications for classroom practice*. Dallas, TX: Texas Instruments.

Clement, C. (1984). *Analogical reasoning and learning computer programming*. Paper presented at the Harvard University Conference on Thinking, Cambridge, MA.

Clements, D.H., & Batista, M.T. (1989). Learning of geometric concepts in a Logo environment. *Journal for Research in Mathematics Education, 20,* 450–467.

Clements, D.H., & Batista, M.T. (1992). Geometry and spatial reasoning. In D.A. Grouws (Ed.), *Handbook of research on mathematics teaching and learning* (pp. 420–464). New York: Macmillan Publishing Co.

Cobb, P., Confrey, J., diSessa, A., Lehrer, R., & Schauble, L. (2003). Design experiments in educational research. *Educational Researcher, 32*(1), 9–13.

Cohen, A.L., & Scardamalia, M. (1998). Discourse about ideas: Monitoring and regulation in face-to-face and computer-mediated learning environments. *Interactive Learning Environments, 6*(1–2), 114–142.

Dienes, Z.P. (1969). *Building up mathematics*, rev. ed. London: Hutchinson Educational.

Diezmann, C. (1997). *Effective problem solving: A study of the importance of visual representation and visual thinking*. Seventh International Conference on Thinking, Singapore.

Drijvers, P. (2003). *Learning algebra in a computer algebra environment: Design research on the understanding of the concept of parameter*. Utrecht, The Netherlands: CD-B Press.

Eisenberg, T., & Dreyfus, T. (1999). Visual information and valid reasoning. In W. Zimmerman & S. Cunningham (Eds.), *Visualisation in teaching and learning mathematics* (pp. 25–38). USA: Mathematical Association of America.

Hembree, R., & Dessart, D.J. (1992). Research on calculators in mathematics education. In J.T. Fey (Ed.), *Calculators in mathematics education: 1992 yearbook of the National Council of Teachers of Mathematics* (pp. 22–31). Reston, VA: NCTM.

Hollebrands, K.F. (2007). The role of a dynamic software program for geometry I the strategies high school mathematics students employ. *Journal for Research in Mathematics Education, 38*(2), 164–192.

Kaput, J. (1992). Technology and mathematics education. In D. Grouws (Ed.), *Handbook of research on mathematics teaching and learning* (pp. 515–556). New York: Macmillan.

Kurland, D.M. (Ed.) (1984). *Symposium: Developmental studies of computer programming skills* (Tech. Rep. No. 29). New York: Bank Street College of Education, Center for Children and Technology.

Kurland, D.M., & Pea, R.D. (1985). Children's mental models of recursive logo programs. *Journal of Educational Computing Research, 1,* 235–243.

Laborde, C., & Laborde, J.-M. (1995). What about a learning environment where Euclidean concepts are manipulated with a mouse? In A.A. diSessa, C. Holyles, & R. Noss (Eds.), *Computers and exploratory learning*. Berlin: Springer-Verlag.

Lesh, R., & Lehrer, R. (2000). Iterative refinement cycles for videotape analyses of conceptual change. In R. Lesh & A. Kelly (Eds.), *Handbook of research design in mathematics and science education* (pp. 665–707). Hillsdale, NJ: Erlbaum.

Mack, A. (2007). *The role of mathematical aesthetic in network-supported generative design: A case study*. Dissertation presented for the completion of requirements for Ph.D. degree.

National Council of Teachers of Mathematics (2000). *Principles and standards for school mathematics*. Reston, VA: NCTM.

Niess, M.L. (1988). Logo learning tools and motion geometry. *Journal of Computers in Mathematics and Science Teaching, 8*(1), 17–24.

Niess, M.L. (1997). Lines and angles: Using Geometer's Sketchpad to construct knowledge. *Learning and Leading with Technology, 24*(4), 27–31.

Niess, M.L. (1998). The computer spreadsheet: A useful tool for learning to solve equations. *Learning and Leading with Technology, 25*(3), 22–27.

Niess, M.L. (2005). Preparing teachers to teach science and mathematics with technology: Developing a technology pedagogical content knowledge. *Teaching and Teacher Education, 21*(5), 509–523.

Niess, M.L. (2006). Spreadsheets as tools for building mathematical connections. *Connections* (AMTE online publication), *25*(2), 12–14.

Niess, M.L. (2007). *Mathematics teachers developing technological pedagogical content knowledge (TPCK)*. Paper presented at the Working Joint IFIP Conference titled Informatics, Mathematics, and ICT: A 'Golden Triangle', Boston, MA.

Niess, M.L., Suharwoto, G., Lee, K., & Sadri, P. (2006). *Guiding inservice mathematics teachers in developing TPCK*. Paper presented at the annual meeting of the American Education Research Association, San Francisco, CA.

Olive, J. (1998). Opportunities to explore and integrate mathematics with the Geometer's Sketchpad. In R. Lehrer & D. Chazan (Eds.), *Designing learning environments for developing understanding of geometry and space* (pp. 395–418). Mahwah, NJ: Lawrence Erlbaum Associates.

Papert, S. (1980). *Mindstorms: Children, computers, and powerful ideas* (2nd ed.). New York: Basic Books.

Pea, R.D. (1985). Beyond amplification: Using the computer to reorganize mental functioning. *Educational Psychologist, 20*(4), 167–182.

Pea, R.D. (1993). Practices of distributed intelligence and designs for education. In G. Solomon (Ed.), *Distributed cognitions: Psychological and educational considerations* (pp. 47–87). New York: Cambridge University Press.

Pea, R.D., & Kurland, D.M. (1984). On the cognitive effects of learning computer programming. *New Ideas in Psychology, 2,* 137–168.

Pea, R.D., Kurland, D.M., & Hawkins, J. (1985). Logo and the development of thinking skills. In M. Chen & W. Paisley (Eds.), *Children and microcomputers: Formative studies* (pp. 193–212). Beverly Hills, CA: Sage.

Roschelle, J. (1996). Designing for cognitive communication: Epistemic fidelity or mediating collaborating inquiry. In D.L. Day and D.K. Kovacs (Eds.), *Computers, Communication & Mental Models* (pp. 13–25). London: Taylor & Francis.

Roschelle, J., & Kaput, J. (1996). Educational software architecture and systemic impact: The promise of component software. *Journal of Educational Computing Research, 14*(3), 217–228.

Ruthven, K. (1990). The influence of graphic calculator use on translation from graphic to symbolic forms. *Educational Studies in Mathematics, 21,* 431–450.

Ryser, G.R., Beeler, J.E., & McKensie, C.M. (1995). Effects of a computer-supported intentional learning environment (CSILE) on students' self-concept, self-regulatory behavior, and critical thinking ability. *Journal of Educational Computing Research, 13*(4), 375–385.

Silver, E., & Metzger, W. (1989). Aesthetic influences on expert mathematical problem solving. In D.B. McLeod and V.M. Adams (Eds.), *Affect and mathematical problem solving* (pp. 59–74). New York: Free Press.

Stroup, W. (2002). *The structure of generative learning in a classroom network*. Paper presented at the annual meeting of the American Educational Research Association in New Orleans, LA.

Stroup, W., Ares, N., & Hurford, A.C. (2005). A dialectic analysis of generativity: Issues of network supported design in mathematics and science. *Mathematical Thinking and Learning, 7*(3), 181–206.

Stroup, W., & Wilensky, W. (2003). *Embedded complementarity of object-based and aggregate reasoning in students developing understanding of dynamic systems*. Paper presented at the annual meeting of American Educational Research Association in Chicago, IL.

Stroup, W., & Wilensky, U. (2004). A guide to participatory simulations activities. http://ccl.northwestern.edu/ps/guide/part-sims-guide.html. Accessed on September 18, 2006.

Suthers, D., & Hundhausen, C. (2003). An empirical study of the effects of representational guidance on collaborative learning. *Journal of the Learning Sciences, 12*(2), 183–219.

van Hiele, P.M. (1986). *Structure and insight*. Orlando, Florida: Academic Press.

van Hiele, P.M. (1959/19850. The child's thought and geometry. In D. Fuys, D. Geddes, & R. Tischler (Eds.), *English translation of selected writings of Dina van Hiele-Geldof and Pierre M. van*

*Hiele* (pp. 243–252). Brooklyn, NY: Brooklyn College, School of Education (ERIC Document Reproduction Service No. 289 697).

Wilensky, U. (2003). Statistical mechanics for secondary school: The GasLab Multi-Agent Modeling Toolkit. *International Journal of Computers for Mathematical Learning, 8*(1).

Wilensky, U., & Stroup, W. (1999). *Learning through participatory simulations: Network-based design for systems learning in classrooms.* Paper presented at the annual meeting of the American Educational Research Association in Montreal, Quebec, Canada.

CHARLES R. BARMAN

# CHAPTER 8
## USING VISUAL DATA TO OBTAIN
## STUDENTS' PERCEPTIONS OF
## SCIENTISTS AND STUDYING SCIENCE

In 1983, Chambers and Schilbeci and Sorenson published their work on the *Draw-a-Scientist-Test* (*DAST*). In using the *DAST*, subjects are asked to reveal their image of a scientist through drawing a picture of a scientist "doing science." The visual data obtained by these investigators indicated that elementary students tended to draw scientists that were aging Caucasion males working in a laboratory. In addition, the elementary students had a tendency to represent scientists as mythical or "Frankenstein creatures."

Shortly after Chambers and Schilbeci and Sorenson reported their findings, a colleague and I began using the *DAST* with our introductory science and teacher education classes. Our primary purpose for using the *DAST* at this time was to have our students examine their beliefs about scientists and to promote a classroom discussion based on their drawings. Although I didn't think about this at the time, it appears that this was my initial use of visual data in my work as a science educator. The remainder of this essay will share my experiences in using visual data to gain information on students' views of scientists and studying science. In addition, I will discuss two other tools which I plan to use in future studies.

### EXPANDING THE USE OF VISUAL DATA

After several years of using the *DAST* with college students, I became interested in determining whether any changes had taken place in precollege students' images of scientists since the studies of Chambers (1983), Schilbeci and Sorenson (1983), and several other investigators (Fort & Varney, 1989; Huber & Burton, 1995; Krause, 1997, Finson, Beaver, & Cramond, 1995). Since the late 1980s, textbook companies made a concentrated effort to represent scientists in many different ways (Barman et al., 1989; Atwater et al., 1993; Heil, et al., 1993). For example, female scientists were featured in the textbooks as well as individuals that represented ethnic minorities. In addition, many of the scientists in the textbooks were also young adults rather than older individuals and these individuals were doing field studies and not only working in laboratories. Therefore, I was interested in finding out whether these efforts were having an impact on how precollege students perceived scientists in the 1990s.

*J.E. Pedersen and K.D. Finson (eds.), Visual Data, 125–131.*

Besides the interest in precollege students' views of scientists, I was interested in finding out their perceptions about how they were studying science in school. Since the 1970s, many of the precollege science curriculum programs were activity-based and the *National Science Education Standards* (NRC, 1996) explicitly recommends teaching science as a process of inquiry. In other words, there was a shared view among curriculum developers and science educators that students should be "doing science" rather than just reading about it. How could data be gathered to see if students perceived themselves doing science in school? It seemed reasonable that these data could also be obtained through student drawings. However, to obtain enough student data from various parts of the United States, it would be necessary to involve practicing teachers in the study. But, before an invitation could be made to teachers, several concerns still needed to be addressed.

## ANALYSIS TOOLS

The first problem was to find a reliable and efficient way for analyzing the data of the *DAST* and the student drawings of themselves studying science. The analysis of the *DAST* was resolved with the development of the *Draw-a-Scientist-Checklist* (*DAST-C*) by Kevin Finson, John Beaver, and Bonnie Cramond (1995). Each item on the *DAST-C* represents a stereotypic characteristic derived from reviews of literature relating to students' images of scientists. During the analysis of a student's drawing, the more items that are checked on the *DAST-C*, the more stereotypes appear on the student's drawing. The analysis of the students' drawings of themselves doing science in school was accomplished by developing a second checklist which had investigators rate whether the students pictured themselves seated at a desk reading a book, seated taking notes, or participating in an activity. Both of these analyses tools were incorporated into the protocol that is discussed in the next section.

## DEVELOPING A RESEARCH PROTOCOL

The next task was to develop and field-test, a research protocol that could be used to obtain uniform data. Maoldomhnaigh and Mhaolain (1990) found that changing the wording in directions given to students can alter the types of drawings produced. These findings underscore the importance of having a standardized procedure, including standardized instructions to follow when administering the protocol. Therefore, the following protocol was developed.

Each student would be individually interviewed. Although the students would be asked a set of standard questions and given a standard set of directions, each interview session would allow the investigator(s) to gain additional information about the students' drawing and to clarify any of their responses. The students' responses would be audio-taped and transcribed for further analysis. The standard set of directions and questions included in each interview would be:

- Will you please draw a picture of a scientist doing science? When you are finished, will you please explain your drawing?
- On another piece of paper, will you please draw a picture of yourself doing science in school? When you are finished, will you please explain your drawing?

To provide an opportunity for students to draw scientists from different ethnic backgrounds, at the beginning of each interview, the investigator(s) were directed to offer the students a set of colored pencils or crayons and tell them to feel free to color their drawing or any parts of the picture that they would like to accentuate.

As the protocol was developed, an additional concern was raised about asking the students to make a forced choice. If you asked students to draw a scientist, would this force them to make a choice between a male or a female? Or, if you asked students to draw two scientists, would this give them the freedom to depict both sexes? To shed some light on this concern, two groups of 10 fifth-grade students were randomly selected. Each group had an equal number of boys and girls. Group A was asked to draw two scientists doing science while Group B was asked to draw one scientist doing science. In Group A, seven students drew two male scientists, two students drew a male and a female scientist, and one student drew two female scientists. In Group B, seven students drew a male scientist and three students drew a female scientist. Because there were no major differences in the results of both groups and because the drawing of two scientists took each student twice as long to complete as one drawing, it was decided that it was sufficient to have the students draw only one scientist.

The next step was to field-test the protocol. This was accomplished with the help of 4 teachers and 100 seventeen fifth grade students (57 males and 60 females) from the Midwestern and Southwestern parts of the United States (Barman & Ostlund, 1996).

INITIATING THE NATIONAL STUDY

Shortly after the analysis tools and the protocol were developed and field-tested, an invitation as well as the research protocol, the analysis tools, and step-by-step directions on how to use the protocol appeared in *Science & Children* (Barman, 1996). In this invitation, K-8 teachers were asked to follow the protocol and obtain information about their students' perceptions of scientists and studying science in school. They were also asked to send their data to a central location where it could be compiled and organized according to specific grade levels (K-2, 3-5, 6-8). These groupings provided a useful mechanism for making comparisons between different aged students, and they made it possible to examine possible trends that may occur as children move from the primary grades to middle school.

The response to this invitation was better than expected. One-hundred fifty-four (154) K-8 teachers from 23 states and the District of Columbia participated in the data collection for this project. Data were collected by these teachers for 1,504 students. Half (50%) of these students were males and 50% were females.

Of the total number of students interviewed, 235 were from grades K-2, 649 from grades 3–5, and 620 from grades 6–8.

## RESULTS

For the most part, the students in the national study drew similar images of scientists to those revealed in previous studies (Chambers, 1983; Schibeci & Sorenson, 1983; Fort & Varney, 1989; Finson et al., 1995; Huber & Burton, 1995; Krause, 1997). For example, most of the scientists were depicted as white males working in laboratories. However, unlike the previous studies, the tendency was to show the scientist in surroundings that were not secretive or dangerous. In addition, the mythical stereotype, such as Frankenstein or the mad scientist was not a predominant feature of the drawings and the scientists were pictured as young adults rather than middle-aged or elderly. These data do show that some progress had been made in how students view scientists. The majority of the students in the national study tended to view scientists as regular people rather than an old crazed person. However, it is clear that a greater emphasis still needed to placed on helping K-8 students develop a more realistic ideas of who scientists are.

The second component of the national study asked the students to draw themselves studying science. These data were more optimistic. The majority of the students pictured themselves doing some type of activity (85% for grades K-2, 84% for grades 3–5, and 88% for grades 6-8) rather than taking notes or reading a book. (For a complete listing of the data from the national study, please see Barman (1997).)

## EXTENDING THE STUDY TO HIGH SCHOOL STUDENTS

Once the data from the national study was published and disseminated to colleagues, several secondary teachers questioned whether similar results would be obtained from students in grades 9–12. Because no data were available to answer this question, a similar study, was organized and conducted with high school students. This time, the help of preservice science teachers was solicited to aid in data collection. Two-hundred ninety (290) high school students (168 from grades 9-10 and 122 from grades 11–12) were interviewed using the same protocol that was employed in the national study. These students' images of scientists were very similar to those in grades K-8. These data substantiate the findings of Driver, Guesne, and Tiberghien (1985) that indicate certain ideas held by students are deeply rooted and very difficult to change.

Unlike the similarity in the drawings of scientists, the high school students' perceptions of themselves studying science was different from K-8 students. As indicated earlier, the majority of K-8 students depicted themselves studying science through an activity. In contrast, fewer high school students drew themselves doing an activity (74% of the 9-10 students and 51% of the 11-12), indicating that a greater percentage of these students perceive school science as either note taking or a reading exercise. (For a complete display of the high school data, see Barman (1999a).)

## REFLECTING ON THE VALUE OF THE DAST STUDY

Both studies provided useful information about K-12 students views of scientists and studying science. However, these studies also provided valuable professional development experiences for in-service and pre-service teachers. These teachers were engaged in gathering data about their students' knowledge of the scientific enterprise, providing them with useful insights into what modifications might be needed in their classroom instruction. In addition, these studies helped demonstrate the value of "action research" as an instrumental component of informing and improving instruction.

To add credibility to the claim that these studies enhanced professional development, a follow-up survey was sent to the K-8 teachers who participated in the national study asking them if they felt their participation was a valuable professional experience and whether they would be interested in doing more action research in their respective classes. The majority of the participants (70%) indicated that this was a valuable experience and that they would be interested in collecting additional data from their students (Barman, 1998). Several of the participants commented on how surprised they were with their students' perceptions of scientists and indicated how these data and additional studies could help inform their current teaching practices.

## LOOKING BEYOND THE DAST

Since my experience with the *DAST*, I have begun to use another tool for gathering visual data called the *Draw-a-Science-Teacher-Test* (*DASTT-C*) developed by Thomas, Pedersen, & Finson (2001). The *DASTT-C* consists of two parts: (1) a prompt asking the subject to draw a picture of themselves as a science teacher at work and (2) a check-list rubric to analyze the drawing (Finson, Pedersen, & Thomas, 2006). Currently, I use only the first part of the *DASTT-C* with my pre-service secondary science teachers. In addition to asking them to draw themselves teaching, I ask them to explain their drawing. I have found these drawings provide valuable insights into a person's idea of what it means to be a teacher and the role a teacher plays in the learning environment. The drawings also provide a useful way to begin a dialogue with my pre-service teachers about teaching science.

Although I have only used the *DASTT-C* as a vehicle to get my pre-service science teachers to think about their role as a teacher, I am planning to incorporate it into the evaluation plan for our secondary science certification program. I plan to use this instrument as a pre- and post-assessment to see whether my teacher education candidates make any shifts in their perceptions of their role as a teacher from the beginning to the end of their certification program.

There is also another tool called *photovoice* (Wang & Burris, 1997) that I feel has real potential in gathering visual data in teacher education. Although I have not yet used this technique, I plan to pilot it in the near future as part of the evaluation plan of my secondary science certification program. I believe that it has the potential of capturing significant events of a prospective teacher's field experiences.

According to one of its developers, Caroline C. Wang and Mary Ann Burris (1997, p. 369):

> *Photovoice* is a process by which people can identify, represent, and enhance their community through a specific photographic technique. It entrusts cameras to the hands of people to enable them to act as recorders, and potential catalysts for social change ...

Individuals who use this technique engage in a four-stage process that allows for data collection and analysis:

1. The investigator requests the participants of the study to take photographs of objects and events they consider important.
2. The photographs that "best" represent the purpose of the investigation are selected by the investigator, the participants, or both.
3. The participants describe the meaning of the photographs to a small group of their peers.
4. The investigator, with the help of the small groups, identifies themes or patterns that have arisen from the visual data and the small group discussion.

As Wang (2005) indicates, the procedure used in photovoice avoids the distortion of trying to fit data into a predetermined paradigm. Through this process, individuals construct what matters to them and what is worth remembering. (For more information on photovoice, refer to this web-site: http://wwwphotovoice.com.)

## SOME FINAL THOUGHTS

As indicated in this essay, my use of visual data evolved over time. However, since I have found how useful this technique can be to my professional work, it has become a natural vehicle to gain insights into the way individuals perceive specific concepts as well as certain aspects of their learning environment. I hope the ideas expressed in this essay will be a catalyst to help you and others find ways to also use visual data as an instructional aid or a research tool.

## REFERENCES

Atwater, M., Baptiste, P, Daniel, L, Hackett, J, Moyer, R., Takemoto, C., & Wislson, N. (1993). *MacMillan/McGraw-Hill Science*. New York: MacMillan/Mcgraw-Hill School Publishing Co.

Barman, C. (1996). How do students really view science and scientists? *Science & Children, 34*, 30–33.

Barman, C. (1997). Students' views of scientists and science: Results from a national study. *Science & Children, 35*(1), 18–24.

Barman, C. (1998). What teachers say about participating in a national study. *Science & Children, 36,* 14–17.

Barman, C. (1999a). Completing the study: High school students' views of scientists and science. *Science & Children, 36*(7), 16–21.

Barman, C. (1999b). Students' views about scientists and school science: Engaging K-8 teachers in a national study. *Journal of Science Teacher Education, 10,* 43–54.

Barman, C. & Ostlund, K. (1996). A protocol to investigate students' perceptions about scientists and relevancy of science to students' daily lives. *Science Education International, 7,* 16–21.

Barman, C., DiSpezio, M, Gutherie, V., Leyden, M., Mercier, C., & Ostlund, K. (1989). *Addison-Wesley Science.* Menlo Park, CA: Addison Wesley Publishing Co.

Chambers, D.W. (1983). Stereotypic images of the scientists: The draw-a-scientist test. *Science Education, 67,* 255–265.

Driver, R., Guesne, E., & Tiberghien, A. (Eds.) (1985). *Childrens' ideas in science.* Milton Keynes: Open University Press.

Finson, K.D., Beaver, J.B., & Cramond, B.L. (1995). Development and field test of a checklist for the draw-a-scientist test. *School Science and Mathematics, 95,* 195–205.

Finson, K.D., Pedersen, J., & Thomas, J. (2006). Comparing science teaching styles to students' perceptions of scientists. *School Science and Mathematics, 106,* 8–15.

Fort, D.C., & Varney, H.L. (1989). How students see scientists: Mostly male, mostly white, and mostly benevolent. *Science & Children, 26,* 8–13.

Heil, D., Allen, M., Cooney, T. Matamoros, A., Perry, M., & Slesnick, I. (1993). *Discover the wonder.* Glenview, IL: Scott Foresman.

Huber, R.A., & Burton, G.M. (1995). What do students think scientists look like? *School Science and Mathematics, 95,* 195–205.

Krause, J.P. (1977). How children see scientists. *Science & Children, 14,* 9–10.

Maoldomhnaigh, M.O., & Mhaolain, V.N. (1990). The perceived expectation of the administrator as a factor affecting the sex of scientists drawn by early adolescent girls. *Research in Science and Technological Education, 8,* 69–74.

National Research Council (1983). *National science education standards.* Washington, DC: National Academy Press.

Schibeci, R.A., & Sorenson, I. (1983). Elementary school children's perceptions of scientists. *School Science and Mathematics, 83,* 14–19.

Thomas, J.A., Pedersen, J.E., & Finson, K. (2001). Validating the draw-a-science-teacher-test checklist (DASTT-C): Exploring mental models and teacher beliefs. *Journal of Science Teacher Education, 12,* 295–310.

Wang, C.C. (2005). *Photovoice.* http://www.photovoice.com.

Wang, C., & Burris, M.A. (1997). Photovoice: Concept, methodology, and use for participatory needs assessment. *Health Education & Behavior, 24,* 369–387.

PATRICIA N. CHROSNIAK

# CHAPTER 9
# SEEING WHAT WE KNOW, KNOWING WHAT WE SEE:
# THE INVOLVEMENT OF VISUAL LITERACY IN
# LEARNING

INTRODUCTION

Standing at the top of the Grand Canyon, we are awestruck by its immensity and grandeur. If we stand at one spot long enough, it seems that the image we first perceived is not the same as the most current one. Indeed, from moment to moment the landscape appears different as the sunlight shifts. Artists such as Ansel Adams have interpreted this effect for us in their photographs, and philosophers such as Wittgenstein and Bertrand Russell have reflected upon perceptual change in their writings about what constitutes reality.

Through our eyes we discriminate and consequently interpret the commonplace and the complicated. The images that we form through our eyes are frequently kinetic and not always absolute. We look at a street sign and automatically know what we are to do, but our interpretations of what we see in other contexts may not be so instantaneous. After a couple years comfortably at home, we may ask ourselves questions such as, "Why did I ever buy that painting?" A father holding his baby son may glance at the baby's face and notice a particular look that is brand new; as time passes the father might comment that he never again saw that same look.

What does our seeing have to do with what we actually know? Do we understand everything that we see to the same degree? And, how does what we know influence what we see and our interpretations of our physical and personal environments? Such are the concerns of the study of visual language and its mate, visual literacy.

VIEW POINTS: VISUALIZATION AS LANGUAGE

In a strict sense, visual literacy refers to understanding texts that are in forms of images (i.e., signs, gestures, diagrams, maps, movies, charts, etc.). These may or may not be accompanied by words or print, and some of these may involve visual *cultural* literacy, that is, visual images that communicate messages from or within a particular culture, current or past. If we think about books or materials that are entirely composed of words, the idea of visual literacy provides an important means for interpreting the words into images as pictures or art, or one of the forms

*J.E. Pedersen and K.D. Finson (eds.), Visual Data, 133–150.*

listed above. In this era of visual barrage, particularly via entertainment media, it is necessary that we consider how visual literacy can be encouraged in youth and utilized for the benefit of all forms of literate acts (i.e., reading writing, listening, speaking), as well as for functioning in the real world.

Visual images, as we perceive and recognize them, enable a distinct language for our interpretations of events, procedures, places and things, as well as our attempts to make human connections in our physical environments. Just as verbal language is an essential vehicle for communication, the things we see are also a means for designating messages and interpreting experiences. Messaris (1994) says, "Language is the most comprehensive system of human communication, the one that comes closest, in principle, to encompassing all of human experience, both the tangible world of objects and events and the intangible world of forces that animates them" (p. 120). Just as there is power in the words we hear and those we use, there is power in the images we see or the images we create. Looking at things in the world around us can catch us off guard, surprise us, make us curious, or raise our concern. It is especially in the current world of visual creativity of expression that we wonder about the intellectual, emotional, and social development of our youth and the enrichment of our own adulthood.

Visual images are sometimes necessary to make sense of written or spoken texts since not all texts enable us to build strong mental interpretations. Verbal language may fail to provide a reader with an adequate description of an event or scene (e.g., the crashing of the two airplanes into the World Trade Center) but a picture, a photograph or film can enable more in depth understanding.

Reflecting upon methods used for the teaching of reading, it is so often the case that children are not involved to any great extent in using visualization for the interpretation of what they read, although there are many authors that encourage teachers to employ techniques that integrate visual expression and visual literacy. Good readers with plenty of experience reading all kinds of texts tend to create their own visual images as they read, and they sometimes develop meanings that may not have been intended by an author. How often have we heard or said, "The book was much better than the movie?" Comparatively, good readers are able to evaluate a film producer's interpretation of a written text against their own interpretations.

## RESEARCH TO UNDERSTAND VERBAL LEARNING

In the latter half of the twentieth century, there was a surge of study regarding verbal learning and verbal behavior as researchers tried to understand people's perceptions of written texts and the structure of memory to provide connections between the world as they know it and the interpretation of the printed word. Drawing from the field of artificial intelligence, cognitive psychologists and psycholinguists focused upon language use and language understanding, given individuals have their own sets of life experiences as well as prior knowledge of how their verbal languages "work" to interpret their world for themselves and to others.

Researchers in the 1970s to the present century have moved in particularly notable directions, building upon a previous body of research that concentrated on the identification and classification of grammars of language as a resource for figuring out how we manipulate spoken and written language forms. They have discovered that there is more to comprehending written texts than just knowing how to use syntax or vocabulary. An example of a precursor to more cognitively situated research is a study by Fredericksen (1977). He explored the responses of children and youth for reading single English sentences and subsequently provided a detailed classification scheme for English grammatical structures according to difficulty of production and comprehension. His work was one of several used by Quigley et al. (1978) to create a *Test of Syntactic Abilities* (*TSA*) consisting of 22 multiple choice tests, one for each major syntactic structure. These subtests could show how students, primarily those who were deaf and had limited proficiency with English, interpreted common to complex grammatical forms, such as personal pronouns or verb tenses as used in single sentences. The TSA and other such materials did not account very well for pragmatics or the world knowledge of students within the content of the test sentences. This is still often the case with standardized reading tests created by publishing houses in the age of *No Child Left Behind*. For example, a story in a 2001 sample document for the New York State ELA tests uses the word *stoop* as a noun. This term is not a common one in most geographic environments in the United States today, and although it may be found in some sectors of New York City, it is not particularly used in upstate New York. The context of that particular sample passage in the New York State test is not sufficient for a child to figure out the meaning of the word *stoop*.

In recent times, researchers in fields allied with cognitive science conduct experiments to try to answer the question of how good readers do so successfully, looking at prior knowledge of the world, language processing theories, and how the mind connects verbal interpretations to prior knowledge of the world. They base their studies on much research from the latter half of the twentieth century. In one classic study, Bransford and Johnson (1972) demonstrated that prior knowledge alone of the way that one's language works may not be sufficient to help interpret a written text or a verbal message. In this experiment they asked subjects to read the following passage and to provide an interpretation.

If the balloons popped the sound wouldn't be able to carry since everything would be too far away from the correct floor. A closed window would also prevent the sound from carrying, since most buildings tend to be well-insulated. Since the whole operation depends upon a steady flow of electricity, a break in the middle of the wire would also cause problems. Of course, a fellow could shout, but the human voice is not loud enough to carry that far. An additional problem is that a string could break on the instrument. Then there could be no accompaniment to the message. It is clear that the best situation would involve less distance. Then there would be fewer problems. With face to face contact, the least number of things could go wrong. (p. 719)

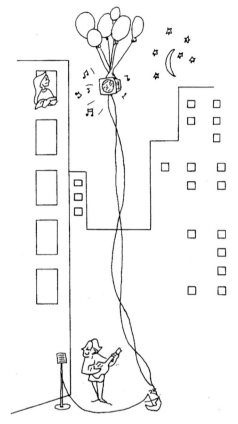

*Figure 1.* A modern-day Romeo scene. (From Bransford & Johnson, 1972)

Of course, no one could explain the paragraph, even though it was written in careful English and the words were not especially difficult. It was necessary to provide the picture shown in Figure 1.

The work of Marvin Minsky (1975) regarding artificial intelligence and creating computer languages that can function just like human languages, raised questions for psychologists and psycholinguists about how the mind creates images, interprets them, and classifies them. Rumelhart (1977), Shank and Abelson (1975), Johnson-Laird (1983), Rosch (1975) and van Dijk and Kintsch (1983), among others, explored related issues about schema activation, use of prior knowledge, and mental images that we create based upon our experiences and abilities to use verbal language and to comprehend it. Scholars such as these studied the classic work of Bartlett (1932) regarding the definition and development of schema. In one article, Shank and Abelson (1975) ask us to attend to our individual schema for the word *restaurant* as part of a larger *dining* schema. The variety of possible images that can be created in our minds indicates that you or I might make a distinct association that no one else would have made, and upon hearing the responses of others our schema for the term grows and changes. Rumelhart

(1980) explains that there are various kinds of schema, including the kind evoked in the single word query, and he explains the importance of schema and prior knowledge to understanding written texts.

## RESEARCH ABOUT VISUAL LANGUAGE

Just as the researchers above manipulated written language and verbal language to understand images we create when we read or listen, there are others who looked at the different ways that we interpret pictures, visual and performing arts, and the physical environment, and how we deal with the world as we see it. Berger (1972) states that "we never look just at one thing: we are always looking at the relation between things and ourselves" (p. 9).

Developmental psycholinguist, Karmiloff-Smith (1980), explored children's verbal interpretations of single pictures and sets of pictures in event sequences. She discovered distinct language interpretation patterns that were different when children looked at one single picture as opposed to going through a set. And, in a large cross-linguistic study coordinated by Chafe, called *The Pear Stories* (1981), linguists who were sent to several countries around the world got very different stylistic oral interpretations of a film (lacking narration) by individuals in each country, demonstrating the effects of one's culture (e.g., Greek narrative style) and specific language forms (e.g., Japanese pronouns) upon the ways that one expresses meaning.

In an article, *Building Visual Communication Theory by Borrowing from Rhetoric*, Kenney (2002) provides very strong parallels between terminology and constructs that characterize rhetorical style and how these things can be used and conceived to describe visual images (e.g., magazine advertisements, photographs). One important point that he makes, citing work by Birdsell and Groarke (1996), is that people can look at visual images and derive meanings because they can relate to immediate visual and verbal contexts, but since visual culture changes significantly over time persons who may lack proficiency in visual cultural literacy would have trouble locating the intended explicit meanings of images not related to their prior knowledge, or their ability to connect their prior knowledge to what they are looking at. For example, if a person had not been to a town for over 20 years and asked for directions from a friend in order to visit that friend's home, the friend might try to describe the current route and landmarks assuming the visitor's prior knowledge. As that visitor proceeds, he might be surprised by the changes in the once familiar setting, even to the extent of hesitating to follow the directions.

Howard Gardner (1990), focusing upon artistic development rather than upon visual literacy per se, makes a case for creating learning environments in which students can be exposed to formal and conceptual knowledge about the visual arts, music, and imaginative writing to enable them to grow in understanding about themselves and their own environments. Through *production, perception, and reflection* Gardner emphasizes that students should naturally make connections and associations to other forms of knowledge with which they need competence. In other words, they should be able to develop broad schema for many areas of learning through a developmentally based program in the arts such as that which Gardner and his colleagues promoted.

Gardner's work brings to mind several illustrator/artists who concentrated on interpreting modern life and aspects of geographical environments. Saul Steinberg, for example, considered himself a "writer who draws" (Smith 2005, p. 30); and, according to the Saul Steinberg Foundation, he defined drawing as "a way of reasoning on paper" (Morrison, 2007). Most noted for his covers and drawings for *The New Yorker*, Steinberg combined his background in philosophy and sculpture to give us his images of the world and our place in it. His famous cover, *View of the World from 9th Avenue* (1976) provides us with what Smith characterizes as some of Steinberg's key trademarks, "mental maps of time and space" (p. 41).

*Figure 2. View of the World from 9th Avenue.*

Just as teachers have to help students develop verbal skills, they also have to help them develop skills in visual literacy. We cannot assume that each student interprets a visual image in the same way, or that every student knows the markers to which he or she must attend in order to figure out meanings. Thinking about Gardner's experiments and the work of Steinberg, I suggest that instruction in the visual arts coupled with elements of visual literacy ought to be done broadly and consistently throughout the curriculum, especially to enhance reading comprehension. Instead of looking at the traditional classroom model where there is a separation of courses (and sometimes the elimination of the arts), I envision an integrated approach to stimulate the development of visual literacy. The most hopeful school programs that I have found are among those documented by the George Lukas Educational Foundation, in the category of project-based learning. In many schools across the United States, there are subject area teachers combining their efforts to help children and youth become aware of connections between what they know and what they see.

## ENCOURAGING VISUAL LITERACY TO SUPPORT LEARNING

Esrock (1994) draws particular attention to the role of image schemas as they pertain to acts of reading literature. She states that image schemata are important because they have a direct and total effect upon how we interpret verbal material. When children and youth are encouraged to explain what they see, whether a visual object or event, or a piece of literature as Esrock proposes, the listener sometimes marvels at the twists and turns and creativity that is used to describe it. And, the listener will most probably modify his or her own mental image for that piece upon hearing another's interpretation.

How important might it be for us, as educator listeners, to go beyond being awestruck by a description, taking advantage of the opportunity to integrate such unique descriptions into a deeper discovery of meaning with the students who created them? Yet, Knobel and Lankshear (2005) caution that we might be tempted to sterilize potentially robust learning experiences if we try to grasp onto a technique or teaching package. This certainly can be true for approaches that integrate visual literacy, just as for other literacies that are addressed by Knobel and Lankshear in their research.

## MY PERSONAL VIEWPOINTS AND MY RESEARCH

I have been particularly intrigued by visual images and visual literacy for a considerable part of my career in the field of deafness, deaf blindness, and language. I have come to know that what may be lacking through the ears can indeed be very much compensated by the eyes. The drawings of many children who are deaf, such as the one below that was given to me on a visit to the Dr. Bela Torok School for the Deaf in Budapest, Hungary, and those of American children with whom I have had contact, provide intriguing and sometimes powerful messages in visual language where speaking may be difficult or incomprehensible. And, it is quite common that deaf persons can interpret human feelings, attitudes, and emotions by studying one's face and one's physical stance. They are truly *visually literate*, in many instances much more than those of us who can hear. Yet, as technology advances (e.g., digital hearing aids, the cochlear implant), many deaf persons are increasingly able to get into the world of sound; and as they experience it, they show much surprise or especially validation for the match between their

*Figure 3.*

interpretations of what they have previously only been able to see and what they now hear.

In one of my experiences as a director of a university reading clinic, a teacher of the deaf asked me to help her with an eight-year-old child (whom I'll call Joey) who had not attended school until the year that I saw him, had very little communication or environmental stimulation in his home, and was fitted for a hearing aid for the first time when he started school. His parents had died and he was being raised by his 16-year-old pregnant sister and her boyfriend in a rural shack with four other young siblings. There was an abundance of love in this home, but little else.

The teacher could not get Joey to learn printed words, even coupled with sign language or speech instruction. For one part of my assessment I wanted to see if he at least had a sense of story that could support his learning. I asked Joey to look over a wordless picturebook, *Tuesday*, by David Weisner (1991). This book has exceptionally vibrant illustrations of frogs. Subsequently, I asked him to follow along the pages and recount the story. I was impressed by the vigor and imagination that Joey put into his retelling. He demonstrated that he could very well interpret the intended meanings in Weisner's book, and to incorporate many of the subtleties that he could see in the pictures.

Observing Joey's successful use of sign and his strong but sometimes unsuccessful efforts to find words, I enabled the teacher to establish routines that connected print to sign and speech instruction. By using Joey's capabilities to handle words with long vowel sounds, the teacher was able to raise Joey's expressive and receptive vocabulary in sign and speech and to connect that to good written texts that had plenty of visual support. After eight months, he was able to tackle books written at the first grade level, a big improvement for him (Chrosniak, 1992).

Children like Joey show us that even with very limited prior knowledge of verbal language or of life experiences, the integration of visuals with the other components required for reading printed texts can be of considerable help for learning. Although Joey and his teacher used signed communication, there is nothing in the instructional procedures that I proposed for him that is distinct only for deaf persons.

In my encounters with individuals who are deaf blind, I have been humbled by their strategic coping with their environments. They have demonstrated visual literacy where vision was virtually nonexistent or extremely limited. One young man that I know, who is profoundly deaf and severely visually impaired, was a most articulate dinner mate conversing with me in a specialized sign language at a conference for families of the deaf blind in New York State. After dinner he escorted his mother and myself to our hotel rooms without any hesitation. He is now an engineer. At another meeting, a professional colleague who is deaf blind gave me directions for driving out of Manhattan to continue on to Buffalo, New York. I had much doubt and was hesitant to trust him, but he was correct. Later, I apologized to him for my dubiousness.

My personal interactions with deaf blind individuals and their families gave me ideas for improving the experiences of preservice teachers in a graduate program for deaf education of which I was the director. A member of the McGowan-Gin-Rosica Family Foundation and the director of the New York State Technical Assistance project provided me with substantial funding to purchase hardware and software that the student teachers could use with deaf blind children. Fortunately, an expert in the field of vision taught courses to these preservice individuals and organized most of the program endeavors with area deaf blind children, youth, and even adults.

Esrock (1994) makes a critical statement about visual literacy and the force of imaging. "... what is important about image schemas is that they structure all of our perceptions and cognitive acts. Image schemas thus have consequences for all forms of human understanding" (p. 112). If individuals with limited sensory capabilities are able to become proficient in acts that are part of what is called visual literacy, then how might we encourage those with intact vision (and hearing) to become just as proficient?


OUR VISUALLY MEDIATED WORLD

It is rather easy to overlook the power that visual images provide. In a century in which there is so much creative energy expended to develop new technologies, consumers take for granted the things that previously were judged as virtually impossible. Bruce and Hogan (1998) comment that within everyday discourse and everyday life, technologies embed themselves to the extent that "The more we look, the more they slip into the background" (p. 270). That which may amuse us and surprise us today in a PIXAR film or on a television commercial becomes commonplace as film producers use even more creative visual techniques in subsequent ventures. Today's youth (and adults) are not satisfied merely with a cell phone that enables them to communicate auditorily. They want to be able to see images, snap and send pictures. They want to be able to access the Internet through their phones and to have the capability of creating presentations through word processing and other software as is possible with *smart* phones. Consumers want to be able to ask, literally, "Do you see what I mean?" as they communicate.

Reading researchers such as Knobel and Lankshear question the effects and potential of new visual literacy media such as manga upon the development of literacy skills, and upon the transfer of fluency for reading traditionally written texts when visual images are the basic text via computer technology and the Internet. More importantly though, they advise that educators need to look at the new social practices that are mediated by new technologies to understand what the world outside of school is like. For example, the popularity of Google's *You Tube* and access to newspapers on the Internet is evidence of new ways that societies are involved in somewhat of a rapid evolutionary process that draws upon the use of visual literacy coupled with sound and verbal language.

There are significant changes apparent in the ways that we communicate today – how we speak, and what we try to communicate because of our visual experiences. Where does this fit in helping youth to become readers and translators of traditional written texts?

## TECHNOLOGY MEDIATED READING RESEARCH

In 1987 I spent two months at the National Technical Institute of the Deaf (NTID) in Rochester, New York completing research for my doctoral dissertation. While at the college, I socialized with the college students in the evenings at which time they usually watched captioned television. Closed captioning on television was still somewhat new at that time, and these students were especially taken by the program, *Dynasty* (Spelling, 1981–1987). As we watched together, I noticed that students who had less fluency, who asked the former to explain what was going on in the episode, would frequently interrupt those who were better readers. The better readers would tell the others to wait until a commercial at which time they would clarify the text. In other words, the less fluent readers who could not keep up reading the captions were hesitant to make assumptions of the story just on what they saw. Both groups had to keep the visual representation in memory as the more fluent readers interpreted the episode during breaks. This experience made me curious regarding the adjustment of deaf individuals to captioned media.

In 1989 I conducted research regarding captioned television and reading comprehension. I wanted to understand how deaf individuals, for whom captioned television was somewhat new, interpreted the visuals while accessing the captions. I also wanted to explore ways to help those whose reading abilities were low to enhance their television watching satisfaction while improving their reading skills. I designed a study using Palincsar's (Palincsar & Brown, 1982) *Reciprocal Teaching* (RT) method to support verbal interactions during the viewing of a television program. I did not want to use RT strategies rigidly, however. I wanted the study participants to lead the way in discussions of what they watched, trying to avoid what I have just recently heard stated by Knobel and Lankshear, that is, to "leachĚmuch of their richness and vitality ..." (p. 25).

I had three groups of participants who were all fluent in American Sign Language. One group consisted of deaf adults who worked in professions that included chemistry, library science, accounting, social work, and computer programming. A second group of deaf adults were high school graduates who were working in blue-collar jobs or had retired from such jobs in which they had little interaction with hearing coworkers. Twelve deaf high school juniors attending a state residential school constituted the third group.

All participants watched six weekly episodes of the situation comedy, *Growing Pains* (Tracy, 1985–1992), at home as scheduled on network television. They used a guide sheet as they watched, and then met with me and one of two graduate assistants on the following evening to discuss their viewing and to repeat the current episode recorded on videotape. At our first meeting, I instructed each group regarding Palincsar's four strategies of prediction, summarization, question asking, and clarification. During our discussions we referred, occasionally, to the guide sheet that reflected each of the strategies, and we stopped the videotape recorder at commercial breaks as suggested. Each group of participants responded in distinct ways depending upon their levels of literacy and the utility they perceived for Palincsar's strategies.

The deaf professionals were intrigued about applying the four strategies to their viewing. Most of all, they appreciated seeking clarification and validation from each other in the group for episode terminology, English expressions, and dialogue. Discussions each week drifted into topics about how they used written material in their professions and the interplay of their bilingualism in American Sign Language (ASL) and English. The second group of adults tended to relate more to the material of the episodes associated with situations and experiences in their own lives than to specific language. One husband and wife pair would humorously chide each other regarding how they, like the parents in the television program, treated their own children. Sharing such as this brought out more jovial conversation among all members of this particular group. The group of adolescents discussed each episode and also wrote an "I learned ..." statement. Analyses of their discussions using the guide sheet and the written "I learned" material revealed some involvement of vocabulary and expressions that were used in the particular episode of the week as well as their association to the teenagers in *Growing Pains*. Those juniors with reading levels at and above grade four tended to get the story line and interpretations of the episode correct; those with reading levels between grades two and four sometimes misinterpreted the episode. Given that the speed of captioning requires about a grade four reading level, it is understandable that the slower readers would not be able to keep up with the match between story line and visuals.

Throughout the study I saw that deaf individuals who previously had had limited opportunities to access closed captions in visual media were able to maintain their gift of visual interpretation while clearing up misconceptions of film using the printed text and sharing with members of a group (Chrosniak, 1990). Many of the adults in both groups offered comments regarding their new appreciation for television programs and captioned films that they could rent and watch via videotape recorder. The study actually propelled some to form a subcommittee to advance the offerings of captioned television by the major network local affiliates as well as by contacts with the film industry through Blockbuster.

## VISUAL LITERACY AND HEARING INDIVIDUALS

The background research for my captioned television study included guidance from the *National Captioning Institute* (NCI) as well as guidance from linguist Gerry Berent of NTID and Bruce Austin, professor of communication and media at the Rochester Institute of Technology. I studied what was being done for hearing as well as deaf persons regarding visual media, language understanding, and closed captioning. Much of the research at NCI regarding reading and captioning had to do with hearing children, some populations with learning disabilities, and English-As-Second-Language (ESL) learners. Austin studied communication and television viewing preferences of hearing adults. Just as I knew that the methods I used to help Joey were not restricted to deaf children, I also concluded that what I had done with reciprocal teaching and captioned television was equally useful for hearing individuals. Although I have not yet had an opportunity to begin an experiment that I have designed to prove the latter, I have encouraged teachers to try using my style of reciprocal teaching with film. With hearing students, a teacher can turn the sound off to urge students to read the captions. The National Captioning Institute currently provides a manual for teachers to use captioned television to improve reading comprehension and vocabulary acquisition (NCI, 2003). This book gives strategies based upon research over the past 20 years.

In some respects Closed Captioning is becoming submerged in a world of synchronic (i.e., real time) interactions among individuals on the Internet. Chat rooms and weblogs are embellished with graphic interfaces so that participants do not have to wait for their turn to share. There are components, such as MUDS (multi-user domains) and MOOS (multi-object oriented domains) that are virtual environments in which one or more forms of visual imaging can be used. (See Knobel and Lankshear for detailed descriptions.) Opportunities seem endless for individuals to communicate using a mix of media on the Internet. Youth who used to be content watching Japanese-inspired anime on the Cartoon Network are now creating their own interpretations. Adults and teens are involved in virtual worlds such as *Second Life* (Baedeker, 2007). The number of such venues as those just stated keep growing and social interactions continue to change and expand.

While supervising a student teacher in a local high school, I met a particularly astute honor student wearing a t-shirt embossed with a manga character. He took time to explain to me why he and others enjoyed manga and its video counterpart, anime. Manga, in Japanese, refers to comic books. In manga, the drawings are quite distinct depending upon the artist, and frames are "read" from left to right and throughout a page. The visual images are extremely complex and not all frames are of equal proportion or size. Anime includes video representations of manga, among other kinds of videos.

My teen friend was especially articulate and he showed me several examples of his favorite manga on the Internet, this in addition to the surrealistic pictures that he had created for an art class using Photoshop. I had the opportunity to observe his art class and I was amazed at the involvement and creativity among all the students, not just this young man. (That is not to say that all were influenced by manga.) Since my conversations with the teenager, I have noticed that a local Barnes and Noble bookstore has increased its stock of manga from one table in 2005 to several shelves in 2007 marked as carefully as is the poetry section or other major section in the store.

My investigations of manga and anime made me think about ways to capture the curiosity and visual experiences of students for the sake of assisting in their growth in visual literacy. This hearkened back to my understandings of Gardner's ideas and artists such as Saul Steinberg. I knew that not all children and youth in America had access to computers for pleasure or study, and that many had no idea about the virtual lifestyles of the Internet, or about weblogs, chatrooms, or manga. Thus, I decided on baseline work regarding visual art and visual literacy.

## VISUAL LITERACY AND VISUAL ART

In 2006 my interests in visual literacy coincided with those of the director of a major nonprofit organization dedicated to literacy and learning. Nancy Rakoff of Common Place in Peoria, Illinois, asked me to review a grant proposal that she was writing to the Starbucks Foundation. Starbucks invited applicants to propose how their nonprofit group might involve the arts and literacy in innovative ways. Given their impressive successes over the past 40 years, Common Place was awarded this grant and it provided funds for many activities for the children, youth, and adults.

The Starbucks project involves 100 individuals, mostly children to age 14, in activities that incorporate the study of the visual arts with everyday visual literacy needs. These children and youth come to Common Place daily for two hours. The first hour is for formal tutoring and the second is for activities that are related to particular themes. Our plan includes training tutors and staff to use any of a set of visual literacy strategies to help the students enhance reading comprehension during activity time. We use books from the *Getting to Know the World's Greatest Artists* series by artist/author Mike Venezia as a focal point to encourage connections between visual art and visual literacy. I am the primary trainer and I help the staff to consider matters of visual literacy that are important to the children, such as knowing how to read maps and charts, deciding upon strategies to solve problems that involved physical dimensions (e.g., getting a cat out of a tree, figuring out alternative routes to places in town). Together we use Venezia's books to learn about specific artists and to create situations that parallel those of the children. For example, students create maps, charts and visual directions (i.e., helping Van Gogh get from Paris to Arles; comparing Jacob Lawrence's environment to one's own; figuring out balance, shapes and size (i.e., how Monet could maintain his materials and painting on his boat in the Seine). Although Common Place has sufficient computer resources, most tutors use simple, practical objects and materials in their activities.

We were fortunate to have a presentation by Mike Venezia in which he stressed to the children the importance of recognizing how visual art helps support visual literacy. He used many examples from his own life and showed us through his works the importance of geography and history. His visit came at the halfway point of the project, and yet, the students were already quite articulate about the artist(s) they had studied up to then. Venezia, who studied at the *Art Institute of Chicago*, has a very perspicuous understanding of the thinking of children. And so, his interactions with them at his visit were admirable, and their questions were very provocative.

At this writing, the Common Place community is still involved in this project. In order to see if there are any gains in reading ability among the participants, we gave them the *Test of Word Reading Efficiency* (Torgesen, Wagner, & Raschotte, 1999) at the beginning of the study and each one will also be retested at the end of the school year. Given this project is coordinated with a nonprofit organization, there are many factors that make it difficult to draw many conclusions for the entire population (e.g., variability of growth due to differences in classroom instruction; variability in the intensity of tutoring required for some children). However, with the help of the Common Place staff, we were able to target seven individuals for more extensive assessment and evaluation that include consultation with their schools and families, analysis of results on the TOWRE and the *Woodcock–Johnson III Diagnostic Reading Battery* (Woodcock, Mather, & Schrank, 2004). We'll be able to complete quantitative and qualitative analyses for these students in late 2007.

INTEGRATING VISUAL LITERACY IN THE CLASSROOM

Although I have described in some detail research and studies regarding visual imaging and visual literacy, I have also tried to share several ideas that can be used in classroom instruction as well as in extracurricular environments. I will share several more instructional and research possibilities here, in this segment of the chapter.

My first suggestion for a teacher is to spoil one's self by visual immersion in a variety of manmade and natural images including paintings, drawings, photography, film, sculpture, pottery, and the natural world. It is by broadening the base of our own visual experience that we can subsequently help children achieve visual literacy. The possibilities are limitless with respect to immersion.

Each artist has a story to tell and gives us impressions that are influenced by personal histories, environments and experiences. I especially appreciate looking at paintings of the Old Masters, contrasting them to avant-garde artistry such as that of the surrealists. Two artists that I find very intriguing for students as well as myself are photorealist Richard Estes and Brazilian American Vik Muniz who creates art from common resources such as sugar, small pieces of trash, and even chocolate. Each artist has a story to tell and gives us impressions that are influenced by personal histories, environments and experiences. One relatively easy way to integrate visual literacy into the curriculum is to integrate visual art into the social studies.

If we are teaching a written text, such as a story that has considerable local color, we might provide a dynamic assignment in which children combine their studies of geography or culture with the setting of the story. Consider, for example, the children's book, *Tar Beach* by Faith Ringgold (1996). On the first page we see the main character flying over New York City and we read Ringgold's beautiful words, "I will always remember when the stars fell down around me and lifted me up above the George Washington Bridge." It might be interesting to help children develop a perspective of the immensity of some New York City high rises and tenement buildings, as well as an understanding of the role of the bridges, by looking at photographs or film clips that involve New York City. To get one of many points across, the children might do a comparative drawing or display of the kind of home in which they live and that of the character in Faith Ringgold's story. Mike Venezia has created a book about Ringgold in his *Getting to Know the World's Great Artists* series. In this book one gets a special view of Ringgold as an author, as a person, and as an important American artist.

Another way to enhance reading comprehension is to use my captioned TV activity with reciprocal teaching. Among the possibilities is one that I suggest for a junior high classroom where a teacher might show a film on the Civil War, for example, with the sound off. Since all televisions from 1991 to the present have caption accessibility, students can read along the presentation. Once this first exposure is done, the sound is turned on and the students can have a follow up discussion on how music and dialogue enhance a depiction of events. Subsequently, reciprocal teaching could be used in the classroom with written text about the Civil War in the fashion first suggested by Palincsar.

Students might be encouraged to create their own films with music and narration. A vivid demonstration of the enthusiasm of children to explore film can be seen in the use of a visual literacy curriculum, The Story of Movies, produced by the Film Foundation in conjunction with Martin Scorcese at the Santa Barbara middle schools (see Project-based Learning at http://www.edutopia.org). In this four week project, students study the power of visualization in segments of the 1962 film, *To Kill a Mockingbird*, based upon the book by Harper Lee (1960). Scorcese explains that children need to know how to interpret the visual information that they experience in daily life carefully and critically. By exploring the use of light and themes in film, students become aware of historical context and how to discern reality and understand social issues. This curriculum is free to teachers through the Film Foundation website.

**Use this paper as you watch the television program.**

At the Beginning of the Program.
Watch the entry material that introduces the program.

A.  At the <u>First Commercial</u> complete the following.

I predict this episode will be about...

B.  At the <u>Second Commercial</u> complete the following.

I am not quite sure about...

C.  At the <u>Third Commercial</u> complete the following.

I would like to ask the following question to the producer:

D.  At the <u>End of the Episode</u> complete the following.

My summary of this program.

Designed by Patricia N. Chrosniak  1989

*Figure 4.*   Captioned TV and reciprocal teaching.

REFERENCES

Baedeker, R. (March 21, 2007). Student exchange without the jet lag. Retrieved March 22, 2007 from Edutopia Online, www.glef.org.

Bartlett, F.C. (1932). *Remembering: A study in experimental and social psychology.* Cambridge, England: Cambridge University Press.

Berger, J. (1972). *Ways of seeing.* New York: Penguin Books.

Birdsell, D.S., & Groarke, L. (1996). Toward a theory of visual argument. *Argumentation and Advocacy, 33,* 1–10.

Bransford, J.D., & Johnson, M.K. (1972). Contextual prerequisites for understanding: Some investigations of comprehension and recall. *Journal of Verbal Learning and Verbal Behavior, 11,* 717–726.

Bruce, B.C., & Hogan, M.P. (1998). The disappearance of technology: Toward an ecological model of literacy. In D. Reinking, M.C. McKenna, L.D. Labbo, & R.D. Kieffer (Eds.), *Handbook of literacy and technology: Transformations in a post-typographic world* (pp. 269–281). Mahwah, NJ: Lawrence Erlbaum Associates, Publishers.

Chafe, W. (Ed.) (1981). *The pear stories: Cognitive, cultural, and linguistic aspects of narrative production.* Norwood, NJ: Ablex Publishing Corporation.

Chrosniak, P.N. (1990). Captioned TV for hearing impaired youth. Alexander Graham Bell Centennial Convention, July 26–30. Washington, DC.

Chrosniak, P.N. (1992). Phonological awareness: A case study of one deaf child. National Reading Conference, December 21–25, San Antonio, TX.

Elkins, J. (2003). *Visual studies.* New York: Taylor & Francis Books, Inc.

Esrock, E.J. (1994). *The reader's eye: Visual imaging as reader response.* Baltimore, MD: The Johns Hopkins University Press.

Film Foundation. *The story of movies.* Curriculum Resources. Retrieved April 2007 from the Film Foundation website: http://www.storyofmovies.org.

Fredericksen, C.F. (1977). Structure and process in discourse production and comprehension. In P.A. Carpenter & M.A. Just (Eds.), *Cognitive processes in comprehension* (pp. 313–322). Hillsdale, NJ: Lawrence Erlbaum Associates Publishers, Inc.

Gardner, H. (1990). *Art education and human development.* Los Angeles, CA: J. Paul Getty Trust.

Gee, J.P. (2003). *What video games have to teach us about learning and literacy.* New York: Palgrave Macmillan.

George Lukas Educational Foundation. http://www.glef.org.

Johnson-Laird, P.N. (1983). *Mental models: Towards a cognitive science of language, inference, and consciousness.* Boston, MA: Harvard University Press.

Karmiloff-Smith, A. (1980). Psychological processes underlying pronominalization and nonpronominalization in children's connected discourse. In J. Kreiman & A.E. Ojeda (Eds.), *Papers on the parasession on pronouns* (pp. 231–250). Chicago: University of Chicago Press.

Kenney, K. (2002). Building visual communication theory by borrowing from rhetoric. In C. Handa (Ed.), *Visual rhetoric in a digital world: A critical sourcebook* (pp. 321–343). New York: Bedford/St. Martin's.

Knobel, M., & Lankshear, C. (2005). "New" literacies: Research and social practice. In B. Maloch et al. (Eds.), *The 54th Yearbook of the National Reading Conference* (pp. 22–50). Oak Creek, WI: The National Reading Conference, Inc.

Lee, H. (1960). *To kill a mockingbird.* Philadelphia: J.B. Lippincott.

Messaris, P. (1994). *Visual literacy: Image, mind, & reality.* Boulder, CO: Westview Press.

Minsky, M. (1975). A framework for representing knowledge. In P.H. Winston (Ed.), *The psychology of computer vision.* New York: McGraw-Hill Publishers.

Morrison, R. (Executive Producer). (2007, March 4). *CBS News Sunday Morning* [Television broadcast]. New York: American Broadcasting Corporation.

Muniz, V. (2005). *Reflex: A Vik Muniz primer.* New York: Aperture.

New York State ELA Sample Tests (2001). New York: Macmillan/McGraw-Hill Publishers.

Palincsar, A.S., & Brown, A.L. (1984). Reciprocal teaching of comprehension-fostering and monitoring activities. *Cognition and Instruction, 1,* 117–175.

Quigley, S., Steinkamp, M., Power, D., & Jones (1978). *Test of syntactic abilities.* Beaverton, OR: Dormac.

Ringgold, F. (1996). *Tar beach.* New York: Dragonfly Books Crown Publishers.

Rosch, E.H. (1973). On the internal structure of perceptual and semantic categories. In T.E. Moore (Ed.), *Cognitive development and the acquisition of language.* New York: Academic Press.

Rumelhart, D.E. (1980). Schemata: The building blocks of cognition. In R.J. Spiro, B.C. Bruce, & W.F. Brewer (Eds.), *Theoretical issues in reading comprehension* (pp. 33–58). Hillsdale, NJ: Lawrence Erlbaum Associates Publishers, Inc.

Rumelhart, D.E. (1977). Towards an interactive model of reading. In S. Dornic (Ed.), *Attention and performance, VI.* Hillsdale, NJ: Lawrence Erlbaum Associates.

Shank, R.C., & Abelson, R.P. (1975). Scripts, plans, and knowledge. In *Advance papers of the Fourth International Joint Conference on Artificial intelligence* (pp. 151–157). Tbilisi, Georgia, USSR.

Smith, J. (2005). *Steinberg at the New Yorker*. New York: Harry N. Abrams, Inc., Publishers.

Spelling, A. (Executive Producer) (1981–1987). *Dynasty* [Television dramatic series]. New York: American Broadcasting Network.

Steinberg, S. (March 29, 1976). View of the world from 9th Avenue. In J. Smith, *Steinberg at the New Yorker* (p. 42). New York: Harry N. Abrams, Inc.

Torgesen, J.K., Wagner, R.K., & Rashotte, C.A. (1999). *Test of word reading efficiency*. Austin, TX: PRO-ED.

Tracy, J. (Executive Producer for 130 episodes) (1985–1992). *Growing pains* [Television Situation Comedy]. New York: American Broadcasting Company. Using captioned television in reading and literacy instruction. (2003). Vienna, VA: National Captioning Institute.

van Dijk, T., & Kintsch, W. (1983). *Strategies for discourse comprehension*. New York: Academic Press.

Venezia, M. (1988-present). *Getting to know the world's greatest artists* [A series of biographies]. Chicago: Children's Press.

Weisner, D. (1991). *Tuesday*. New York: Clarion Books.

Wilmerding, J. (1993). *Richard Estes*. New York: Pomegranate Communications.

Woodcock, R.W., Mather, N., & Schrank, F.A. (2004). *Woodcock–Johnson III diagnostic reading battery*. Itasca, IL: Riverside Publishing.

MICHAEL ANGELOTTI AND MARK LETCHER

# CHAPTER 10
# IMAGES AS VISUAL DATA IN THE WORLD OF
# ENGLISH TEACHING AND LEARNING:
# A LOOK AT THE EFFECTS OF STUDENT
# PRODUCED ART AND INTERPRETATIONS OF
# THE POPULAR MEDIA

## INTRODUCTION

Humankind has always lived in a universe of images – some created by the brain from within, some captured by the brain from without. History suggests also that over time we have been disposed to express those images in more and more complex ways – on cave walls, as sculpture and paintings, on film, over the world wide web, and, of course, as words. For every image there was a maker and a reader. In the historical moment of this paper, the imaging catch phrase is "multi-modal-media." We may, for example, simply think a picture in our heads. Or, wondering about our ability to conjure such visual data, we may "google" or "wiki" the www to gather information on a topic such as "image." In fact, using "Google" to explore "image" December 31, 2006 took us to "The Free Dictionary" website, which, in turn, offered "mental image" as a more defined option, obtainable in more detail at "Wikipedia," the free web encyclopedia site. There we discovered several referenced pages of helpful information key to our search, such as the following excerpts from page one: "A mental image is a term used in philosophy and communication studies to describe the representation of an idea in a person's mind .... According to some biologists, our experiences of the world around us are stored as mental images which we can then associate and compare with other mental images and we can synthesize as completely new images, for example when we dream or imagine. This theory states that this process allows us to form useful theories of how the world works based on likely sequences of mental images, without having to directly experience that outcome, for example through the process of deduction." And on page three, "Researchers generally agree that ... our brains do form and maintain mental images as image-like wholes. The problem of exactly how these images are stored and manipulated within the human brain, particularly within language and communication, remains an fertile area of study" (Rohrer, forthcoming 2007).

Embedded within that Wikipedia find are the two perspectives on visual data offered by the authors of this chapter: we explore first how educators might help students manipulate their capacities to generate mental images to manage

*J.E. Pedersen and K.D. Finson (eds.), Visual Data, 151–165.*

language and communication more effectively through a process called "paint-write" – an "inside-out" approach to literacy growth developed collaboratively with secondary school English teachers during graduate courses and in their own classrooms (e.g. Courtney-Smith, 2005; Gasparino, 2006). We then examine how educators might help students apply their perceptions of the external world of images as expressed in the media and popular culture to their own social and cultural advantage – an "outside-in" strategy. Throughout our narrative we call upon our students and secondary teaching colleagues to help us describe how our respective approaches to paint-write and popular media studies translate into viable practice in the preparation and professional development of secondary English teachers and English teacher educators.

## ORIGIN, DEVELOPMENT, AND CURRENT STATUS: A BRIEF PERSONAL HISTORY OF PAINT-WRITE-MIKE ANGELOTTI

For much of my life I have fancied myself a poet, exploring with some passion methods of writing better poems. A decade or so ago, I became interested in strategies for stimulating the free flow of ideas to my writing and intensifying the images expressed in my writing. To that end, I enrolled in "free writing" workshops conducted in Taos, New Mexico, by Natalie Goldberg, author of *Writing Down the Bones: Freeing the Writer Within* (1986) and other books. The workshops featured individual growth in writing through personal writing (often stream-of-consciousness) shared in small and whole group discussions to encourage self-growth and nurturing feedback. This relatively risk-free, write-talk, word driven, egocentric format and method was highly motivational and comfortably served my free writing needs. In that my private writing agenda emphasized a focus on more effective verbal images in poetry and personal narrative, I also was able to move those wants forward to some degree; that is, as far as self-development in writing would take me. While in Taos, I also discovered that Michelle Cassou, co-author with Stewart Cubley of *Life, Paint, and Passion: Reclaiming the Passion of Spontaneous Expression* (1995), offered spontaneous painting workshops in that place, which invited non-painters as well as experienced painters into the same venue, and promised a nondirective model similar to that of Natalie Goldberg described earlier. Supposing that I could improve my verbal images multi-dimensionally by self-directed, creative visual play with the colors and shapes that painting offered, I participated in the Cassou Taos program. Over the three-year period of free painting in Cassou's workshops, I noticed that the combination of writing and painting did indeed strengthen the general aesthetic of my writing and motivation to write, as well as my sensitivity to the colors, shapes, and art present in ordinary life – all of which served to validate my perceptions of self as an accomplished writer and developing painter.

The notion that at some level there is within each of us a common creative core that serves equally well those verbal and visual arts we choose to explore (Dunn, 1995; Foster & Prevallet, 2002; Walsh-Piper, 2002) proved to be true for me. I wondered what the effect might be on others interested in improving the quality of their writing by interacting painting and writing and soon developed a working assumption that anyone open to paint-write could profit from the earnest exercise of it. It would be my role as teacher to devise means to encourage that openness among my students. Personally, I was able to interact writing and painting to the benefit of both, and wondered next what applying that approach to teaching and learning in my graduate teacher education classes would do for those teachers in practice seeking effective strategies for engaging their students in the development of reading and writing abilities, particularly those students less able and/or less motivated, That is, I was curious about the portability of paint-write benefits from teacher as student to the secondary students in their charge.

Frankly, I believed that paint-write could work in educational settings because it is so simple in practice, obvious in concept, and likely as old as the first humans finger tracing clouds in the sky or making red clay drawings on cave walls. Further, in more recent human history, accounts and artifacts suggest that artistic uses of image and word interactively was common, particularly with the Greeks, who identified the act of making verbal art from visual art as *ekphrasis*:

> In its earliest, most restricted sense, *ekphrasis* referred to the verbal description of a visual representation, often of an imagined object such as the shield of Achilles in the Illiad. With its principle of *ut pictura poesis* (poetry as a speaking picture and painting as mute poetry), Horace's *Ars Poetica* expressed the ekphrastic ideal of giving voice to painting. From Ben Jonson to William Blake to the Romantics, many poets, most famously Keats with his urn and Shelley with his fallen statue, have allowed art to tease them "out of thought." (Blackhawk in Foster and Prevallet, p. 1). Looking at art calls upon us to observe, taking in the particulars before the whole scene and its encompassing feeling. The act of writing imaginatively, whether poetry or prose, likewise first demands close observation – training the eye and getting the details right – before leaps of imagination can be made ... (Edgar in Walsh-Piper, p. xi) Plato writes of it in *Phaedrus*, observing that paintings and poems, when put together, "seem to talk to you as if they were intelligent." Listening to works of art and participating in a conversation with them can produce exciting and shifting responses in each of us: poems, stories, self-portraits, essays, and other creative works are generated that "talk back" to the visual stimulus. (Foster and Prevallet, p. xv)

What I have done with paint-write, then, as a contemporary writer-painter-professor, is to transform the classical *ekphrastic* idea of using *established* art and literature as the prompts for student response to using *student-produced* art and writing as prompts for *student-produced* art and writing. The classroom is their studio and the learning is owned immediately because the locus of its content and process is within them. It is theirs to begin with. Engagement and motivation to continue naturally follow.

My experience with students and teachers in our paint-write experiment, thus far, suggests that if we can establish routines whereby students will put to paper rough renderings of that which they are visualizing as images in mind (e.g., while reading text or listening to conversation), even abstracts spontaneously generated without much, if any, forethought, then we can use those personally created, immovable depictions (as opposed to countless, most often irretrievable, mental pictures that flash by at incredible speeds during such languaging acts as reading and writing) as points of departure for expressive language that can be manipulated to encourage self and teacher-directed developmental learning. Simply put, the working assumption here is that except in the case of some rote emanations, images are necessary precedents to words and strings of words humans produce to interpret and communicate thought, and we, as teachers, can use that human propensity to construct viable learning contexts.

"Paint-write" evolved from that line of thinking. The term describes a process whereby individuals spontaneously apply paint to paper, then spontaneously write from that "paint" as prompt, or similarly use a "write" (e.g., a self-composed poem) as prompt for a spontaneous paint. The process can remain spontaneously driven in the realm of free writing to encourage verbal fluency or engagement in a learning process, or gravitate to essay, fictional narrative, impressionistic painting, or other more product-driven ends more consistent with particular learning-teaching goals. In the end, paint-write practices seem to affect most significantly student and teacher interest and growth in reading, writing, and aesthetic understanding of the visual and verbal arts.

As I was to discover, the primary values of paint-write were embedded in my focus on the teachers' perceptions of self as accomplished writer and developing painter. They had to observe their own growth largely driven by their own personally effective and satisfying adaptations of concepts and applications initiated by professor or peers and, equally as important, their own inventions of strategies not presented or practiced in the college classroom setting. They had to accept risk, create paints spontaneously, dismiss aesthetic judgments, buy into process, write and talk spontaneously about their own paints and those of others, be collaborative, be honest, trust themselves as intuitive painters and writers, and totally give in to play as a learning tool prerequisite to more accomplished writing and painting. In brief, teachers had to struggle through and experience success with (and deeply own) that which they would introduce to their own students in their own unique teaching situations in their own ways. They had to physically do it, observe others doing it, intellectualize about it, and talk about it, more or less socially, with others going through the same thing. And our experience suggests that the sheer physicality of putting paint to paper, thinking about the process, and actively participating with their peers in the class culture made it stick, made them believers in themselves as growing writers, developing painters, and teachers able to help students help themselves as developing writers and painters, and, in the end, more confident human beings. Each teacher-graduate student, then, intuitively created a working model for self-growth in personally significant paint-write manifestations and addressed not only their own needs but some of every English teacher's most distressing challenges: student motivation and demonstrated improvement in reading and writing competence and performance in a contemporary culture of increasing diversity.

To be more specific, one of my summer courses, "Creative Teaching of Composition," is a dedicated paint-write course. It is an intensive, two-week, five-hours-per-day workshop course that blends personal growth in free painting and writing with teacher applications of the approach to secondary English classrooms. Its students typically are a mix of advanced English and English education undergraduates and experienced secondary English teacher-graduate students. Students paint, write, talk, collaborate, help each other, and examine their own learning processes, and those they observe, for possible applications to their own teaching, writing, and painting. They each contribute a sampling of work to a course anthology and compile a portfolio of self-selected work for peer-review and as an assessment tool for the professor.

Course texts most often available to students are the Goldberg and Cassou books previously mentioned, Charles Dunn's *Conversations in Paint* (1995), Foster and Prevallet's *Third Mind* (2002), and Kathleen Walsh-Piper's *Image to Word* (2002). These works are all accessible, conversational, and effective course texts, especially for writers unsure of the quality of their own writing and anxious about their abilities as painters. For example, *Writing Down the Bones* persuades students that they can write productively. Once they establish fluency and confidence in writing, they are enabled to move to more accomplished writing. *Conversations in Paint* demystifies painting and seems to greatly diminish the intimidation of painting for non-painters, even convincing some to pursue the art as a personal study. It not only connects painting and writing conceptually, but also shows students how to move from free paints to more accomplished paintings. In *Image to Word* Walsh-Piper carefully demonstrates strategies for helping secondary school English students engage paintings, literature, and writing in the same lesson, while at the same time informing readers of the aesthetics of those visual and verbal expressions she uses. She also includes a high quality, true-color CD of 67 well-known paintings that form the crux of her teaching lessons in the book. One of her motives is to make non-visual artists comfortable with some of art's technical elements. *Image to Word* also serves as an easy transition from paint-write to the more conventional *ekphrastic* strategies alluded to earlier. Including both paint-write and *ekphrasis* in combination provides a powerful arts-based package for literacy growth.

This is an important point to iterate here because most of my students, like me, are more skilled as writers, not a painters, and, like me, again, have observed personal growth in both areas to certain levels of personal satisfaction using the same techniques I teach; therefore, I am persuaded that anyone reading this document can apply this image and word approach to self or students of whatever subject they teach. That I have such room for growth in both the verbal and visual arts is an advantage. I grow with my students each time, and, maybe, that is part of the success of what I am doing. In regard to these particular choices of course texts, I suspect, in retrospect, that they have been extraordinarily helpful to students because they have been extraordinarily helpful to me. And we have the same mountain to climb.

Nevertheless, most students do walk away from the course energized to practice and apply paint-write. In fact, a number of them also have researched the
paint-write process further and adapted versions of the approach to public and
private middle, secondary, and college English classrooms. Jenna Gasparino,
for example, addresses some effects of paint-write on her ELL students in her
Master's thesis, "An Analysis of Creativity in One Twelfth Grade Public School
Classroom Through the Use of Art: Visual and Verbal" (2006). Her comments
suggest paint-write encouraged meaningful student language learning through
active participation in class activities and conversations:

> As students read their writing, some went on to explain the source of their
> inspiration. The majority of them related their work to the painting they had
> completed. Matt, for example, explained how his poem was a direct response
> to the "free form" that he felt Lana had illustrated in her painting. (See my
> Figure 1/Jenna's Figure 8) While sharing her painted response to Matt's poem,
> Lana said she felt it was a result of the "free creative playfulness" that she
> used when she painted. This explanation offered the class insight to both in-
> spirations. On the other hand, some students simply shared their work, both
> painting and writing, with no explanation.
>
> This (paint-write) also provided a safe sharing environment for many of my
> ELL students. Many of them do not feel comfortable sharing in front of the
> class because of their verbal communicative skills. This allowed them a creative
> outlet to express themselves without the threat of being judged. It also became
> a way for them to play with vocabulary. One Mexican student wrote his free
> response to his painting in both English and Spanish. He chose to read his
> poem to the class in both languages while he showed his painting. In his post
> paint/write reflection he wrote, "No teacher has ever let me use English and
> Spanish in my writing. When you told me I had the freedom to write whatever
> I wanted it made it easier to express my thoughts by using both languages."
> Regardless of what students said about their paintings, it was obvious in every
> example that there were significant connections in both visual and verbal works
> of art and learning was happening. (Gasparino, 2006, pp. 24–26)

Another former student, Kelly Courtney-Smith, wrote of her experience with
paint-write and a tenth-grade literature unit featuring Herman Hesse's 1951 novel,
*Siddhartha*, in the July, 2005 *English Journal*. In her piece she often captures students in the act of paint-write and includes several reflective pieces of her students.
One example is that of Jonathan, who seems to indicate he has realized deeper
insights into poetry, audience, and humanity, itself, through his participation in
Kelly's approaches to paint-write:

> It is a strange feeling being asked to take someone else's poetic tapestry and
> weave it into your own painting .... During the process, you almost go from
> interpreting some individual's poem, to interpreting yourself as an individual.
> What their cryptic artistic words meant and represented no longer mean the
> same thing, for now they are being seen through another set of eyes, with a

Lana's Paint

Matt's Free Write:
Free form
Free write
The paint used to create
The pawn used to play
Free play
Free speech
The hand that moves to create
The hand moves to play
Behind it
It's master
The mind used to imagine
The mind used to exist
Without it
It's master
No paint to create
No pawn to play
No hand to move
No hand to move

Lana's Free Paint – response to Matt's free write

*Figure 1.* Lana Ngyun's Free Paint followed by Matt Mulligan's Free Write followed by Lana's Free Paint in response to Matt's Free Write.

different life or history and experience. It's like it is being run through a filter of an entirely different composition. In the end, the meaning may no longer be the same, and that's the beauty of art. It's the artist's backdoor key to people's inner soul. Through your work and expression you open people up to new ideas and thoughts, all surprisingly of their own subconscious. (Courtney-Smith, 2005, p. 60)

In one of her own reflections in the article, Kelly writes, "What emerged from these painting and writing interactions was an illumination of several different texts: the novel, the poetry, the paintings, and the students themselves" (Courtney-Smith, 2005, p. 60). Both Jenna and Kelly organized their commentaries around analyses of dozens of student paints and writes included in their respective narratives – each demonstrating possibilities of paint-write for a wide range of teaching goals and students.

Paint-write may or may not grow to capture the fancy of the English teaching community, which typically centers on traditional read-write approaches to studies in literature, language, and composition. Almost paradoxically, as the next segment of this chapter will suggest, the field has also demonstrated an affinity to field-test new features of the popular culture as they emerge, particularly those media-based. In the twentieth century, for example, English teachers invented ways to integrate such mediums as newspapers, film, photography, computers, television, and the arts into lessons designed to advance student abilities in literature, language, and composition, and, to some degree, the mediums themselves. Already in the twenty-first century digital photography, text messaging, and the contemporary arts are providing ready tools to engage and facilitate literacy growth of students increasingly savvy of current communications technology. Ironically, teachers are playing technological catch-up at the same time they are experimenting with age-old arts techniques such as incorporating pencil drawings of scene and character as part of literature studies to foster engagement and deepen literary understandings. These classroom applications of the visual in terms of more commercial products such as paintings, photographs, and film to supplement word-driven (oral and print language) studies in literature, language, and composition are, in large part, manifestations of the classical *ekphrastic* approach described earlier; that is, students are being led to make words from pre-existing art (external images), which has unquestionable classroom value. What we are just coming to terms with, however, and the focus of paint-write in this piece of the chapter, is the potential of human predispositions to create mental images as it relates, in concrete educational applications, to not only language and literacy learning, but all learning. Once the issue is raised, it appears to be an obvious point, perhaps too obvious, according to those English education students who enroll in my courses and English teachers who participate in my national conference sessions. They seem to agree, upon discussion of the possibilities for student mental imaging, that in our preoccupation with explicit study of the word and wording in English teaching, we have overlooked the potential of student composed internal and external images as powerful links to their personal histories and, therefore, their engagement in English learning. In missing this point, we may be missing a set of key teaching strategies that encourages student engagement at all levels, as well as growth in thinking, reading and writing across the curriculum. Paint-write, then, and approaches like it using different mediums, is both a reminder and an example of how we, as a teaching-learning community might address that omission.

Where I am in regard to exploring this question at the moment is still deeply involved in related classroom practices, still teasing out the theory embedded in what appears effective in nurturing writing and painting development, now chasing previous research that has been done by others, particularly in brain research and art therapy, to find grounding, similarities, disparities. To this point, as Jenna reports in some detail in her study, the behavioral patterns of individuals we and Kelly have each engaged in paint-write are predicted by the findings of brain (Benson & Proctor, 2003), art therapy (Adamson, 1984; Malchiodi, 1998), and other researchers such as Gardner, 1993; and those yet to be encountered. In brief, now that I have seen it at work, I need to know more precisely what "image" is, particularly as a phenomenon of the human brain, and how, specifically, it influences language growth. And then, of course, to put that knowledge to work in the education of students, their teachers, and, as I can, in the development of my own writing and painting.

## BRINGING VISUAL DATA AND THE LITERACIES OF MEDIA AND THE POPULAR CULTURE INTO THE TEACHER EDUCATION CURRICULUM-MARK LETCHER

While the earlier portion of this chapter dealt with students and teachers exploring and working with images from their own minds, this section will focus on how students and teachers manage the images that come to them from outside sources, namely media and popular culture. This section will include the rationale for developing a new methods course within our undergraduate and graduate teacher preparation programs, developed in response to the exploding need for increased media literacy among our students and teacher candidates. Also described will be some of the reactions to the course, and how teachers hope to incorporate their new knowledge into their classroom teaching practices.

Teaching within a College of Education, our responsibility is to prepare future Language Arts teachers for secondary school positions, and teacher educators to train the next generation of secondary teachers. Traditionally, such preparation has included methodologies and models of teaching literature, composition and language. In recent years, however, the field of visual literacy has made its presence felt in our field of Language Arts Education. Teachers, both pre-service and practicing, must now be aware of a wider variety of communicative genres and literacy practices. To speak of "literacy" in the 21st century now means not only the decoding and interpretation of black lines on a white page, but also moving images, static images. These new and continually evolving definitions of literacy are reflected in the standards that guide our preparation of future teachers. The following objectives are taken from the joint National Council of Teachers of

English (NCTE) and International Reading Association (IRA) Program Standards for the Preparation of Teachers of Secondary English Language Arts, Grades 7–12 (2003):

- Create opportunities and develop strategies that permit students to demonstrate the influence of language and visual images on thinking and composing.
- Engage students in activities that provide opportunities for demonstrating their skills in writing, speaking and creating visual images for a variety of audiences and purposes.
- Use a variety of ways to assist students in creating and critiquing a wide range of print and non-print texts for multiple purposes and help students understand the relationship between symbols and meaning.
- Understand media's influence on culture and people's actions and communication, reflecting that knowledge not only in their own work but also in their teaching.
- Use a variety of approaches for teaching students how to construct meaning from media and non-print texts and integrate learning opportunities into classroom experiences that promote composing and responding to such texts.
- Help students compose and respond to film, video, graphic, photographic, audio, and multimedia texts and use current technology to enhance their own learning and reflection on their learning.

Given such standards for teacher education, and the fact that our state standards for secondary education also include sections on visual literacy, it is relatively easy to see the need for teachers to become better prepared to deal with media and popular culture images, among other forms, as they move into their own classrooms.

With a doctoral student as my co-teacher for the course, I began to conceive the general outline and methodology for the class. This was certainly no easy task, for several reasons: the course was a new offering within our program and college, I myself had what I could best describe as a tentative grasp of multimodal literacies in the classroom, and there appeared to be far too much suitable material to comfortably fit into a summer course syllabus. I knew that selection and focus would be key, and in order to gain focus I would need to determine what my own goals for the course would be.

The basis for this course, as well as others I design, was a strong belief that language and learning are socially constructed entities (Vygotsky, 1978). With this social element in mind, we can begin to look at literacy as a socioculturally mediated practice (Gee, 2000). We then needed to take a much broader conception of the possible modes for learning. In our field of Secondary Language Arts, the printed word has been, and continues to be, the dominant mode of communication and learning in classrooms. However, as we read further in the literature, we came to the realization that "a multimodal approach to learning requires us to take seriously and attend to the whole range of modes involved in representation and communication (Kress & Jewitt, 2003, p. 1). In planning a new course, this gave us a great amount of freedom, and not a little trepidation. Where to begin? We agreed that we would work to cover multiple forms of media literacy within the scope of the course, including film, television, music, graphic novels and computer technology (such as online video, blogs and chat rooms).

This approach to new literacies in the classroom was, I was happy to find, in line with what Gunther Kress (2003), one of the leading scholars in media literacy education, has noted in describing "the broad move from the now centuries-long dominance of writing to the new dominance of the image and, on the other hand, the move from the dominance of the medium of the book to the dominance of the medium of the screen" (p. 1). It would likely be an interesting shift for the pre-service and in-service teachers enrolled in the course: from the comfortable paper page, to images displayed on screens large, small, and everywhere in between.

On the first day of the course, the students were asked to explain what the term "media literacy" meant to them. The results were varied, and indicated a somewhat narrow view of both parts of the term. Many of the students drew on their own experiences with non-print texts as students. Several class members remembered media such as films being used in the classroom, but usually only as "a filler of dead time," and "the stereotypical 'treat' at the end of a unit so as to bribe students to remain attentive and give the teacher a break from planning lessons." Even though some of these students had graduated from high school only several years prior to the class, there was still an indication that the use of new literacy technologies had not made its way into their secondary classrooms.

However, the class did express, even on the first day of our class together, a view that media was a large part of their students' lives. More than one described today's secondary students as "media savvy," and all indicated that younger students have much more confidence with these new forms of communication than they do. As one student commented during the initial class meeting, "There is still a difference, though, between a student knowing how to use all of this stuff, and knowing how to decode the messages in it, knowing how to read what they're seeing." This acknowledgement became one of the tacit foundations for our time together in the class: while we, as teachers, recognized that our students would undoubtedly be much more knowledgeable about new media forms than we would be, it would fall to us to teach our students the skills they needed to become critical readers and consumers of those media. In the words of one class member, "Demonstrating to students the value (or lack thereof) behind such texts transforms them from passive to active audience members." This was the shift we needed, to move from the recognition of media *consumption* among today's adolescents, toward a sense of greater media *literacy*.

Through theoretical and practice-based readings, class activities and discussions, and teaching demonstrations, we began to conceive of different and engaging ways that teachers (in all discipline areas, not just English/Language Arts) could incorporate the images that students see, and the sounds that they hear, into curricular materials and goals. The students created lessons that analyzed political advertisements, popular song lyrics, *The Simpsons* parodies of classic literature, advertisement deconstruction, and virtual tours of museums and art galleries. In the span of three short weeks, the class had developed their original, narrow definitions of "media literacy" into broader, more encompassing stances on how various media could be used with their own students.

As one of the final assignments for the class, the students revisited their first-day writings, and reflected on how (if at all) their definitions and conceptions had changed over the course of several weeks. The following excerpts from students' essays indicate how their perceptions shifted as they moved through the course.

As educators, it is essential that we are able to understand that while the printed word is a valuable vehicle for education, we are living in a time that literature has morphed into new forms just as worthy of examination. Further, we have a responsibility to our students to prepare them for a world where technology and multimedia are pervasive; they will require the skills to be able to access, read, and produce these messages in multiple forms. Teachers should strive to produce students that are critical and independent thinkers who are capable of a sophisticated appreciation of art forms across the spectrum of media.

Students must know how to live in a culture engulfed in the media, and schools should share at least part of the responsibility of making sure their students learn these skills. Mediums such as television and the internet are becoming (or already are) more widely read than print; this is our future and young people should be equipped to live in it. The English classroom is a great place to incorporate media literacy because it is already focused on reading, analyzing and creating written messages; now it is time to broaden the subject area to include messages from all mediums. Literacy is the responsibility of English teachers, and if the definition of literacy has expanded it is our job to expand the curriculum to accommodate today's new literacies.

Within my own field of reading education, I have discussed in several classes with classmates the need for change with a reading program and after taking this class, I think incorporating media into the reading program is a fantastic idea. I love the way it creates such active learning in the classroom and gives the students a variety of ways to see print, not just in a textbook, but by using ads, cartoons, comic books, TV and movies. It also creates the connection between school and the world the students live in to promote interesting and active learning. Learning can be fun and engaging, but still connect with the curriculum and I need to find ways to bridge the gap between them and know my justification for incorporating media into my teaching.

A number of these final reflections also noted how teachers, as a whole, must adapt to the changing times, and incorporate media forms that their students understand and perhaps utilize on a daily basis. The responses also hint at the trepidation that many teachers experience when they are asked, or forced. to move beyond their comfort zones:. As another student wrote:

In America, we cannot escape the media. The Kaiser Family Foundation Report (2005) shows that on the average youth spend an estimated 44.5 hours per week inundated with media. This research also reports the capability of students to multi-task with various media. Young adults are smart and media-savvy. If we, as educators, can channel this energy into their personal learning, amazing accomplishments will happen in education. This is a significant reason to integrate media literacy into the school setting. I am motivated to bring more media in the classroom as a source for student learning, and the students will be the leaders with some of the technology. Teachers must be willing to give up their roles as "all-knowing experts." Media literacy is the "language" of our students; they understand through ways that connect prior knowledge and hold personal relevance to their lives.

The ability to incorporate multiple media and popular culture into the classroom is becoming increasingly more emphasized and yet there remain unanswered questions in how to implement such instruction. Educators seem unsure on how to go about teaching students to "read" various forms of literature and those that have come up with innovative techniques exist on the fringes of teaching practices. What is needed is a reframing of how teachers perceive new literacies; educators must first educate themselves on how to keep up with what is relevant for today's students to learn and how to keep students engaged with the curriculum. Pop culture is increasingly finding its way into the classroom and skeptical educators are not sure where it fits in the curriculum.

In all, I was very impressed with the open attitude these teachers took to new literacies instruction; it is not easy to break free from long-held beliefs and biases, and media forms such as music videos and popular film certainly can leave themselves open to their share of criticism, and debate over their place in today's curriculum. However, the purpose of this class was to examine exactly how adolescents in today's digital culture engage with multiple forms of literacy, and how adults can gain a greater perspective on those literacy practices. Donna Alvermann (2004) reminds us that, "By embracing a rapidly changing digital world, the so-called millennial adolescent is proving quite adept at breaking down century-old distinctions between age groups, among disciplines, between high- and low-brow culture, and within print and digitized text types. But such embracing is not done uncritically; neither is it done for the sole purpose of compartmentalizing digital technologies as tools for learning, entertaining, or knowledge production" (pp. viii–ix). For such reasons, it is vital that today's teachers begin to look beyond the traditional views of literacy and learning, as some of the class responses suggest.

While our next generation of teachers is generally more comfortable with new technologies, there is no certainty that teachers and other adults will be able to "keep up" with the new literacies adopted by adolescents. There should also be no expectation that teachers should keep up. Adolescent culture will, as it usually does, determine which new literacies will be adopted, and which older literacies will be appropriated in new ways. Teachers' roles will be to learn from their students, and seek to integrate multiple literacy forms into the curriculum. Perhaps then, rather than the ubiquitous film at the end of a unit of study, without clear ties to instruction, our curriculum can approach what Kist (2005) sought in his case studies of classrooms: spaces where new literacies became more of the rule than the exception. Kist asks some probing questions about new literacies, which we discussed often in the class. Can new literacies be taught in a traditional school environment? What will happen to new literacies in the schools? Will something "authentic" become "non-authentic" once it gets into schools? We don't yet have the answers to these questions. But through conversations such as ours, and with open minds from teachers, we can begin to explore our possibilities with students. That in itself is an exciting prospect.

## ACKNOWLEDGEMENTS

Student Contributors: Matt Mulligan and Lana Ngyun of Santa Monica High School, CA (Figure 1).

## REFERENCES

Adamson, E. (1984). *Art as healing.* United Kingdom: Nicolas Hays.

Alvermann, D.E. (Ed.). (2004). *Adolescents and literacies in a digital world.* New York: Peter Lang.

Benson, H., & Proctor, W. (2003). *The break-out principle.* New York: Scribner.

Blackhawk, T. (2002). Ekphrastic poetry: Entering and giving voice to works of art. In T. Foster & K. Prevallet (Eds.), *Third mind: Creative writing through visual art* (pp. 1–14). New York: Teachers & Writers Collaborative.

Cassou, M., & Cubley, S. (1995). *Life, paint and passion: Reclaiming the magic of spontaneous expression.* New York: Tarcher/Putnam.

Courtney-Smith, K., & Angelotti, M. (2005). To search for enlightenment: Responding to Siddhartha through paint and poetry. *English Journal, 94*(6), 56–62.

Dunn, C. (1995). *Conversations in paint: A notebook of fundamentals.* New York: Workman Publishing.

Edgar, C. (2002). Foreword. In K. Walsh-Piper, *Image to word: Art and creative writing.* (pp. xiii–xiv). Lanham, MD and London, UK: Scarecrow Press.

Foster, T., & Prevallet, K. (2002). Introduction. In T. Foster & K. Prevallet (Eds.), *Third mind: Creative writing through visual art* (p. xv). New York: Teachers & Writers Collaborative.

Gardner, H. (1993). *Creating minds: An anatomy of creativity seen through the lives of Freud, Einstein, Picasso, Stravinsky, Eliot, Graham, and Ghandi.* New York: Basic Books.

Gasparino, J. (2006). *An analysis of creativity in one 12th-grade public school classroom through the use of art: Visual and verbal.* Master's thesis, University of Oklahoma, Norman.

Gee, J.P. (2000). The new literacy studies: From "socially situated" to the work of the social. In D. Barton, M. Hamilton, & R. Ivanic (Eds.), *Situated literacies: Reading and writing in context* (pp. 180–196). London: Routledge.

Goldberg, N. (1986). *Writing down the bones: Freeing the writer within.* Boston: Shambhala.

Keats, J. (1919). Ode on a Grecian urn. In A. Quiller-Crouch (Ed.), *The Oxford book of English verse: 1250–1900* (#625). Oxford: Clarendon.

Kist, W. (2005). *New literacies in action: Teaching and learning in multiple media.* New York: Teachers College Press.

Kress, G. (2003). *Literacy in the new media age.* London: Routledge.

Kress, G., & Jewitt, R.C. (2003). Introduction. In C. Jewitt & G. Kress (Eds.), *Multimodal literacy* (pp. 1–18). New York: Peter Lang.

Malchiodi, C. (1998). *The art therapy sourcebook.* Lincolnwood, IL: Lowell House.

Rohrer, T. (2007). The body in space: Embodiment, experientialism, and linguistic conceptualization. In T. Ziemke, J. Zlatev, & R. Frank (Eds.), *Body, language, and mind,* Vol. 1 (pp. 339–376). Berlin: Mouton de Gruyter.

Rotenberg, T. (2002). The verbal-visual nexus. In T. Foster & K. Prevallet (Eds.), *Third mind: Creative writing through visual art* (pp. 154–163). New York: Teachers and Writers Collaborative.

Shelley, P. (1875). Ozymandias of Egypt. In F.T. Palgrave (Ed.), *The golden treasury of the best songs and lyrical poems in the English language*. London: Macmillan.

Vygotsky, L.S. (1978). *Mind in society: The development of higher psychological processes*. Cambridge, MA: Harvard University Press.

Walsh-Piper, K. (2002). *Image to word: Art and creative writing*. Lanham, MD and London, UK: The Scarecrow Press, Inc.

ADRIENNE HYLE

# CHAPTER 11
# VISUAL DATA AS INSTRUCTIONAL JOURNEY: TEACHER AND STUDENT EXPERIENTIAL LEARNING AT SEA *

Education graduate program research methodologies have traditionally been taught in teacher-centered classrooms over multiple week-long semester courses. Instruction is delivered through lecture format with limited hands-on activities (Fink, 2003; Silverman & Casazza, 2000). In these courses, students are asked to transfer what they learn about traditional qualitative data collection strategies (i.e., interview and observation) to the writing of their research projects. It is no wonder then why institutions of higher education have been prompted to realign their methods from an instructional paradigm to a learning paradigm-from teacher centered to learner centered – an emphasis on student learning and not on pedagogy. In terms of teaching graduate students, adult learning theory literature has continuously pointed out adults learn best when engaged in experiential, collaborative (Giddens, 1991; Granello, 2000; Hopkins, 1999; Miller, 2000) lessons. As individuals involved in the graduate education instructional process as both students and instructors, we have sought opportunities to provide experiential and student centered learning settings.

Such an opportunity for experiential, collaborative learning presented itself during the 2005 summer semester, The *"I"/Eye of the Researcher: Strange and Familiar Contexts and Qualitative Research*. We designed and taught the doctoral-level, qualitative research course for 16 students in the educational leadership program at a land-grant institution. We met for two Saturday courses to discuss the philosophies, structures, and components of qualitative research and students' specific assignments. We then took a seven-day cruise to Mexico and Latin merica with three port calls. During the cruise, we met daily in class and worked within teams to collect and analyze data and to compose their specific studies. One group of students investigated the culture of a Belizean junior college; the other examined the learning process of the other group. In concluding the class, we met for follow-up sessions and an educational conference where students presented their research projects.

---

* The following students in EDLE 6870, *The "I"/Eye of the Researcher: Strange and Familiar Contexts and Qualitative Research*, helped make this possible: Kathy Seibold, Jovette R. Dew, Tena J. Fry, Jody L. Jones, Tom C. Messner, Linda L. Rider, Janet Wansick, and Jessie Young.

*J.E. Pedersen and K.D. Finson (eds.), Visual Data, 167–177.*
© 2009. *Sense Publishers. All rights reserved.*

By expanding the walls of the traditional classroom and by revisiting foundational anthropological research methods, we were able to provide students with
learning focused on research data collection and appreciation of the unfamiliarity
of a new environmental context with qualitative methods that usually do not receive attention in typical graduate education research coursework. Our argument
was, and still is, that to see within a strange setting using different techniques
would lead them to better see the world around them. We wrote in the course
syllabus:

> Sometimes to get a clearer view of ourselves, we must step outside our envi-
> ronment and turn an eye upon something different. In the process of observing
> and reflecting upon how others function, we gain insight into our practice. The
> action of qualitative processes pushes researchers into these "strange" and "for-
> eign" contexts, and the reflection of them opens the scope beyond the study and
> the observed to that of the researcher and the universal. Janesick (2004) posits
> that qualitative inquiry allows "researchers to know themselves better." (Hyle
> & McClellan, 2005, p. 3)

Ultimately, we wanted students to collect and analyze data, and to capture,
through the use of the researcher's eye, a depiction and an understanding of a
particular culture. As Eisner (1998) puts it, "We *learn* to see, hear, and feel. This
process depends upon perceptual differentiation, and in the ability to see what
is subtle but significant" (p. 21). First students must be engaged in *seeing* as a
method of inquiry before they can become acquainted with "writing as a method
of inquiry" (Richardson, 2003, p. 501).

In addition to our students' learning how to use the *eye*, we wanted them to
recognize their influence as researcher, the role of the *I*. In their seminal work,
Boud, Keogh, and Walker (1985) posit that experiential learning should be accompanied by reflective observation. Giddens furthers that in turn the "the self
becomes a reflexive project" (1991, p. 32). And as Richardson (2003) argues,
"Self reflexivity brings to consciousness some of the complex political/ideological
agendas" (p. 520) that cause the "researcher subjectivity to be both producer
and product of the text" (p. 522). In becoming reflective about their own research process and the influence they have on the meaning-making, our students
confronted the complexity and interpretative act of inquiry.

## WHY VISUAL DATA?

A recent article in *National Geographic Magazine* (2007) illustrates the problem
that many new and veteran qualitative researchers have during observations. In an
attempt to capture the setting sun across the Caribbean, an amateur photographer
snapped the photograph from her cruise ship. The same photograph, that she later
submitted to the magazine, shows the setting sun across the green waters. In the
center of the frame, a flying finned fish is caught in mid-air, black eye smiling
into the camera. As explained by the photographer in her submission: "I had no
idea the fish was there. Only until I received the printed photos did I realize it was

there." As the photographer in the story reports, even though we think we capture the scene, data reveal what might have been missed by mere observation.

Videos and photography help researchers "see a scene and provide the raw material for interpretation and analysis" (Eisner, 1998, p. 188). As charts and histograms visually portray the data of the quantitative researcher, pictures provide data that led to the qualitative researcher's interpretation. The use of photography in our course allowed students to prolong their observations. They used the visuals as raw data to which they returned when drawing inferences.

From their readings, students heard from Eisner (1998) that visual methods "can say things that not only would require pages and pages of words to describe, but in the end could not be adequately described with words" (p. 187) and that in time as we learn more about how our minds work, the use of visual data will become more prevalent. Eisner also points out that just as audio recordings recalls an interview, visual data records details that make for a credible study. Practically put, the camera is a tool that we used to gather data and to help our students develop as qualitative researchers.

As teachers of research, we felt supported in our choice of assigning visual data collection by Janesick (2004) who wrote in a photography exercise for qualitative researchers:

> Of all the exercises that I use with learners, this one seems to inspire the most confidence, an awareness of one's limitations, and the most enthusiasm for finding out what kind of qualitative researcher one might become. (p. 93)

We believed that this strategy would result in our students coming away from our class with both confidence and self-awareness as qualitative researchers.

In our class, students used qualitative data collection methods to complete their course projects. To assist students in accurately recording their encounters with the contexts and in collectively analyzing observations, photographs were taken and other visual texts collected. To investigate self reflection and insight about texts and observations, reflective journals and field notes were also used.

We turned to photography initially for pragmatic reasons. Although newcomers to the use of visual data, we decided that by collecting, sequencing, and collectively analyzing photographs and other visual texts, our students could capture a scene for further observation and collective analysis. As Collier and Collier (1986) note, "Photography offers the stranger in the field a means of recording large areas authentically, rapidly, and with great detail, and a means of storing away complex descriptions for future use" (p. 16).

When referring to the collection and use of visual data in our course, we used a blended term inspired by Harper's (2003) description of visual methods. Harper claims that visual data make statements about social realities. Because our students would only have a brief encounter with the Belizean culture, we realized that they would have to rely upon the images as a *visual sociology*. Through photography, students would construct a visual sociology of their visit. And, through reflective journaling and collective analysis of data, we believed students would be able to see the benefits of visual sociology for understandings "strange" contexts as well as their personal influences on the research process – the "eye" and the "I." Both sets of activities were designed to provide a broader picture of the learning process. Reflective journals were used to examine personal feelings and thoughts throughout the learning process. Field notes and visual sociology were used to determine the growth in participants' knowledge associated with the study of qualitative research. And, we believed that these documents would give us a unique picture of each student's experiential learning.

## THE LEARNING EXPERIENCE

To develop students' understanding of the qualitative process and data collection, a series of readings were required of students before cruise departure. Our hope was that these readings would inform and prepare students with the necessary tools and strategies needed for organization, conceptualization and general analysis in dealing with their visual data (see Appendix A).

The eye of researcher. A great deal of attention was given by students to preparation intended to assist in the collection of visual and textual data. Class members were assigned duties and roles – group leader, scribe, photographer, videographer, librarian, etc. From these roles and duties emerged technology requirements-computers, cameras, video-cameras, CDs, etc. Clearly, the focus of the students was on capturing the realities of life and education in the Caribbean. The *eye* was being trained and well-equipped for the tasks of data collection.

Visual sociology in the form of photographs and video recording documented the pictorial experiences of the members. Textual data was documented through the use of individual reflective journals written during the planning process, their time on the ship, and at various ports of call. Journals were used to gain a better understanding of participants' thoughts and beliefs before, during, and after the process. The focus areas in the journals were both the cultural context as well as the learning process associated with visual sociology.

Visual and textual data was collected from each of the 16 participants and compiled for use in analysis. This task was essential given that

> Raw field notes and verbatim transcripts constitute the undigested complexity of reality. Simplifying and making sense out of that complexity constitutes the challenge of content analysis. Developing some manageable classification or coding scheme is the first step of analysis. Students used content analysis to identify, code, categorize, classify, and label the themes and patterns of data. (Patton, 2002, p. 463)

Journals, field notes, photographs and texts of on-line discussions were stripped of identity markers, collapsed, and organized chronologically. The data was then reported by date and participant number. The result was a massive amount of data to be examined.

"I" of the researcher. Our hope was that students would begin to see the interplay between the documentation of what was observed and their own constructions of those observations. However, we found that to gain an understanding of the emerging patterns, group members examined the data collected using content analysis methods to help reduce the data set to a manageable size for analysis (Ryan & Bernard, 2003). Their focus for analysis was almost entirely on the textual data. They had no real plan for the review or analysis of the visual data collected.

The students reported that after reading through the journals a number of times, they were able to discern patterns related to the learning process of the participants. As the patterns began to emerge, the students began to formulate related patterns into sub-themes. The visual data, so integral to their experiences with the *strange* were merely supplements to what they had previously learned about the analysis of interview texts and field notes.

In their journals and reflections they neglect to cite anything related specifically to visual data and focus solely on text. For example, they note that

> The fieldworker must also consider how a selected theme can be related to other apparent themes. A theme that allows the researcher to make linkages to other issues noted in the data is particularly promising. Finding new ways of linking themes together allows for the possibility that some of the themes that might have been seen as unrelated and possibly dropped can in fact be reincorporated as sub-themes. (Emerson, Fretz & Shaw, 1995, p. 158)

And, continue with Patton's recommendation to look for "statements about which things appear to lead to other things . . . " and "when careful study of the data gives rise to ideas about casual linkages, there is no reason to deny those interested in the study's results the benefit of those insights" (2002, p. 479). This textual content analysis strategy helped to provide the students with numerous sub-themes but did not facilitate awareness of or application of analytical strategies related to visual data. The students divided the tasks of textual analysis into teams activities; one group focused on the entire set of data, another focused on data prior to the cruise, another focused on data entered while on the cruise, while another focused on data related to the excursion dates and yet another focused on data from the online discussions. At the time, no one focused exclusively on the visual data or noted strategies designed to get at visual data specifically.

## RESEARCHER CONFIDENCE AND AWARENESS

Initially, the most commonly expressed concern was a lack of experience in qualitative research. "I am not confident in my understanding of the process" was a common assertion. Journal writing was another concern. Some students came to the project with little experience with journal writing. Others were concerned about sharing their private thoughts.

> I had an epiphany this evening that in my professional life. . . . I do quite a lot of qualitative research in the evaluation and treatment. So why I am I having such as hard time with notes now when I don't in my documentation (on the job)? I think it's because my scope of inquiry with (in my job) is limited to just that and not everything that is going on in the public.

As the course moved onto the ship, students felt uneasy about their skills in qualitative research. One student wrote of the "collective uncertainty" seen in the group. As novice researchers, students felt unorganized and uncomfortable. Many questions were in need of answers. Specifically, students recorded the difficulty they had when working with visual data especially when trying to take notes and photographs. One student wrote about challenge of mastering visual data collection techniques.

The logging of photos was much more complex than I thought. It seemed like a simple process to write basic information for the photos I was taking, but it soon became overwhelming. In order to get the feel of the moment, I was diligent about writing (or logging) information for each photo when I took it. You wouldn't believe the looks I was getting as I stopped to write in my little notebook every time I took a picture. There was an overwhelming amount of information and I was having difficulty focusing on anything well enough to thoroughly cover it. I found my 15 min. field note exercises I was trying to focus on too much. In class this evening, we discussed this same issue and talked about how this will make us better researchers in Belize. I also believe this is one of those instances where we had to learn for ourselves the best approach. In the material I read, it was mentioned not to try to cover too much material. However, until I had the opportunity to practice, their suggestions didn't sink in. I found myself time and again wishing for a tape recorder to record my thoughts throughout the day.

By the third and fourth day of the trip, students began to write of their gained knowledge in qualitative research. One student wrote, "I think we are all learning a lot about qualitative research strategies." Many still struggled with field notes and dealing with the overwhelming amount of information, but they seemed to be learning new ways to organize their observations. Many wrote that learning visual sociology was challenging and fun. One student wrote that the experience gained in the class will aid in future research projects. Most commented on how hard they had worked during the course. They seem to share an appreciation about the amount of work that goes into a qualitative research project. Many wrote that they had learned more in this course than any other research course they had taken on campus. "Today has given me some of the best instruction into the world of research that I have received to date." The field-based research experience gained by the participants was incredibly rigorous and yet rewarding for the majority of the class.

At the end of the project, students held a much deeper appreciation of their own personal strengths and weaknesses. They understood the challenges of playing a variety of roles within a research group made up of individuals with widely varied personalities, skills, motivations, and talents. All participants gained deeper understanding of qualitative data collection, field work techniques, and data analysis – but only as it pertained to document collection and analysis. Awareness of visual data analysis and management techniques and strategies was missing. Students did not comment about or appear to realize that visual data collection and analysis was different than textual collection and analysis.

## 1. WHAT WE'LL DO DIFFERENTLY

Despite the difficulties that students face when using visual data, we will continue to assign the use of it. We concur with Grady (2004) who claims, "Visual data collection is ideally suited for the classroom, making it like a lab or workshop because images can be collected and analyzed collectively" (p. 19). We will offer practical advice. Students should take care of their equipment. They should have the camera ready to shoot before they ask to take a photograph, and they should know the type of shot they want to take before asking. They should start simply. There should be more than enough time to take the picture. They should take the time to record details about the data they collected and specifics about the mechanics of the picture immediately after the shot. And, they should be prepared to fail.

Besides practical advice and in anticipation of students' difficulty of collecting and recording their visual data, we will recommend to students that they develop skills that will help them with collection (adapted from Grady, 2004). For example, we will prompt them to be more methodical, to list and record systematically the details that they are intentionally recording. By producing specific lists of items being captured by the camera, they will identify what points of focus they intended to store and how they perceived the setting at the time of collection. In recording these specific lists, students then may become more cognizant of what and how they see and how they are recording data – a merging of *eye* and *I*. This awareness, we hope, will lead students to a more thorough collection of images. The collection should become more sequential and more narrative in nature. Then, to encourage students to undertake a rigorous inquiry of their visual data, we will schedule time for a collective analysis of everyone's photographs. We will ask them to sequence their photographs and to explicate in narratives what observable facts they have recorded about the setting.

In addition to helping students with collecting and recording visual data, we will follow Collier and Collier's (1986, pp. 171–180) basic model for analyzing their photography. Table 1 delineates these stages of analysis.

By providing these schemata and practical guides, we hope our students might acquire a more thorough understanding in the use of visual data collection and achieve fuller comprehensions of what they have observed. Furthermore, by using these processes, we hope students will become more cognizant of how the *I* may influence their *eye*, thus developing a keener sense of the complexity of culture and how the researcher must work at uncovering these multiple levels of contextual meaning.

## SUMMARY

What we wanted for our students was an awareness of their role and impact upon qualitative research. We now know that despite their initial apprehension at working with qualitative data, students do gain a confidence and awareness of qualitative research. Despite this awareness and confidence, however, they need

TABLE 1

Collier and Collier (1986) basic model for analyzing visual data.

| First Stage | • Look at the data as a whole |
|---|---|
| | • Listen to all its overtones and subtleties |
| | • Connect and contrast its patterns |
| | • Identify and note your perceptions about the data |
| | • List questions the data bring to mind |
| | • Respond to the visual data as statements of cultural drama |
| | • Form a context emerging from the data |
| Second Stage | • Inventory and log evidence so that it helps visualize context |
| | • Categorize your data and your reflection |
| Third Stage | • Structure Analysis |
| | • Generate questions about the evidence that will direct your attention |
| | • Measure distance, count heads, compare movements, identify group/ relationships |
| | • Graph (often in statistical form) what you see |
| | • Detail how one situation as seen in the data compares with another |
| Fourth Stage | • Return to field records and identify overtones and significance |
| | • Respond to the data with openness in search of a complete context replete with significance in patterns |
| | • Reestablish context |
| | • View the sequencing and narration of all photographs |
| | • Write conclusions influenced by final viewing |

additional assistance from the literature and us in order that they become aware of their impacts upon the research they are doing and their management of visual data. We also realize that our students had a propensity to engage more easily with textual collection and analysis and were less adept at visual collection and interpretation.

This summer we will travel with a new group of students. The course design will be the same; readings have been expanded to include texts and articles focusing with greater detail on visual sociological methods. Students will be encouraged to undertake only one research project thereby offering a more focused discussion and critique of our locale and the visual data collection methods used. This stronger frame for visual data collection, including "steps and 'rules of thumb' for visual data collecting," and visual data analysis (as offered by Collier and Collier) can lead to a more in-depth discussion of postmodern "reality" and the cultures that slide in and out of focus. We want our students to acknowledge that "visuals are complex and have layered meaning and that visual data may appear objective but remains highly subjective." This should cause students "to pay close attention to the explanatory potential of various kinds of data and not just on the techniques for manipulating and interpreting data" (Grady, 2004, p. 18).

We believe our class not only pushes students outside the traditional boundaries of the classroom but does the same with their research methodologies. By blending discourse analysis methods, those that we use to "re/present as documented simulations of the real" (Davison, 2006, p. 134, paraphrasing Denzin, 1997), with visual methods, we transition students out of the modernist view of representing and translating subjective experiences (Davison, 2006) into the postmodern conundrum that reality is "unrepresentable" (Jay, 1994) in text or in image. Awareness of the "I/eye" of the researcher is essential.

## CONCLUSION

In the artistic movements of the early nineteenth century, the camera changed painters' attempt to capture reality. Realism, as defined by the visual and literary arts, was the artist's attempt to capture reality. Paintings and language were attempts to replicate what the eye observed. When the camera confronted realism, artists turned to how the mind makes reality. They discovered that looking is not seeing. In research, the scientist and the sociologist have often debated the idea of reality.

Philosophically, for qualitative researchers, reality is not fixed but is shaped through the changing perceptions and enlightened insights of the viewer. The traditions of "scientific methods" are founded upon "objective reality." Qualitative research has inherited this tradition. At the same time, however, it asserts that reality is constructed through perception, objectivity does not exist. In our graduate level qualitative class we will continue to prompt our students to recognize that reality is only a point of view and that they are integral to the data collection and analysis processes because of their place within and their view of "reality," the I and the eye. We want them to recognize that "the very act of observing is interpretive, for to observe is to choose a point of view" (Harper, 2003, p. 183).

In our future qualitative research classes, we will sharpen our instruction of the collection, organization and analysis of visual data. Through the use of photography and other visual media, we challenge our students to "choose a point of view by aiming the camera and by choosing the focal length of the lens" (Harper, 2003, p. 183). By sequencing their photographs, students will construct a "visual narrative, consistent with symbolic interaction based on interpretation" (Harper, 2003, p. 186). Most importantly, with the use of their photographic sequences and categories, students will begin to translate their data into a study of complex, multi-layered social patterns, larger social constructs, and culture.

APPENDIX A: COURSE READINGS

Ellis, C., & Bochner, A.P. (2003). Autoethnography, personal narrative, reflexivity: Researcher as subject. In N.K. Denzin & Y.S. Lincoln (Eds.), *Collecting and interpreting qualitative materials* (2nd ed.) (pp. 199–258). Thousand Oaks, CA: Sage.

Harper, D. (2003). Reimagining visual methods: Galileo to Neuromancer. In N.K. Denzin & Y.S. Lincoln (Eds.), *Collecting and interpreting qualitative materials* (2nd ed.) (pp. 176–198). Thousand Oaks, CA: Sage.

Janesick, V.J. (2004). *Stretching exercises for qualitative researchers* (2nd ed.). Thousand Oaks, CA: Sage.

Rager, K.B. (2005). Self-care and the qualitative researcher: When collecting data can break your heart. *Educational Researcher, 34*(4), 23–27.

Ryan, G.W., & Bernard, H.R. (2003). Data management and analysis methods. In N.K. Denzin & Y.S. Lincoln (Eds.), *Collecting and interpreting qualitative materials* (2nd ed.) (pp. 259–309). Thousand Oaks, CA: Sage.

REFERENCES

Boud, D., Cohen, R., & Walker, D. (Eds.). (1985). *Using experience for learning.* Buckingham, England: Society for Research into Higher Education & Open University Press.

Collier, J., & Collier, M. (1986). *Visual anthropology: Photography as a research method.* Albuquerque, NM: University of New Mexico.

Davison, K.G. (2006). Dialectical imagery and postmodern research. *International Journal of Qualitative Studies in Education, 19*(2), 133–146.

Denzin, N.K. (1997). *Interpretative ethnography.* London: Sage.

Dwyer, B. (2002). Training strategies for the twenty-first century: Using recent research on learning to enhance training. *Innovations in Education and Teaching International, 39*(4), 265–270.

Eisner, E.W. (1998). *The enlightened eye: Qualitative inquiry and the enhancement of education practice.* Columbus, OH: Prentice Hall.

Emerson, R.M., Fretz, R.I., & Shaw, L.L. (1995). *Writing ethnographic fieldnotes.* Chicago: The University of Chicago Press.

Fink, L.D. (2003). *Creating significant learning experiences: An integrated approach to designing college courses.* San Francisco: Jossey-Bass.

Giddens, A. (1991). *Modernity and self identity: Self and society in the late modern age.* Stanford: Stanford University Press.

Grady, J. (2004). Working with viable evidence: An invitation and some practical advice. In C. Knowles & P. Sweetman (Eds.), *Picturing the social landscape [electronic source]: Visual methods in the sociological imagination* (pp. 18–29). New York: Routledge.

Granello, D.H. (2000). Contextual teaching and learning in counselor education. *Counselor Education & Supervision, 39,* 270.

Harper, D. (2003). Reimagining visual methods: Galileo to Neuromancer. In N.K. Denzin & Y.S. Lincoln (Eds.), *Collecting and interpreting qualitative materials* (2nd ed.) (pp. 176–198). Thousand Oaks, CA: Sage.

Hopkins, J.R. (1999). Studying abroad as a form of experiential education. *Liberal Education, 85*(3), 36–42.

Hyle, A.E., & McClellan, R. (2005). EDLE 6870 Syllabus: *The "I"/eye of the researcher: Strange and familiar contexts and qualitative research.* Unpublished document. Stillwater, OK: Oklahoma State University.

Janesick, V.J. (2004). *"Stretching" exercises for qualitative researchers* (2nd ed.). Thousand Oaks, CA: Sage.

Jay, M. (1994). *Downcast eyes: The degeneration of vision in twentieth-century French thought.* Berkeley, University of California Press.

Miller, N. (2000). Learning from experience in adult education. In A.L. Wilson & E.R. Hayes (Eds.), *Handbook of adult and continuing education* (pp. 71–86). San Francisco: Jossey-Bass.

Patton, M.Q. (2002). *Qualitative research & evaluation methods* (3rd ed.). Thousand Oaks, CA: Sage.

Richardson, L. (2003). Writing: A method of inquiry. In N.K. Denzin & Y.S. Lincoln (Eds.), *Collecting and interpreting qualitative materials* (2nd ed.) (pp. 499–541). Thousand Oaks, CA: Sage.

Ryan, G.W., & Bernard, H.R. (2003). Data management and analysis methods. In N.K. Denzin & Y.S. Lincoln (Eds.), *Collecting and interpreting qualitative materials* (2nd ed.) (pp. 259–309). Thousand Oaks, CA: Sage.

Silverman, S.L., & Casazza, M.E. (2000). *Learning and development: Making connections to enhance teaching*. San Francisco: Jossey-Bass.

Breinigsville, PA USA
02 March 2010
233264BV00003B/28/P